D1548083

CATHOLIC THEOLOGIANS IN NAZI GERMANY

Catholic Theologians in Nazi Germany

by

ROBERT A. KRIEG

continuum
NEW YORK • LONDON

2004

The Continuum International Publishing Group Inc
15 East 26 Street, New York NY 10010

The Continuum International Publishing Group Ltd
The Tower Building, 11 York Road, London SE1 7NX

www.continuumbooks.com

Copyright © by Robert A. Krieg

Printed in the United States of America

Library of Congress Cataloging-in-Publication Data

Krieg, Robert Anthony, 1946-
    Catholic theologians in Nazi Germany / by Robert A. Krieg.
        p. cm.
    Includes bibliographical references and index.
    ISBN 0-8264-1576-8 (hardcover : alk. paper)
    1. Theologians—Germany—Biography. 2. Catholic
Church—Germany—History—1933-1945. 3. Church and
State—Germany—History—1933-1945. 4. Christianity and
politics—Germany—History—20th century. 5. National socialism.
6. Germany—Church history—1933-1945.—I. Title.
    BX4683.K75 2004
    230'.2'092243—dc22
                                                    2004000549

Contents

Preface

THE CATHEDRAL OF COLOGNE STANDS ON A RISE OVERLOOKING the Rhine River. From its Gibraltar-like foundation, it soars to a height of 515 feet (157 meters)—almost as high as the Eiffel Tower. Begun in 1248, this edifice embodies the Gothic architecture that was new for its day; it emerges in vertical lines that arc into the sky. Although as massive as a medieval castle, it is as dynamic and graceful as a German oak. Its towers reach, as Konrad Adenauer said in 1926, into the heavens like hands raised in an oath. Each day its grand portals welcome thousands of men, women, and children who stream into its sacred space and then return to the outside world, renewed by the cathedral's majestic interior movement upward into sunlight and shadows.

Cologne's cathedral, or *Dom*, is a multivalent symbol. It is a manifestation of the Christian belief that has matured among the German-speaking peoples since the 400s—the belief that nurtured the mind of Albert the Great, the soul of Martin Luther, the music of Johann Sebastian Bach, and the art of Albrecht Dürer. This faith also tolerated, however, the anti-Semitism that brought about the death of six million Jews. Yet the cathedral itself condemns religious intolerance and racism by enshrining the relics of the Three Magi, who are symbols of God's love for all people.

The *Dom* is also an expression of German Romanticism. It stood unfinished in 1560 and would have likely remained so had not J. W. Goethe and Friedrich Schlegel campaigned in the early 1800s for its completion. They argued that the cathedral radiated the grandeur of the creative spirit. The construction of the towers resumed in 1842, and, in 1851, the composer Robert Schumann lauded the cathedral in his Third, or *Rhenish*, Symphony. The *Dom* was finished in 1880.

Cologne's cathedral symbolizes even more, however, than Christian belief and German Romanticism. It conveys, too, the notion of a hierarchical religious institution—a theological notion whose acceptance in the West coincided with the emergence of Gothic architecture. Its vertical lines suggest that grace streams down from God through the pope, bishops, and clergy to the laity, who look passively upward. The cathedral's pillars and high walls imply that the Christian assembly, under the leadership of ecclesiastical authorities, protects all who seek shelter from the world's cares, commerce, and politics. While this institutional ecclesiology has merit, it is also incomplete. Just as the Gothic form is not the only kind of architecture, so too the notion of the church as an organization does not express all aspects of the Christian life. The church is also a community and, further, a servant of truth and justice. All three models of church—institution, mystical communion, and moral advocate—influenced pastoral leaders' political statements and decisions during the Third Reich. Yet one ecclesiology predominated, namely, the church as a hierarchical institution intent on preserving itself so that God's grace would be immediately available to its members.

As far as the Nazis were concerned, Cologne's *Dom* had only one value: it provided towers for military reconnaissance. But the cathedral withstood Hitler's nihilism. Amid the Führer's fog and darkness, it was a source of hope and light. In this sanctuary in March 1944, Archbishop Joseph Frings declared that the Third Reich's persecution of Jews was "an injustice that cried out to heaven."

This book analyzes the impact of religious ideas on the political decisions of Pope Pius XI, Pope Pius XII, and Germany's bishops and theologians from 1933 to 1945. It shows how differing notions of the church and the church's mission in the modern world shaped the attitudes and actions of pastoral leaders as they tried to provide a Christian response to the Third Reich. Theology has social and political consequences, and nowhere is this more evident than when the church struggles with totalitarianism.

My work on this monograph received financial support from the University of Notre Dame's Department of Theology, Institute for Scholarship in the Liberal Arts (ISLA), and Nanovic Institute for European Studies. It was also made possible by grants from the Eastern Province of the Congregation of the Holy Cross, with which I was affiliated until four years ago. This study crystallized during the 2001–2002 academic year, when I was able to concentrate full-time on it thanks to a Henry Luce III Fellowship in Theology from the Henry Luce Foundation, Inc., and the Association of Theological Schools. I owe a debt of gratitude to those whose generosity made my work possible. I dedicate this book to my former confreres in the Holy Cross Congregation.

While writing this study and making changes in my life, I benefitted from the encouragement and good counsel of my family, friends, and colleagues. I wish to thank all of them, especially Judith Anne Beattie, C.S.C., Hugh W. Cleary, C.S.C., and Thomas F. O'Meara, O.P. Finally, I am grateful to my wife, Elizabeth, who helped me bring this work to completion.

1

The Bishops' Accommodation with Hitler in 1933

THE CATHOLIC BISHOPS OF GERMANY FOUND THEMSELVES at a political crossroads on January 30, 1933, when President Paul von Hindenburg gave the nation a new chancellor, Adolf Hitler.[1] They had not previously felt threatened when a chancellor was named, for each leader had shown respect for the Protestant and Catholic churches. But the bishops came to a fork in the road on January 30 because they had condemned Hitler's ideology. The leader of the National Socialist German Workers (Nazi) party had denounced the churches and preached racist and neopagan ideas in his party's platform of 1920 and in his book *Mein Kampf* (1925).[2] Hence, the bishops had banned Catholics from joining the party. President Hindenburg's appointment created a dilemma for the bishops: should they maintain their opposition to Hitler because of his teachings, or should they seek an accommodation with him? They eventually decided to withdraw their opposition to Hitler and to find ways to work with the Nazi regime. I wish to recall how they reached this decision and explain its theological rationale, that is, the religious ideas by which the bishops came to their decision.[3]

The bishops did not know in January 1933 that during the next twelve years they would be required to make decisions with life-and-death consequences for millions of people. These twenty-five men were the official religious leaders of roughly one-third of Germany's total population, that is, of approximately twenty-two million Catholics, half of whom participated in mass every Sunday. The bishops were assisted by over twenty-one thousand priests and approximately one hundred thousand members of religious orders of women and men.[4] Depending on the

1

geographical location of their dioceses, some of the bishops belonged to the Fulda conference of bishops, which was led by Breslau's Cardinal Adolf von Bertram, while others were members of the Bavarian conference of bishops, whose president was Munich's Cardinal Michael von Faulhaber. In the spring of 1933, the two groups united into one conference with Cardinal Bertram as its leader. As the bishops' spokesman, Bertram was charged with representing the church before the state, and for this reason he worked closely with the Vatican's papal nuncio in Berlin, Monsignor Cesare Orsenigo.

Catholic bishops, priests, and lay leaders had criticized National Socialism since its inception in the early 1920s. They had called attention in sermons, public addresses, and newspaper editorials to its racism and neopaganism. On September 30, 1930, amid Germany's economic crisis, a priest in Hesse condemned membership in the National Socialist party. When he was publicly challenged by pro-Hitler Catholics, he received the backing on October 30 of his bishop, Ludwig Maria Hugo of Mainz. This was the first official stand by a bishop against participation in Hitler's party. Bishop Hugo soon won the public support of both conferences of bishops. In a pastoral letter from the Bavarian bishops, Cardinal Faulhaber wrote on February 10, 1931, that "[t]he bishops as guardians of the true teachings of faith and morals must issue a warning about National Socialism, so long as and insofar as it maintains cultural-political views that are not reconcilable with Catholic doctrine."[5] In March, Cardinal Bertram, along with Cologne's Archbishop Karl Josef Schulte and the bishops of the upper Rhine, publicly agreed with Faulhaber's statement. Six months later, on August 17, Cardinal Bertram issued a pastoral letter on behalf of the Fulda bishops' conference that stated: "All ordinaries [bishops] have not permitted membership in this party because parts of its official program contain false teachings. . . . National Socialism actually stands in the most pointed contradiction to the fundamental truths of Christianity and with the institution of the Catholic church created by Christ."[6]

In their condemnations, Faulhaber and Bertram spoke for most Catholics. Although many Catholics lacked confidence in the

Weimar Republic, only one out of seven of them voted for the Nazi party in July 1932, whereas two out of five non-Catholics voted for Hitler's delegates in that same election.[7] Reflecting this consensus, many pastors refused communion to anyone who wore a Nazi uniform at mass, and some pastors even denied a Catholic burial to members of the Nazi party. Catholics stood united against National Socialism until 1933.

After Hitler became the chancellor on January 30, 1933, the bishops judged that they were required to reassess their political stance. They recognized that the Nazi leader had come to power by apparently legitimate means and assumed that he would henceforth voice more moderate political and religious views. Hitler himself seemingly indicated this shift when he promised in a national radio speech on February 1 to uphold Christian values. He and his vice chancellor, the Catholic Franz von Papen, also made it known that they wanted to establish amicable ties with the bishops and the Holy See. These political signals invited a softening of the church's opposition to National Socialism. If the church and the new government could attain a modus vivendi, they could work together to restore order in German society.

Germany seemed to be falling into chaos in 1933, as street riots between National Socialists and Bolshevists became more frequent and more violent. The Nazi party's Storm Troopers were even beating up prominent Catholics like Adam Stegerwald, a conservative leader of the Catholic Center party, because of his opposition to National Socialism. When fire destroyed the parliament building, or Reichstag, on February 27, Hitler pressured President Hindenburg into immediately issuing his Edict for the Protection of People and State, which in effect set aside the Weimar Constitution, thereby suspending all civil rights and making it legally possible for the chancellor to incarcerate his political opponents without judicial hearings. The Nazi terror was well under way by March. Given the strength of the National Socialist state, the bishops reconsidered their stance against membership in the Nazi party.

Catholics were still not ready, however, to give Hitler their political support. On March 5, the Nazi party won 40 percent of the votes in the national election for the Reichstag. This was substantially more than any other single party. But this political success had come about without the backing of Catholics: in the election, 5.5 million Catholics had voted for the Catholic Center party, while the remaining 7 million Catholics had divided their votes among the other seven political parties. In any case, the new government required that all employees of the civil service (e.g., school teachers, professors, railroad workers, postal clerks) belong to the Nazi party. This decree meant that Catholics in the civil service would lose their jobs if they continued to obey the ecclesiastical bans against Nazi membership, and the loss of their jobs would be disastrous, since one-third to one-half of the nation's work force was unemployed.[8]

Influential Catholic laity urged the bishops to reverse their stand against Hitler. Meeting with Cardinal Bertram on March 18, Vice Chancellor Papen argued that the church should drop its prohibitions against membership in the Nazi party and work with the new chancellor for the good of both the church and the nation. Papen was simultaneously establishing an association of wealthy Catholics, called *Kreuz und Adler* (Cross and Eagle), to knit ties between Catholicism and National Socialism; he formally founded it on April 3. During February and March, he was also likely involved in confidential discussions with Monsignor Ludwig Kaas, the leader of the Catholic Center party, about the possibility of a concordat between Rome and Berlin, an agreement that would give the church official protection while requiring the dissolution of the Catholic Center party. Kaas was a confidant of the Vatican's secretary of state, Cardinal Eugenio Pacelli, and knew that Pope Pius XI and Pacelli wanted to secure a treaty with Germany's national government.[9]

In his address to the parliament, or Reichstag, on March 23, 1933, Hitler himself reiterated his seemingly new respect for the Protestant and Catholic churches. Acknowledging that Christian belief is the "unshakeable foundation of the moral and ethical life of our people," he promised that he would honor the Holy See's concordats with individual German states, that he would maintain government support for church-related schools, that he would uphold religious education in the public schools, and that he would secure a good working relationship with the papacy.

After the chancellor's speech, the Reichstag passed the Enabling Act, thereby approving President Hindenburg's edict of February 28. In other words, the parliament formally set aside the Weimar Constitution and authorized a dictatorship.

In light of Hitler's speech of March 23 and the Reichstag's approval of the Enabling Act, the bishops urgently needed to clarify their stance toward the new government. On March 28, Cardinal Bertram announced that the bishops had dropped their prohibitions against Nazi membership. They had made their decision, Bertram explained, because of Hitler's public assurances of his respect for the church. Bertram wrote:

> It has now to be recognized that public and solemn declarations have been made by the highest representative of the national government, who at the same time is the authoritative leader of that movement, through which due acknowledgment has been made of the inviolability of Catholic doctrinal teaching and of the unchangeable tasks and rights of the Church. In these declarations the nationalist government has given explicit assurances concerning the validity of all provisions of the Concordats concluded by individual German states with the Church. Without repealing the condemnation of certain religious and moral errors contained in our earlier measures, the episcopate believes it may trust that the above-mentioned general prohibitions and warnings need no longer be considered necessary.[10]

With this announcement, the bishops reversed the position that they had publicly held for two years, thereby avoiding an overt confrontation with Hitler. They were now on record as willing to give the new chancellor a chance to show his trustworthiness. In withdrawing their earlier position, they neglected, however, to praise and thank the clergy and laity who had previously supported the episcopal bans against Nazi membership; nor did they insist that Hitler's regime protect these men and women from abuse by Storm Troopers. Moreover, they did not remind the government that it was expected to respect the human rights of all people, including Jews. The episcopacy remained silent when on April 1 the Nazi party called for a national boycott of Jewish businesses. It said nothing on April 7, when Hitler decreed the reorganization of the civil service with its "Aryan

Clause" excluding Jews from all employment related to the government. The bishops' decision on March 28 had, however, a significant consequence: it opened the way for a concordat between the Holy See and Hitler's government.

The bishops announced on April 6 that negotiations toward a concordat between the Holy See and Germany would soon begin in Rome. The next day, Vice Chancellor Papen and Reich Minister Hermann Göring headed to Rome and met Monsignor Kaas on the train. (It still remains unclear whether the meeting was planned.) Papen and Kaas started deliberations with Secretary of State Cardinal Eugenio Pacelli on April 10. When Pacelli was the Vatican's nuncio in Munich (1918–21) and then in Berlin (1921–29), he had included bishops, clergy, and laity in the deliberations for the concordats between the Holy See and the states of Bavaria (1925), Prussia (1929), and Baden (1932). But in April and May 1933, he worked out the details of a treaty in discussions only with Papen and Kaas, thereby following the centralized procedure used by Pius XI in his successful negotiations with Italy's fascist leader Benito Mussolini for the Lateran Treaty of 1929.

The bishops saw a draft of the Reich Concordat on May 30, 1933, when they assembled for a joint meeting of the Fulda bishops' conference and the Bavarian bishops' conference. Bishop Wilhelm Berning of Osnabrück and Archbishop Conrad Gröber of Freiburg—both of whom held favorable views of Hitler—presented the document to the bishops. In general, the bishops were inclined to endorse it, since they wanted to give the church legal protection and to stand in unity with Cardinal Pacelli and Pius XI. They expressed concerns, however, about the draft's sharp reduction of the church's social and political programs. Although they did not object to the dissolving of the Catholic Center party, they raised questions about the concordat's article 32 forbidding the clergy and members of religious orders from commenting on political and social issues. The strongest critics of the concordat were Cologne's Cardinal Karl Joseph Schulte and Eichstätt's Bishop Konrad von Preysing, who two years later became the bishop of Berlin. Schulte and Preysing pointed out that because the Enabling Act had established a dictatorship, the church lacked any legal recourse if Hitler failed to respect the concordat.

Nevertheless, the bishops approved the draft and delegated Gröber, who was a friend of Cardinal Pacelli and Monsignor Kaas, to present the episcopacy's concerns to Pacelli and Kaas. On June 3, the bishops issued a statement, which Gröber had drafted, that announced their support for the concordat and, while reiterating their love of Germany, also warned against the state's disregard for human rights and infringement on the church's rights.

During June 1933, Nazis waged a strong anti-Catholic campaign. In mid-June, they disrupted a national meeting in Munich of the Kolping Society—a Catholic organization devoted to assisting the poor—by assaulting its members on the street. They also attacked priests and Catholic lay leaders who had opposed the Nazi movement and vandalized the offices of Catholic newspapers, charitable organizations, and social clubs. In late June, the police imprisoned almost two thousand members of the Bavarian People's party, an affiliate of the Catholic Center party. They released these "political dissidents" only after the Bavarian People's party and the Center party permanently dissolved themselves in early July. Hoping that the concordat would prompt Hitler to end the Nazi persecution of Catholics, Vice Chancellor Papen and Secretary of State Pacelli made their final revisions of the concordat on June 30 and July 1, and Pope Pius XI approved it on July 2. After getting Hitler's endorsement, Papen and Pacelli signed it on July 20, and the pope ratified it on September 10.

The Concordat of 1933 gave the Holy See and the German government what each had set as high priorities.[11] It gave Pius XI the formal guarantees that he wanted in order to preserve the autonomy of ecclesiastical institutions and their religious activities. Article 14 recognized the church's authority to appoint pastors and bishops; article 21 authorized religious instruction in the public schools; and article 22 recognized the church's control over the Catholic schools. The concordat assured Hitler that the church would end so-called political Catholicism. Article 16 required bishops to make an oath of loyalty to the state. It read:

> Before God and the holy gospels I swear and promise loyalty, as befits a bishop, to the German Reich and the Land [state]. I swear

and promise to respect and cause my clergy to respect the legally constituted government. In dutiful concern for the welfare and interest of the German state, I shall in the exercise of my spiritual office labor to preserve it from any harm that might threaten it.[12]

The oath's significance was ambiguous; it remained unclear whether the bishops would violate their oath if, out of national loyalty, they publicly opposed the Nazi government's policies and actions. Article 31 acknowledged that while the church would continue to sponsor charitable organizations, it would not support political organizations or social and political causes. Article 31 was supposed to be supplemented by a list of protected Catholic agencies, but this list was never agreed upon. As a result, the bishops could not appeal to the concordat as the Reich eventually closed Catholic social organizations and charitable agencies. Since the Catholic Center party and Bavarian People's party had dissolved themselves in early July, they were not mentioned in the concordat. The concordat did not offer protection to Catholic newspapers, journals, and publishing houses. Finally, despite the concerns voiced by the bishops in late May, article 32 excluded clergy and the members of religious orders from political and social activities.

The signing of the Reich Concordat on July 20 brought no lessening of Nazi actions against the church organizations and their members. Storm Troopers continued to harass Catholic leaders, and, on July 14, the regime instituted its sterilization law, even though Cardinal Bertram protested that the law violated the church's teaching as formulated in Pius XI's encyclical *Casti Connubii* (December 31, 1930). Nevertheless, some prominent Catholics held that the concordat had secured the church's freedom in the Nazi state. Abbot Ildefons Herwegen, O.S.B., of Maria Laach Abbey had declared on May 26 that "[t]he people and the government were again being united through the activity of the leader Adolf Hitler."[13] He had his assessment reinforced on July 22, when Vice Chancellor Papen addressed the members of the Association of Catholic Academicians who had gathered at the abbey. Papen described the Reich Concordat as "the final conclusion of the Kulturkampf in Germany."[14] Within a year, Abbot Herwegen regretted his initial decision to support the new chancellor; he eventually had to go into hiding because of his public criticism of the Reich. Seeing the concordat as a victory in public relations, Hitler announced that the Holy See had formally recognized the Nazi state; he subsequently disregarded the concordat. Summarizing a speech by Hitler to Nazi officials, Joseph Goebbels publicly asserted on August 7, 1933: "We shall become a church ourselves."[15]

The Nazi persecution of Catholics intensified during the autumn of 1933, as Hitler pursued his goal of a "total state." The Bavarian bishops issued a public statement in November expressing their sorrow at the recent "events and decrees" and calling attention to the state's violations of the concordat. In December, Cardinal Faulhaber preached a series of Advent sermons at St. Michael's Church in Munich upholding both the Jewish origins of the Christian faith and the necessity of the Old Testament for Christian belief. In doing so, he implicitly opposed the teachings of the Protestant "German Christians" and the neopagan German Faith Movement, teachings that presented an "Aryan" Jesus. As 1933 came to an end, it was becoming clear that the bishops' two political decisions—the rescinding of the prohibitions against Nazi membership and the approval of the Reich Concordat—had not achieved what Pius XI, Cardinal Pacelli, and the bishops had intended.

The Church's Self-Understanding after Vatican I

The German bishops viewed Hitler's government within a theological horizon determined by the First Vatican Council (1869–70) and by the papal teachings from Gregory XVI (d. 1846) to Pius XI (d. 1939). In particular, they took for granted the ecclesial self-understanding contained in the notion of the church as a "perfect society."[16] The notion of a *societas perfecta* was used in Scholastic thought to describe autonomous or self-sufficient organizations such as the state and the church. As applied to the church, it conveyed the sense of the church as a medieval castle or Gothic church—like Cologne's cathedral—providing spiritual and moral security for all people within its walls amid society's rebel-

lion against divine and ecclesiastical authority. The theology of
societas perfecta had originated in Robert Bellarmine's *Disputationes de Controversiis Christianae Fidei adversus huius temporis
Haereticos* (1586–93), published at a time when Catholic leaders
sought to clarify the church's identity in response to the Protestant Reformation.[17] This ecclesiology gained greater specificity
during the nineteenth century as ecclesiastical officials defined
the church in relation to an increasingly secular society and to
governments committed to the separation of church and state.
The perfect-society ecclesiology was concisely expressed in the
first schema or draft of the Dogmatic Constitution on the Church
prepared for the First Vatican Council: "The Church has all the
marks of a true society. Christ did not leave this society unde-
fined and without a set form. Rather, he himself gave its existence, and his will determined the form of its existence and
constitution. The Church is not part nor member of any other
society and is not mingled in any way with any other society. It is
so perfect in itself that it is distinct from all human societies and
stands far above them."[18] Implicit in this statement is an understanding of the church as (1) a hierarchical institution that
(2) stands apart from modernity, (3) safeguards the truth by
means of neo-Scholasticism, and (4) prizes those governments
that establish Catholicism as the state's religion.[19]

During the early 1900s the dominant ecclesial self-understanding was reiterated by theologians like Bernhard Bartmann and
Ludwig Koester, S.J. Bartmann taught in 1911 that "Christ himself
founded the church, and to be sure as a visible, united, religious
community, clearly distinguished from all other communities
with the goal of realizing in itself the kingdom of God on earth."[20]
Koester explained in 1933 that "Jesus Christ himself had founded
the visible, religious society, under hierarchical . . . and monarchical authority," which is the church. The church is "the perfect
society, subordinate to no other, possessing its own supernatural
goal—God's kingdom—and its own means—the threefold powers (of sanctifying, teaching, and governing)."[21] These reflections
rely on the model of the church as a society or institution, that is,
as a formal association of men and women with a set of rules,

officeholders, and formal lines of decision making.[22] Four elements here require comment: the church's goal, its composition, its governance, and its status in the world.

The church's mission is to bring God's saving grace to all people, "to communicate to the ends of the earth the salvation for all people gained for us by Jesus Christ."[23] As Pius XI asserted in *Quas Primas* (December 11, 1925), the Catholic church is "the kingdom of God on earth" (art. 1).[24] Called to continue the work of Jesus Christ, the church is intent upon one task: the reconciliation of all men and women with God in Jesus Christ. People come to know and love Jesus Christ by participating in the church. According to Vatican I's schema on the church, "[i]t is an article of faith that outside the church no one can be saved. . . . Who is not in this ark will perish in the flood."[25] In Bartmann's words, "Membership in the church is necessary for all people who want to obtain salvation."[26] In the church, believers experience the "truth and grace, the teaching, and the sacraments," all of which are the means to salvation. Pastors lead believers to salvation by means of their "threefold powers" of administering the sacraments, teaching, and governing.[27]

The church's membership consists of two groups: the clergy and the laity. Vatican I's schema states that "the church of Christ is not a community of equals in which all the faithful have the same rights. It is a society of unequals, not only because among the faithful some are clerics and some are laymen, but particularly because there is in the church the power from God whereby to some it is given to sanctify, teach, and govern, and to others not."[28] This view is reiterated in the Code of Canon Law (1917): "By divine ordination, clergy and laity in the church are distinct" (canon 107). Through the sacraments and the gospel, the priests make the saving grace of Jesus Christ available to the laity. The laity do not directly participate in the church's mission or in its governance. They are the recipients of grace and benefit from the guidance and governance of the pope, bishops, and priests.[29] In sum, it was taught that the church possessed "a strong differentiation between the clergy and the laity, in which obedience to the hierarchy was required as *the* basic unifying and identifying ecclesiastical posture."[30]

The church's governance occurs from the top down. Jesus Christ himself organized the church to be a hierarchical, juridical institution. Indeed, the church is "the visible religious institution, under hierarchical . . . and monarchical authority."[31] St. Peter and his successors administer the believing community as a king governs a kingdom. Standing at the apex of the organizational pyramid, the pope speaks and acts for Christ. As taught by the First Vatican Council in *Pastor Aeternus* (July 18, 1870), the pope, empowered by God, teaches in faith and morals with infallibility when he formally chooses to do so, and in general he directs and instructs the bishops who in turn delegate their priests to act on the bishops' behalf. The relations and lines of authority in the church are determined by the Code of Canon Law.

The church is a wholly self-sufficient or self-contained institution in the world. Called into existence by Jesus Christ, it has only one allegiance, namely, to Christ in glory. As a consequence, it stands apart from the contemporary world and from all human authorities. This understanding was reiterated by several modern popes. In his *Syllabus of Errors* (December 8, 1864), Pius IX condemned the view that "the Church is not a true and perfect society, entirely free; nor is she endowed with proper and perpetual rights of her own, conferred upon her by her Divine Founder; but it appertains to the civil power to define what are the rights of the Church, and the limits within which she may exercise those rights" (art. 19).[32] Leo XIII declared in *Immortale Dei* (November 1, 1885) that the church is "a society chartered of divine right, perfect in its nature and in its title, to possess in itself and by itself, through the will and loving kindness of its Founder, all needful provision for its maintenance and action" (art. 10). Pius X maintained in *Pascendi Dominici Gregis* (September 8, 1907) that the so-called modernists had wrongly reduced the church to a human institution, dismissing its divine origins and subordinating it to civil society and the state: "What, then, is the Church [for the modernists]? It is the product of the *collective conscience*, that is to say of the society of individual consciences which by virtue of the principle of *vital permanence,* all dependent on one first believer, who for Catholics is Christ" (art. 23). In establishing the feast of Christ the King, Pius XI stated in *Quas Primas* that "the

Church, founded by Christ as a perfect society, has a natural and inalienable right to perfect freedom and immunity from the power of the state" (art. 31). The popes of the 1800s and early 1900s reinforced the idea that the church is a wholly autonomous institution that makes God's grace available to all people who stand within its walls.

The ecclesial self-understanding that operated among the German bishops in the early twentieth century came about during the 1800s in reaction to modernity. The modern epoch—which began with the Enlightenment, the American Revolution of 1776, and the French Revolution of 1789—shattered the symbiosis of church, state, and society.[33] Whereas the medieval and baroque periods took Christendom for granted, the period that began in the 1700s separated church and state and made society secular, that is, independent of the Christian faith. This secular age, with its emphasis on freedom, was condemned by the papacy from the early 1800s until the mid-1900s, and prompted popes to urge a return to medieval Scholasticism as presented by its baroque commentators. The papacy was intent upon a restoration of Christendom.

Modernity rests on a belief in personal freedom or emancipation.[34] It holds that human life should be marked by independence, by the absence of constraint or coercion upon individuals and communities by external authorities, whether the state or the church. It defines freedom as self-determination, that is, as the ability to reason, judge, and act for oneself. Representative of this belief is John Stuart Mill's *On Liberty* (1859), with its stress on individuality, on a person's continuing self-development. This idea of freedom, or personal autonomy, shapes modernity's understanding of human reason, the personal subject, and history. Human reason should enjoy free rein to inquire into all aspects of reality; every human being possesses a dignity and basic rights that demand the respect of society, the state, and the church; all human beings have the potential to improve their lives. These three aspects of the modern project are characterized, especially by their critics, as "subjectivism," "individualism," and "progress."

Although modernity has produced liberalism and modernism, it remains distinct from them. Liberalism is the mentality that "has favored a minimum of restrictions on individual liberty in private and public life, and defended a maximum of freedom for the individual in his social, economic, and religious existence and in his relations to the state."[35] It frequently opposes the church, which it regards as an opponent of personal independence. For this reason, it not only upholds the separation of church and state but also wants to abolish the church as an institution in the public realm so that religious belief becomes a wholly private or subjective matter. Modernism is the attitude that reduces all aspects of life to rational principles that the human mind is capable of knowing by its own powers.[36] As defined by Pius X in his encyclical *Pascendi Dominici Gregis*, modernism rests on a rejection of both metaphysics (especially proofs for God's existence) and the objectivity or supernatural character of divine revelation. It was associated with George Tyrrell, Friedrich von Hügel, and Maude Petre in England; with Alfred Loisy, Édouard le Roy, and Lucien Laberthonnière in France; and with Franz Xaver Kraus and Hermann Schell in Germany. The distinction between modernity, on the one hand, and liberalism and modernism, on the other, is important, because it was frequently overlooked by popes, bishops, and theologians prior to the Second Vatican Council (1962–65).

The popes from the early nineteenth century to the mid-twentieth century held that modernity itself is an act of human self-assertion in defiance of God and the church.[37] In his encyclical *Mirari Vos* (August 15, 1832), Gregory XVI attacked modernity by condemning the conviction

> that the liberty of conscience and of worship is the peculiar (or inalienable) right of every man, which should be proclaimed by law, and that citizens have the right to all kinds of liberty, to be restrained by no law, whether ecclesiastical or civil, by which they may be enabled to manifest openly and publicly their ideas, by word of mouth, through the press, or by any other means.[38]

Pius IX rejected in his *Syllabus of Errors* the idea that "[t]he Roman Pontiff can, and ought to, reconcile himself, and come to terms with progress, liberalism, and modern civilization" (art. 80); he also condemned religious freedom by denouncing the proposition that "[e]very man is free to embrace and profess that religion which, guided by the light of reason, he shall consider true" (art. 15). While Leo XIII spoke against the evils of modern society in his first encyclical, *Inscrutabili Dei* (April 21, 1878), he showed an openness to contemporary issues and ideas when he defended the rights of laborers in his encyclical *Rerum Novarum* (May 15, 1891). Pius X campaigned against modernism in his decree *Lamentabili Sane Exitu* as well as in his encyclical *Pascendi Dominici Gregis*, condemning the idea of faith as "religious sentiment" and theories on the development of doctrine. On September 1, 1910, he enforced his teachings by instituting the Oath Against Modernism (*Sacrorum Antistitum*), which was required of all clergy until Paul VI rescinded it in 1967. Benedict XV broke with his predecessors by taking a more benign view of modernity. In particular, he ended Pius X's antimodernist crusade in his first encyclical *Ad Beatissimi* (November 1, 1914), in which he also appealed for peace in the world. In trying to mediate world peace, Benedict XV advanced the model of the church as a moral advocate, while reinforcing the notion of the church as a hierarchical, juridical institution by approving the Code of Canon Law in 1917.[39] Pius XI presented in his first encyclical, *Ubi Arcano Dei* (December 23, 1922), a vision of the West moving toward a new Christendom and thereby overcoming secularism, liberalism, and communism; Pius XII maintained this vision as he tried to serve as a mediator for international peace. Nevertheless, Pius XII condemned the influence of modern ideas on theology in his encyclical *Humani Generis* (October 12, 1950).

The papacy's stance against the modern age gained support from neo-Scholasticism.[40] Beginning in the early 1800s, scholars such as Bruno Liebermann at Strasbourg and then at Mainz judged that the emphasis on independent reason, the knowing subject, and history threatened the intellectual foundations of Christian belief. Hence, they set out to provide an independent basis for Catholic thought by recovering the philosophical and theological wisdom of the medieval and baroque universities. By the mid-1800s this renewal of Scholasticism was under way throughout Europe under the leadership in Rome of the Jesuits Carlo Maria Curci, Matteo Liberatore, Serafino Sordi, and Luigi Taparelli. Drawing on scripture and tradition, especially papal teachings and the works of baroque theologians, the neo-Scholastic scholars assumed that these diverse sources contain a unified body of unchanging thought which they called after Leibniz the *philosophia perennis*.[41] It was further assumed that at the center of the "perennial philosophy" was the Thomism of Thomas Aquinas (d. 1274), Francisco Suarez (d. 1617), and John of St. Thomas (d. 1644). In his preparations for the First Vatican Council (1869–70), Pius IX relied on the work of the German theologian Joseph Kleutgen, S.J., who spoke for neo-Scholasticism when he declared that modernity is "an impudent revolt against authority."[42] Along with influencing Vatican I's constitutions *Dei Filius* and *Pastor Aeternus*, Kleutgen also wrote the first draft of Leo XIII's encyclical *Aeterni Patris* (1879) on Thomism as the foundation of philosophy and theology.

Neo-Scholasticism dominated Catholic thought until the Second Vatican Council. Writing in 1935, the medieval scholar Martin Grabmann defined neo-Scholasticism as

> that orientation that has emerged since the mid-nineteenth century and is usually found in Catholic theology and philosophy; it takes up again the traditional links with (medieval and baroque) ecclesiastical Scholasticism that were broken by the Enlightenment; it searches to make fruitful for contemporary problems the thought world of medieval Scholasticism, particularly that of Thomas Aquinas.[43]

This definition accurately calls attention to a merit of neo-Scholasticism, namely, its aim of remaining anchored in medieval thought, thereby giving clergy a sense of the church's identity.[44] It fails to note, however, the limitations of neo-Scholasticism that had become evident in the 1920s. Motivated by *Aeterni Patris*, scholars began to examine medieval and baroque texts and to note the divergences among them: for example, between the Neoplatonic orientation of Bonaventure and Duns Scotus, on the one hand, and the Aristotelian orientation of Thomas Aquinas, on the other. They also called attention to the differences between Aquinas himself and his baroque commentators. These studies eroded the assumption that the Christian tradition had generated a *philosophia perennis.*

Another limitation of neo-Scholasticism that emerged by the early 1900s was its inability to understand modernity and to make the wisdom of scripture and tradition available to twentieth-century minds.[45] Scholastic thought relied on a metaphysics of unchanging substances or essences, a metaphysics that dismissed both the notion of a person as a knowing subject located within a specific time and place, and also the idea of history as a changing reality that shapes human life and thought. Further, the Scholastic method required that scholars take up solely the classic or perennial questions in theology and that they answer them by means of fixed categories and the deductive method, derived from Aristotle's *Posterior Analytics.* In this endeavor, they employed propositions or theses that were generated in medieval and baroque theological texts. This method produced a "theology of conclusions" whose relevance to the church in the twentieth century remained unclear.[46] Romano Guardini noted in 1909 that neo-Scholasticism stifled Catholic intellectual life; because Guardini himself disregarded the scholastic method, he was not regarded as a significant theologian until after Vatican II.[47] Pinpointing how neo-Scholasticism distanced the church from modernity, Cardinal Walter Kasper has written, "Catholic theology barred itself for so long against a reception of modern thinking in theology, judging and rejecting modern anthropocentrism in highly critical terms as apostasy, a revolt against Christian theocentricism. Neo-Scholasticism, with its conservative mentality, was certainly incapable of taking up the positive intention of the modern era in a creative way."[48]

Thus, the theological horizon of the papacy and episcopacy in the early 1900s was determined by the notion of the church as a hierarchical institution, the rejection of modernity, and the reliance on neo-Scholasticism. Concomitantly, the ideal polity was seen as the confessional state in which Catholicism is the established religion. Shaken by the French Revolution of 1789 and its aftermath, Gregory XVI and his successors until John XXIII (d. 1963) promoted the restoration of unitary religious states throughout Europe similar to those formed after the Peace of Westphalia in 1648. In short, they opposed the emergence of a secular society and tended to see democracy as an expression of godlessness or as a fruit of Protestantism.[49] Determining the popes' view of the relationship between church and state was their interpretation of "the Gelasian dyarchy," the ancient papal teaching that "this world is ruled by two powers."[50] The Gelasian dyarchy is the understanding of the church–state relationship that was derived from the letter of Pope Gelasius I to Emperor Anastasius in 492. It holds that God entrusts spiritual or religious authority to the church, while simultaneously granting civil authority to the state with the intention that the church and the state will oversee their respective realms and cooperate with each other for the well-being of the people. Because of its responsibility for the supernatural realm, the church has superiority over the state in overlapping matters; in other words, it possesses "indirect power" over civil authority. As explained by Pius X in *Pascendi Dominici Gregis*, this principle holds that it is appropriate "to subordinate the temporal to the spiritual and to speak of some questions as *mixed*, allowing to the Church the position of queen and mistress in all such, because the Church [is] regarded as having been instituted immediately by God as the author of the supernatural order" (art. 24).

This interpretation of the Gelasian dyarchy manifested itself in papal teachings for over one hundred years. Gregory XVI in *Mirari Vos* condemned Félicité de Lamennais's calls for the separation of church and state and for religious freedom. The pope declared: "It is certain that that concord which always was favorable and beneficial for the sacred and civil order is feared by the shameless lovers of liberty" (art. 20). (Nevertheless, German Catholics at the Frankfurt National Assembly in 1848 pushed for the separation of church and state.) In his *Syllabus of Errors*, Pius IX condemned the propositions that "[t]he church ought to be separated from the state, and the state from the church," and that "it is no longer expedient that the Catholic religion should be held as the only religion of the state, to the exclusion of all other forms of worship" (art. 55, art. 77). In response to the question why the state should not grant legal protection to non-Catholic churches, Henré Sauvé, a French advisor at the First Vatican Council made a statement that subsequently held sway among church officials for almost one hundred years: "Error has no rights."[51] Although Leo XIII stated in *Immortale Dei* that the Catholic church could adapt to any political system, he wrote in *Longinqua Oceani* (January 6, 1895) to the U.S. bishops that American Catholicism would be richer if the Catholic church enjoyed the favor of the civil laws and promotion by the state. In *Pascendi Dominici Gregis*, Pius X condemned the view that "[t]he state must, therefore, be separated from the Church, and the Church from the citizen" (art. 24). While Benedict XV did not explicitly address the church–state issue, Pius XI made clear, when he established the feast of Christ the King in 1925, that government officials should "not neglect the public duty of reverence and obedience to the rule of Christ," including civil support for the Catholic church (*Quas Primas*, art. 18). Pius XII implicitly upheld the establishment of religion in his first encyclical, *Summi Pontificatus* (October 20, 1939), but he implicitly compromised it when he acknowledged the merits of parliamentary democracy in his Christmas message of 1944.[52]

The papacy's understanding of the Gelasian dyarchy in the 1800s and 1900s created both theoretical and practical dilemmas for the church. Church officials could not accept in theory any form of government that upheld religious freedom and the separation of church and state. For this reason, the popes and most European bishops remained suspicious of democracy with its political parties and consensus-seeking processes. At the same time, they opposed communism because of its avowed atheism and rejection of the church.[53] Having in principle dismissed both democracy and communism, the papacy found it difficult to specify what form of government it favored apart from a monarchy. In *Quadragesimo Anno* (May 15, 1931), Pius XI criticized capitalism and proposed "corporatism" as the way to remedy the world's economic ills. Was he proposing a possible third way, a kind of government that was neither democratic nor communist? Perhaps a form of socialism? It is not clear what Pius XI concretely meant by his notion of a corporate state.[54] He showed in his negotiations with Benito Mussolini for the Lateran Treaty that he was not uncomfortable negotiating with authoritarian regimes that conveyed a public respect for the church.[55] This political stance was noted by many Catholics. For example, influenced by *Quadragesimo Anno* and Pius XI's collaboration with Mussolini, some German Catholics such as the philosopher Josef Pieper (d. 1997) initially saw Hitler in 1933 as the political leader with whom Pius XI could build a new kind of corporate, or communal, society in Germany.[56]

On the level of day-to-day politics, however, the popes adjusted to social and political realities. They recognized that while they held the ideal (the "thesis") of the unitary religious state, they needed simultaneously to resign themselves to what could be realistically attained (the "hypothesis") in the actual situation.[57] Three specific ways in which this adaptation occurred are noteworthy. First, Leo XIII taught in *Rerum Novarum* that, given its respect for natural law, the church needed to promote just wages and a humane way of life for all people regardless of their religious beliefs. Further, Pius XI and Cardinal Pacelli negotiated concordats with governments that upheld the separation of church and state in order to secure legal guarantees for some of their specific commitments, for example, that the state should support Catholic schools and should not interfere in the church's appointment of bishops. Finally, Pius XI perceived that the laity should share in the church's mission by promoting Christian values in secular society with the ultimate aim of leading non-Christians to Christ and into the church. Such was the goal of Joseph Cardijn's Catholic Action movement, which Pius XI endorsed. Although these three concrete steps were inconsistent with the ideal of the church as the established religion, they enabled the church to cope with the political and social realities of the modern world.

The papacy's interpretation of the Gelasian dyarchy, and hence its uneasiness with democracy, only officially changed when Pope John XXIII issued his encyclical *Pacem in Terris* (April 11, 1963) and the Second Vatican Council adopted in 1965 its Pastoral Constitution on the Church in the Modern World (*Gaudium et Spes*) and its Declaration on Religious Liberty (*Dignitatis Humanae*). As a result of the work of John Courtney Murray, S.J.,

(d. 1967) and other theologians, the Gelasian dyarchy is now interpreted to mean that the Christian is both a child of God and a member of the human community as a citizen of the state; in each capacity he or she is endowed with a set of rights.[58] These teachings brought about a radical shift whereby today's popes and bishops view the church in relation to the contemporary world. But Pius XI, Pius XII, and the German bishops had previously espoused the theology of church that came to expression in the First Vatican Council's schema on the Dogmatic Constitution on the Church. Operating within the ecclesiology of *societas perfecta*, they ensured that the church "remained an overwhelmingly anti-democratic and inward-looking institution, intolerant of internal and external debate."[59]

The Theology in the Bishops' Political Decisions

The German bishops in 1933 had grown up during or shortly after Otto von Bismarck's Kulturkampf (1870–80) and amid the rise of imperial Germany as an international industrial giant. When Germany went to war in August 1914, these clerics were already priests and in some cases bishops, and they—along with most Germans—were shocked and saddened when Kaiser Wilhelm II and Bavaria's King Ludwig III abdicated their monarchies in November 1918. The bishops were middle-aged men when they had their first experience of parliamentary democracy, the Weimar Republic, and most were in their fifties or older when, in 1933, Hitler became Germany's chancellor at the age of forty-three. Cardinal Bertram, who headed the bishops' conference throughout Hitler's rule, was seventy-five in 1933 and was eighty-seven in 1945. The bishops' formal education was in the philosophy and theology of neo-Scholasticism; they became ecclesiastical leaders and skilled administrators through their pastoral service and informal apprenticeship to older, accomplished pastors and bishops. Although many bishops were trained in canon law, only Bishop Preysing had earned a diploma in German civil law. Along with most German Catholics, the bishops maintained two loyalties: the first to the papacy, which was at the zenith of its ecclesiastical power, and the second to the relatively new nation that Kaiser Wilhelm I and Bismarck had formed at Versailles out of the German states on January 18, 1871.[60]

When the German bishops reconsidered their stance toward Germany's National Socialist regime in the winter of 1933, they did so within the perfect-society ecclesiology. Faced with the issues of whether to rescind their bans against Nazi membership and then to approve the concordat, they operated in a conceptual framework determined by their notion of the church as a hierarchical institution, their distrust of democracy, and the ideal of Catholicism as the state's established religion. Moreover, they received little guidance from theologians because neo-Scholasticism had distanced these scholars from contemporary life and thought.

Decision making in the church moved away from the dioceses to the papacy during the 1800s and 1900s. Grounded in the ecclesiology of *societas perfecta*, Vatican officials gradually took control of the religious ideas and practices in dioceses around the world. This concentration of authority brought about uniformity of ecclesiastical teachings, conduct, and ritual amid the growing diversity of ideas and values in contemporary society. It meant, too, that the church presented a single, united defense against outside interference from civil governments; for example, in the selection of bishops and in the appointment of theology professors at universities.[61] This organizational form significantly influenced the German bishops' political actions during 1933.

The bishops' decision to change their positions on Nazi membership came about through their top-down process of governance. Even though they had publicly forbidden participation in the party since 1931, they reversed their stand on March 28, 1933, without soliciting the advice of clergy and laity. The bishops apparently discounted the election results of July 1932 and March 1933 that showed Catholics' antipathy to Hitler. Even if they had not carefully studied the election results, they likely knew "that the higher the proportion of Catholics in an electoral district, the lower tended to be the level of support for the [Nazi party]."[62] In any case, as a result of their reversal, they put in jeopardy those priests and lay leaders who—as pastors, directors of church organizations, editors of Catholic newspapers, and officials of political parties—had spoken out against Hitler.[63]

Accustomed to ecclesiastical authority, German Catholics accepted the bishops' decision to reverse their bans against Nazi membership. Many Catholics had lost confidence in the Weimar Republic because of the economic crisis and its attendant street violence and were looking for an alternative form of government. Nevertheless, a good number were demoralized by the bishops' announcement of their accommodation with Hitler, and some expressed their disagreement to their bishops.[64] The pastoral leader Konrad Algermissen reported to Cardinal Bertram on March 31 that "the announcement has not lifted the general depression of the past weeks 'but in many cases has given the impression of a yielding by the church.'" On April 10, Francis Stratmann, O.P., who was a chaplain to students in Berlin and the head of the German Catholic Peace Union, wrote to Cardinal Faulhaber: "The souls of the well-intentioned are deflated by the National Socialist seizure of power, and I speak nothing but the truth when I say that the bishops' authority is weakened among countless Catholics and non-Catholics because of their quasi-approbation of the National Socialist movement."[65] Some Catholic critics of National Socialism saw that their lives were now at risk and soon emigrated from Germany; among them were Waldemar Gurian, Dietrich von Hildebrand, and Hans A. Reinhold.

The bishops themselves did not, however, have the final say about the church in Germany, for they were subordinate to Pius XI and Cardinal Pacelli. In fact, they may have come under pressure from the Vatican during February and March 1933 to rescind their prohibitions against Nazi membership.[66] In any case, they found themselves in a secondary role during April and May while Cardinal Pacelli, Vice Chancellor Papen, and Monsignor Kaas negotiated the Reich Concordat. Having briefly discussed a draft of the concordat in its final stages, they were nevertheless responsible for implementing it. While the top-down leadership that shaped the church's stance toward Hitler is consistent with the model of the church as a hierarchical institution, it did conflict with Pius XI's principle of subsidiarity. In *Quadragesimo Anno*, the pontiff advocated decision making on the local level: "Just as it is gravely wrong to take from individuals what they can accomplish by their own initiative and industry and give it to the community, so also it is an injustice and at the same time a grave evil and disturbance of right order to assign to a greater and higher association what lesser and subordinate organizations can do" (art. 79). If Pius XI, Cardinal Pacelli, and the German bishops had followed the principle of subsidiarity in the winter of 1933, they, with the support of German Catholics, might have taken a stronger stand against Hitler.

The German bishops made accommodations with Hitler in part because they felt little loyalty to the Weimar Republic. They perceived Germany's first parliamentary democracy to be an embodiment of modernity, of a world in rebellion against God. Emerging out of the abdications of Wilhelm II and Ludwig III, the Weimar Republic manifested a spirit of personal autonomy and of self-determination that challenged centralized forms of civil and ecclesiastical decision making.[67] This spirit moved women to pursue independent lives, to attain diplomas at the universities, and to exercise their new right to vote in civil elections. It also opened German society to such Jews as Hugo Preuss, who drafted the Weimar Constitution, and Walther Rathenau, who served as its minister of reconstruction (1921) and then as its foreign minister until he was assassinated by nationalists in 1922. Because the Weimar Republic gave a public role to Jews, it was often called the Jewish Republic by nationalists. The Republic's social and cultural pluralism went contrary to the Idealist's vision of a unitary society.[68] The Republic's political leaders questioned the long-standing practice of the state providing Protestant and Catholic religious education in the public schools; they insisted that civil law should not provide a special status to the Protestant and Catholic churches. This official toleration of all religions offended the German bishops, who regarded it as implicitly a rebellion against God, the church, and even the German tradition.

Some bishops judged that the Weimar Republic had come about by illegitimate means, namely, the overthrowing of the monarchies of Kaiser Wilhelm and King Ludwig. Pope Gregory XVI had declared in his bull *Sollicitudo Ecclesiarum* (1831) that, while the church would cooperate with a new government after a revolution, it would not support a revolution as such because such action goes against legitimate civil authority and hence against God.[69] Furthermore, adhering to papal teachings, the bishops opposed the separation of church and state. They had expressed their opposition to it in a pastoral letter on November 1, 1917, one year before the end of the monarchies. In this same letter, they asserted that public schools should continue to provide religious education for the Protestant and Catholic churches. As Heinz Hürten has noted, it was not until after 1945 that the German bishops reconsidered the political philosophy expressed in their pastoral letter of 1917.[70]

Taking a positive view of the Weimar Republic, some influential lay Catholics publicly disagreed with the bishops in what came to be known as the "constitution controversy."[71] At the national Catholic conference (*Katholikentag*) of 1922 in Munich, Cardinal Faulhaber declared that the Weimar Republic was a "perjury and betrayal" because it had come about by the overthrow of the legitimate civil authorities, namely, the monarchies, and had incorporated in its constitution the separation of church and state. These remarks upset Catholics who were committed to the Weimar Republic and who were also aware that Faulhaber had praised the monarchy a few months earlier at the funeral of King Ludwig. Among these lay leaders was Cologne's forty-six-year-old mayor Konrad Adenauer (d. 1967). In an address to the entire assembly, Adenauer pointed out that the majority of Germany's Catholics supported democracy and, implicitly referring to Faulhaber's comments, said that "[t]he feelings of the moment should play no decisive role in civic life, even though they in themselves may be worthy of great respect."[72] The controversy about the constitution flared up again in 1930 at a gathering of Catholics at the University of Münster. After listening to participants' comments, Clemens August von Galen, who was the cathedral's pastor and the next bishop of Münster, sharply criticized democracy because of its separation of church and state. In response, Josef Mausbach, S.J., (d. 1931), a professor of Catholic ethics, publicly argued for the validity of democracy. He pointed out that the Weimar Republic respected the church's autonomy and that it was in fact allowing Catholics to attain the economic, social, and educational objectives that they had pursued with little success during the reign of Kaiser Wilhelm II.[73]

If the German bishops could not in principle support a parliamentary democracy, what form of government did they prefer? They opposed communism, especially as realized in Stalin's Bolshevism. They also distrusted socialism and became alarmed in 1918 when Prussia's Socialist party called for the separation of church and state in the new Germany. Moreover, they were shocked by what occurred in Bavaria in 1919. After dethroning King Ludwig III in November 1918, Kurt Eisner had established a socialist republic and made himself its prime minister. After Eisner was assassinated on February 21, 1919, a communist revolution broke out in April. During a tumultuous few weeks, the revolution's leaders closed churches and parochial schools. At one point, a group broke into the residence of the Vatican's nuncio, Monsignor Eugenio Pacelli, and held him at gunpoint. The rebellion was violently suppressed by the German army and Free Corps, and a democratic government was established that brought Bavaria into the Weimar Republic. This traumatic experience strengthened the conviction of the bishops and Pacelli that neither a democratic nor a socialist state could withstand communism, only an authoritarian state could stop the "red tide."[74]

The papacy and the German episcopacy judged in 1933 that their first responsibility was to defend the church against Hitler. They held that since Jesus Christ had established the church as a self-sufficient institution with the mission of bringing divine grace to the faithful, the church's leaders are responsible for safeguarding this institution for the salvation of God's people. As José Sánchez has noted, Pius XI and Pius XII were clear about a pope's "first obligation": "As head of an institutional church, he is charged with protecting that church; according to Catholic theology, the Church is the necessary means of providing the sacraments which give the grace needed for salvation. Without the priests to administer the sacraments and the freedom to receive them, Catholics can be hindered in their search for salvation."[75] Standing beside the papacy, bishops had this same obligation to preserve the church. Hence, Pius XI, Cardinal Pacelli, and the German episcopacy were intent on ensuring that the state would not close parishes and imprison pastors, as it had during the Kulturkampf, and they wanted to secure the state's support for Catholic schools and for religious instructions in public schools. All of these aims were promised in the Reich Concordat.

In his comments on the concordat, Cardinal Pacelli stated on July 27, 1933, that "the Code of Canon Law is the foundation and essential legal presupposition of the concordat." The concordat involved "not only official recognition [by Germany] of the legislation of the Church, but also the adoption of many provisions of this legislation and the protection of all Church legislation."[76] In arranging the treaty between Rome and Berlin, the Vatican secretary of state was fulfilling his duty of providing German Catholics with the sacraments and religious instruction. Two weeks later, in mid-August, Pacelli explained to the British minister to the Vatican, Ivone Kirkpatrick: "The spiritual welfare of twenty million Catholic souls in Germany was at stake and that was the first and, indeed, only consideration" in agreeing to the concordat. The Holy See "had to choose between an agreement on Nazi lines and the virtual elimination of the Catholic Church in the Reich."[77]

The Theologians and Hitler

Theologians serve the believing community by mining the wisdom of the Bible and the Christian tradition and by making it available to the church as it seeks to be true to its identity and mission in various cultural, social, and political situations.[78] Nineteen faculties or departments of Catholic theology existed in Germany in 1933.[79] Seven of these faculties were within universities, namely, the universities of Bonn, Breslau, Freiburg, Münster, Munich, Tübingen, and Würzburg. Twelve departments of

Catholic theology belonged to academies or schools, "Hochschulen," which housed solely faculties of philosophy and theology. These schools were located in Augsburg, Bamberg, Braunsberg, Dillingen, Eichstätt, Frankfurt, Freising, Fulda, Mainz, Paderborn, Passau, and Regensburg. During the Weimar Republic, the number and size of faculties of Catholic theology had increased because the Catholic Center party had pressured the government into opening higher education to minorities. The nineteen theology departments in 1933 held a total of approximately two hundred regular professors, more than one hundred instructors, and about four thousand students.[80] Twelve years later, when Nazi Germany surrendered to the Allied powers, sixteen of the original nineteen faculties were still functioning, though with almost no students. The Reich's minister of education, Bernhard Rust, had shut down the University of Munich's faculty of Catholic theology in 1938, and the war on Germany's eastern front had closed the academy at Braunsberg and the University of Breslau.[81]

Most of the professors of Catholic theology offered few ideas in public on how the church should relate to Hitler. They addressed the classic questions of the medieval and baroque texts by means of Scholastic categories and the Scholastic method of deduction. Even when scholars like Bernhard Bartmann at Paderborn modified the conventional method to include a history of church teachings, they generally stayed within the scope of topics determined by medieval and baroque Scholasticism. They assumed that they were investigating a subject matter that had no immediate relevance to current events and ideas and that there were essentially no fresh questions and hence no new answers in the church's reflection on God's revelation as known in the Bible and the Christian tradition.[82] Thus, the majority of theologians remained silent in the face of Nazism.

As institutional units, the nineteen faculties of Catholic theology adopted an ambiguous stance toward the Third Reich. On the one hand, they acquiesced as the Reich's minister of education dismissed colleagues who had been active in the Catholic Center party or were Jewish by race. On the other hand, the majority of theologians remained impervious to Nazi ideology.

Of the two hundred or so professors of Catholic theology in 1933 fewer than ten became members of the Nazi party. Committed to Christian belief, they were not drawn to the National Socialist rhetoric about Hitler as Germany's savior and about Jews as the embodiment of evil. For this reason, Nazis such as Hitler's assistant, Martin Bormann, looked forward to the day when the Reich would close the faculties of Catholic theology. The fact that sixteen faculties of Catholic theology were still functioning in 1945 attested to the church's institutional resistance to the totalitarian state.

However, not all theologians remained silent about Hitler's regime. After the bishops announced on April 6, 1933, that Cardinal Pacelli, Vice Chancellor Papen, and Monsignor Kaas were negotiating a concordat in Rome, some theologians spoke out in support of collaboration between the church and the Nazi state, while others urged caution.[83] Those who favored a rapprochement came to be known as the bridge builders, for they looked for points of contact between Catholicism and National Socialism. Among these scholars were Karl Eschweiler, who taught fundamental theology at Braunsberg in east Prussia; Joseph Lortz, who was a church historian also at Braunsberg; and Karl Adam, who lectured in dogmatic theology at Tübingen. Other theologians were publicly critical of Hitler and paid a personal price for their dissension. Among these men were Romano Guardini, who taught Catholic thought at Berlin, and Engelbert Krebs, who taught dogmatic theology at Freiburg. As a result of their opposition to the Reich, both were eventually dismissed from their professorships by the minister of education.

Those theologians who spoke out—whether for Hitler or against him—shared one conviction that was not held by their neo-Scholastic colleagues. They believed that theology must somehow be explicitly engaged in the issues and ideas of the day. Influenced by the renewal movements in scripture and liturgy and by the youth programs of the 1920s, these scholars took an interest in contemporary thought. In short, they were relatively progressive theologians in a day when "Catholic theology understood itself . . . not in terms of modern science, the Enlightenment, historical consciousness, and democratic revolution but in terms of the defense against modernity."[84] Eschweiler, Lortz, Adam, Guardini, and Krebs agreed that theology should not take a wholly defensive position toward the twentieth century. Was it their very openness to modernity that disposed some theologians to support Hitler in 1933? In recent years, some commentators have noted that progressive theologians were attracted to the Third Reich. With varying degrees of emphasis, these scholars have observed that the theological effort to reconcile the Catholic church and the Third Reich was undertaken mostly by the so-called liberal theologians.[85] This claim is, however, too sweeping. Analysis shows that some of the theologians who urged the church's accommodation with Hitler were liberal or progressive in that they adopted a theological orientation outside of neo-Scholasticism, but they were simulatenously reactionary in that they disdained modernity, including democracy. They envisioned Hitler bringing about what Hugo von Hofmannsthal (d. 1929), the Austrian dramatist and poet, had called the "conservative revolution."[86]

2

Karl Eschweiler

Claiming the Church's Authority

THE THEOLOGIAN KARL ESCHWEILER PUBLICLY PROMOTED
cooperation between the church and Hitler's regime beginning in
the spring of 1933. After the German bishops had dropped their
bans against membership in the Nazi party and announced that
the Holy See and the Reich were negotiating a concordat, he published an article entitled "Die Kirche im neuen Reich," in which
he argued that Catholicism and National Socialism should work
together for the regeneration of Germany.[1] Eschweiler was
widely respected in academic circles. Seven years earlier, in 1926,
he had sparked a lively discussion among theologians concerning human knowledge of God in his book *Die zwei Wege der
neueren Theologie* [The Two Ways of the New Theology], which
represented for its time "the most basic and stimulating effort" in
fundamental theology.[2] He disappointed many of his colleagues,
however, when he came out in support of Hitler.

Karl Eschweiler was born on September 5, 1886, in Euskirchen,
near Cologne.[3] Desiring to become a priest, he studied at
Cologne's seminary and then at the University of Munich, where
he earned a doctorate in philosophy in 1909. He wrote his dissertation on the aesthetic elements in St. Augustine's philosophy of
religion.[4] He returned to the seminary and was ordained a priest
for the Archdiocese of Cologne in 1910. After a few years in
parish ministry, he undertook full-time doctoral studies in theology at the University of Bonn.

During the Weimar Republic, the University of Bonn was a
center for Catholic scholars with "progressive ideas."[5] Some of
these men resided in or near Bonn, while others frequently came

31

to the city to participate in conferences and discussions. There were almost a dozen creative scholars with whom Eschweiler would have come into contact. Alois Dempf (d. 1982), a professor of philosophy, specialized in the philosophy of history and became a sharp critic of National Socialism. Albert Ehrhard (d. 1940), a professor of patristics at Bonn from 1920 to 1927, concentrated on the history of ideas and also criticized Nazism. He had ignited a controversy in 1902 with his book *Der Katholizismus und das zwangzigste Jahrhundert im Licht der kirchlichen Entwicklung der Neuzeit* [Catholicism and the Twentieth Century in Light of the Ecclesial Development in Modern Times], in which he argued that "there is no absolute contradiction between Catholicism and the modern world."[6] Because of this thesis, he was viewed with suspicion by church authorities. Romano Guardini, to whom we turn in chapter 5, wrote his Habilitationsschrift (second doctoral dissertation) at Bonn from 1920 to 1923; he had previously won international recognition for his well-known book *The Spirit of the Liturgy* (1918). He too became a critic of Hitler. Waldemar Gurian (d. 1954), a Jewish convert to Catholicism, was an independent scholar intent on bringing about a mutually beneficial exchange between Christian belief and modernity; he vigorously opposed such right-wing movements as Integralism and the Action Française. An outspoken critic of Nazism, he fled to Switzerland in 1934 and then emigrated to the United States in 1937.[7] Gottfried Hasenkamp (d. 1990) was an accomplished poet and an editor at Aschendorf publishing house in Münster. Paul Ludwig Landsberg (d. 1944) was a professor of medieval philosophy at Bonn. A convert to Catholicism, he was incarcerated by the Gestapo because of his Jewish race and died at the Oranienberg concentration camp. Karl Muth (d. 1944) was the Munich editor who in 1903 founded the journal *Hochland*, dedicated to bringing about a conversation between Catholicism and contemporary culture, especially world literature and the arts. Wilhelm Neuss (d. 1965) was a professor of church history at Bonn and a leader in the Catholic scholars' resistance to Hitler. Erik Peterson (d. 1960), a convert from Protestantism to Catholicism, became a professor of theology at Bonn in 1922. Bonn's philosopher Hermann Platz (d. 1945) reflected on culture, especially Romanticism. Carl

Schmitt (d. 1985), a professor of law at Bonn and then Berlin, specialized in constitutional law and eventually became a legal advisor to the Third Reich.

Karl Eschweiler apparently valued Bonn's progressive spirit in scholarship. In his doctoral dissertation of 1920 on theological rationalism from the Enlightenment to the [First] Vatican Council, he argued that the modern turn to the knowing subject in the work of Descartes had also occurred in the writings of baroque theologians like Francisco de Suárez, S.J., and John de Lugo, S.J.[8] In 1922 he completed his Habilitationsschrift on the Enlightenment theologian Johann Michael Sailer, S.J., who brought Catholic thought into a creative dialogue with such thinkers as Christian Wolff, Leibniz, and Kant. Concentrating on human knowledge of God, he maintained that Sailer's "experiential theology" had fostered "fideism in pre-conciliar theology."[9]

Remaining at the University of Bonn as an instructor, Eschweiler wrote on various themes in foundational theology. He published an article in 1922 on the phenomenology of religious experience as developed by Max Scheler (d. 1928) in his book *On the Eternal in Man* (1921). According to Eschweiler, while Scheler correctly distinguished between religious belief and metaphysics, he failed to highlight the rational character of Christian faith. The act of faith is an assent of the mind as well as of the heart, as is evident in the work of Thomas Aquinas.[10] In 1924 Eschweiler examined "the crisis of the neo-Scholastic philosophy of religion." Drawing on a similar analysis by the progressive scholar Erich Przywara, S.J. (d. 1972), he maintained that Catholic scholars needed critically to engage modern ideas.[11] Turning in 1925 to the plight of the "natural man" in industrial society, Eschweiler explained that, although twentieth-century men and women find themselves burdened by society's complexity and functionalism, they still have a deep-seated desire for "truth and faith," as manifested when they gather to celebrate marriages, anniversaries, and holidays. This innate longing for a transcendent reality and rich human experience is the starting point for God's grace in people's lives. In the words of St. Thomas Aquinas, "grace does not destroy nature but rather perfects it." As people attain healthier, fuller lives, they are more and more disposed to God.[12] Eschweiler eventually appealed to this idea in his attempt to build a bridge between Catholicism and National Socialism.

Eschweiler gave a public lecture at the University of Bonn in 1925 that germinated into his most important contribution to the theology of his day. Speaking in the University's series of events celebrating a millennium of Western civilization in the Rhineland, he analyzed two contemporary forms of theology that he saw evident in the works of Georg Hermes (d. 1831) and Matthias Scheeben (d. 1888), both of whom had been priests in the Archdiocese of Cologne. Hermes, who was a professor at Bonn, had employed the ideas of Kant and Fichte in his treatment of the rational character of Christian faith. While not denying the supernatural origins of belief, he tried to show the intellectual preconditions of assent to divine revelation. He did not live to see the publication of his three-volume *Christkatholische Dogmatik* (1834–35), which the Holy Office condemned in 1835 because of its alleged semi-rationalism.[13] Whereas Hermes drew on the ideas of his day for his theological inquiries, Scheeben relied on the work of Thomas Aquinas as presented by the baroque theologian Dionysius Petavius (d. 1652). Teaching at Cologne's seminary, Scheeben focused on the supernatural basis of faith by explaining that faith begins as the human heart trusts in God, and also that Christians make their act of belief within the church. Scheeben explored these themes in his books *Nature and Grace* (1861) and *The Mysteries of Christianity* (1865). According to Eschweiler, Hermes and Scheeben represented two distinct ways of doing theology in the twentieth century, ways that Eschweiler proposed be combined into a third way.

This lecture was so well received that Eschweiler developed it into his book *Die zwei Wege der neueren Theologie*. According to Eschweiler, the work of St. Thomas as interpreted by his baroque commentators confirms "the spirit of modernity in Catholic theology."[14] The turn to the subject which began with Descartes was implicit in the baroque scholasticism of Suarez, Petavius, and de Lugo, especially in their tracts on faith. What came about in the Enlightenment had already occurred in Scholasticism, namely, a recognition of the role of the human intellect in all knowledge. In other words, "the self-conscious person who characterizes the modern period has been at work also in Catholic theology. Such a person has plunged into modernity not from the outside, somehow through the Reformation or the Enlightenment. Rather this person has matured to [the recognition of the knowing subject] through scholastic theology."[15] It is possible, therefore, to reconcile Catholicism and modernity. While the two outlooks on life differ in their understanding of the relationship between faith and reason, they could move toward each other if they appreciated St. Thomas's understanding of the relationship between nature and grace. Catholicism can support modernity's emphasis on attaining full human life, but it sees that life in relation to God's saving activity. Men and women are capable of responding to God because God has freely given them the *potentia oboedientialis*, the potential to respond in faith to the divine overture. This encounter with God involves an assent of the human mind and heart empowered by grace. Hermes highlighted the role of the mind, and Scheeben stressed the importance of the heart. A theology is needed that unites the emphases of Hermes and Scheeben. In making this point, Eschweiler also criticized Luis de Molina, S.J., (d. 1600) for accentuating the role of human free will in the knowledge of God to the neglect of the role of grace.

Eschweiler also clarified that Hermes and Scheeben worked out two separate "ways" of doing theology. Hermes fashioned a contemporary account of Christian belief, for he tried to show the reasonableness of faith in God. Beginning with a deliberate act of "imaginative doubt," he argued on the basis of man's intellectual inquisitiveness that human questioning eventually leads to the question of God's existence. Hermes's method is "the way of apologetic self-consciousness," which brackets the act of faith and highlights the capabilities of the human intellect in search of the truth. While Hermes developed a "theology of critical reason," Scheeben crafted a "theology of faith."[16] That is, he located the act of faith—and hence knowledge of God—primarily in volitional assent and only secondarily in intellectual assent. In his view, although belief engages the mind, it originates in the heart. Christian faith is similar both to the trust of children in their parents and also to the love between spouses. Faith and theology are anchored in trust and simultaneously draw on the intellect to clarify what the heart already intuits. This trust is not blind, however, since it occurs in response to God as known in the church. Recognizing the limits of the human mind, faith and theology acknowledge both God's authority and the church's authority. In sum, Scheeben's method is "the way of dogmatic self-consciousness."

The reconciliation of Hermes's "apologetic consciousness" and Scheeben's "dogmatic consciousness" could come about, Eschweiler argued, by beginning with Scheeben's starting point, namely, the act of faith in God as known in the church. A person encounters God through a self-surrender in response to grace. Still this trust in God is not irrational, as it involves the mind as well as the heart. True faith is "the natural and normal fulfillment" of a person's yearning for God. It begins with the *potentia oboedentialis*. This potential involves the whole human being and requires the use of the intellect to shed light on faith's object, God. Thus, reason operates within the relationship that faith establishes between the believer and God. Furthermore, this faith is possible only within the church: "The universal and absolute consciousness of faith . . . is the one, holy, catholic and apostolic church. This is the 'basic experience,' out of which scholarly theology thinks and acknowledges [God]."[17]

Die zwei Wege der neueren Theologie prompted a debate among theologians concerning the experiential, rational, and volitional aspects of faith. It also sparked a reconsideration of Molinism, the seventeenth-century theory that stressed the role of human free will in response to grace.[18] These discussions failed to note, however, that this book was idiosyncratic. That is, although Eschweiler appealed to the thought of Thomas Aquinas, he made in fact only a limited number of references to the Angelic Doctor's texts. Moreover, he worked apart from the Thomists of the late 1800s and early 1900s. For example, he did not cite the transcendental Thomists such as Joseph Maréchal, S.J., and Pierre Rousselot, S.J. Although he occasionally referred to the writings of Ambrose Gardeil, O.P., Reginald Garrigou-Lagrange, O.P., and Jacques Maritain, he did not consistently engage their respective works. He was most dependent on Scheeben's understanding of

Thomas Aquinas, and with Scheeben he stressed that faith involves trust in ecclesiastical authority.[19] This stress on religious authority may have led to Eschweiler's emphasis on civil authority.

On Church and State

In 1928 Karl Eschweiler was appointed to the faculty of theology at Braunsberg in Prussia (now Kaliningrad, Russia). Although he wanted to reside in the Rhineland, he could not refuse the opportunity to become a professor of apologetics and dogmatic theology, albeit at a Hochschule close to Germany's eastern border. Given his studies in philosophy, he likely appreciated his proximity to the University of Königsberg, which is where Kant had taught. Separated from the Archdiocese of Cologne, he was now affiliated with the Diocese of Ermland, whose center was Frauenberg. Today, what was the Diocese of Ermland is divided into Russia's Diocese of Kaliningrad and Poland's Dioceses of Elbalg (Elbing) and of Lyck (Elk). Braunsberg's Hochschule in philosophy and theology had been established by the Jesuits in 1565 in order to provide diocesan seminarians with the education required by the Council of Trent (1545–1563).[20] The academy was taken over by the Prussian state in 1811 as part of its secularization program. Ten years later, it again became a Hochschule for Catholic seminarians, thanks to the efforts of Bishop Joseph von Hohenzollern. Henceforth, the school's professors and administrators were formally accountable both to the Prussian state and to the Diocese of Ermland. In 1919, the school was named the Staatliche Akademie.

At the academy, Eschweiler pursued the theme of authority that he had explored in *Die zwei Wegen der neueren Theologie*.[21] In 1930 he published *Johann Adam Möhlers Kirchenbegriff: Das Hauptstück der katholischen Auseinandersetzung mit der deutschen Idealismus* [Johann Adam Möhler's Notion of the Church: The Cornerstone of the Catholic Dialogue with German Idealism], in which he argued that according to Möhler (d. 1838) the church is an objective reality similar to the state.[22] In Eschweiler's judgment, beginning with the Enlightenment, theologians had not upheld this notion of the church. Either they did not grasp modernity's skepticism about the church because they were influenced by Scholasticism, or they relied on the categories of Kant or Schleiermacher, which reduced the church to a mere way of life or spiritual communion that deemed it a subjective matter. Möhler himself had accentuated the church's subjectivity or personal character in his book *Unity in the Church* (1825). Stressing that the Holy Spirit unites believers in the body of Christ, he did not expound on the church's objective character as expressed in its doctrines, liturgy, and institutional structures. However, Möhler remedied this inadequacy in his *Symbolism* (1832), in which he emphasized that the church is "the ongoing incarnation" of Jesus Christ. It is the divine-human institution in which Jesus Christ is present and active in history, and in which Christ's authority is exercised.[23]

According to Eschweiler, Möhler used categories derived from Hegel in order to stress the church as an ontological reality. Whereas Hegel spoke of the state as God's objective manifestation and the church as his subjective manifestation, Möhler argued that the church exists on a par with the state. "That the state and the church are two distinct and in themselves independent realms in one ethical reality . . . was not doubted by Möhler," as Eschweiler put it.[24] The state and the church should exercise authority in their respective arenas, and simultaneously they should respect and reinforce each other's authority (the Gelasian dyarchy). Moreover, since the authority appropriate to the state cannot be secured in a democracy, the nation needs to be sovereign in a highly structured society. In this polity, the church should uphold the state's authority: "the task of the individual as well as the church is to obey the legitimate (civil) authorities." The church should support this shift from democracy to an authoritarian state. "Accommodation to such changes in the state and society should occur as long as they do not attack the essence of the church." At the same time, the new state should respect the church. That is, it should demonstrate "a receptivity to and acceptance of the ongoing Christ [in the church]." If these conditions were met, the state and the churches could work together for the well-being of the "extended empire [*Reich*]."[25]

In his essay "Politische Theologie" (1931), Eschweiler reflected further on the church–state relationship. Drawing on Carl Schmitt's book *Politische Theologie* (1922), he asserted that political theology should not focus on human rights or on conscience as it does in the "vague theology of liberalism."[26] Political theology should instead emphasize that the relationship between church and state rests on the principle that the church has received authority from God to care for the spiritual realm, while the state possesses authority from God to govern the civil arena. According to Schmitt, this division between religious and civil authorities is conveyed in the Gospel when Pilate interrogates Jesus and asks, "What is truth?" (John 18:38). With this question, Pilate has implicitly recognized the limit of the state in relation to true religious authority. The state cannot answer the question, What is ultimate truth? It must respect the church's answer to this question. "It is crucial that the state poses daily and officially [to the church] the question of Pilate. This is the victory of the truth revealed in Christ for the state. In relation to this truth, the Enlightenment and political liberalism, along with their dangerous errors and effects, must be regarded as rubbish."

This "political theology" also showed that the constitution of the Weimar Republic was seriously flawed, since article 137 on religious freedom declares that "there exists no state church." In particular, the article grants freedom to all "religious organizations," that is, to all organizations "that have as their mission the communal cultivation of a world view." This, of course, misrepresents the churches by including them in a vacuous category of social groups. While some organizations may promote a noble ideal, Eschweiler maintained, the Protestant and Catholic churches witness to God's revelation. Moreover, groups such as the Freemasons are often intent on gaining influence over the state, whereas the church recognizes the appropriate autonomy of civil authority. Article 137 should be changed so that the constitution, differentiating between the divine and human organizations, recognizes the unique public status of the churches in German society.

Finally, political theology must affirm that, according to the Gelasian dyarchy, the church possesses "indirect power in the temporal realm." While the state is ultimately accountable to

God, it is indirectly accountable to the church as God's proper representative on earth. The church does not stand at odds with the state but in fact cooperates with it so that civil authorities and religious authorities fulfill their divinely determined roles. The Catholic view of this complementarity rests on Thomas Aquinas's theology of nature and grace. Just as nature and grace do not compete with each other but work together, so too the state and the church are not meant to compete with each other but to work together in God's presence. The state must acknowledge that both civil authority and ecclesiastical authority come from God. In this regard, the Gospel is again instructive. Jesus tells Pilate: "You would have no power over me if it were not given to you from above" (John 19:11). Therefore, if Germany is to flourish, its civil leaders must acknowledge that because their authority ultimately comes from God, they must be accountable to the church.

Toward an Authoritarian State

Karl Eschweiler reflected in the late 1920s on ecclesiastical and civil authority while Germans were looking for stronger political leadership. They wanted a more authoritarian state in part because the Wall Street crash of October 1929 had devastated their economy. Loans from the United States and elsewhere had been withdrawn from the Weimar government and German businesses. Unemployment rose from 1.3 million in September 1929 to over 3 million by September 1930. By the end of January 1933—when Hitler was named the nation's chancellor—over 6 million Germans were unemployed, one-third of the work force. Germans remembered the harsh conditions of the postwar period, when families lived on the streets and died of hunger. Exploiting this situation in the early 1930s, Communists and Nazis held public demonstrations often accompanied by street violence, and the Weimar Republic seemed powerless amid this economic, social, and political chaos.

Amid the crisis of the late 1920s and early 1930s, Catholic intellectuals proposed partial or even drastic changes in the Weimar

Constitution. Karl Muth in *Hochland* observed that the Weimar Republic could overcome its paralysis only by somehow extending "its roots into the ground of ethics and religion."[27] The moral theologian Gustav Gundlach, S.J., observed in May 1932 that the Weimar Constitution needed a major revision so that democracy could survive in Germany.[28] The theologian Kurt Ziesche asserted that Christians should urge government leaders to resist liberalism and deliberately promote Christian values in German society.[29] The political commentator Friedrich Muckermann, S.J., called for the reestablishment of some form of the Holy Roman Empire (*Reich*) in which the state and the churches would work together. In his judgment, this kind of polity was so much a part of Germany's history and culture that it was needed once again.[30] Muckermann struck a deep chord among Germans who longed for a return to the political and juridical structure that had existed in Germany until 1806, when it was officially dissolved by the Austrian emperor Francis I. Napoleon had demanded in 1803 that the three hundred German states be reorganized into larger units and also be secularized so that the Protestant and Catholic churches would not have legal control over schools, libraries, farms, and vineyards. Since the crisis of the Weimar Republic seemed to result from the ethnic, moral, and religious diversity of democracy, some Germans judged that the crisis would be remedied only by an authoritarian state in which the churches were given an official status. They even promoted a *Reichstheologie*, a religious theory according to which German people were being called by God to form a polity reuniting the state and the churches and dedicated to bringing about a moral revival in the West.[31]

Catholic voices calling for a new Holy Roman Empire reached a crescendo as Hitler became the nation's leader. Damasus Winzen, O.S.B., at Maria Laach Abbey, wrote that "the themes—leadership, organic and universal solidarity, and national effort—manifested an emergent sense of a new Reich." He added: "If they are grasped and lived by the German people, they can mean the overcoming of the French revolution. . . . The decisive victory of the German idea of Reich will however depend on whether these three themes resolutely lead back to their ultimate ground in the living God."[32] Robert Grosche, a progressive theologian and chaplain at the University of Cologne, argued that since the Christian tradition generated the idea of close cooperation between church and state, it reinforced the idea of a "Third Reich." Catholics could "work toward the construction of this state without a false anxiety about a totalitarian state. Indeed, this polity could be the outcropping of God's kingdom if it were a state of genuine authority and genuine values."[33] The essayist Albert Mirgeler also maintained that Germans needed to reverse the French Revolution of 1789 by restoring the Holy Roman Empire. A new empire could come about only if political parties were eliminated and the national government took a greater control of the fragmented German states.[34] These Catholic proponents of an authoritarian government were neither Nazis nor committed to Hitler's rule; most saw his regime as a transitional one.[35] Commenting on the theologians who emerged as the bridge builders between the church and the Nazi state, Vincent Berning has pointed out that Karl Eschweiler, Joseph Lortz, Karl Adam, Max Pribilla, S.J., and Michael Schmaus "hoped not for a totalitarian state but for a contemporary reincarnation of the medieval German empire."[36]

The ideal of a new Holy Roman Empire served, too, as the basis for criticizing Hitler. Disillusioned by Nazi rule, Friedrich Muckermann became such an outspoken critic of the new state that he would have been imprisoned or murdered if he had not fled Germany in 1934. Alois Dempf, Bonn's professor of philosophy, appealed to the religious vision of a new Germany in his criticism of the reconcilers of Catholicism and National Socialism. Since it was already dangerous in 1934 to voice political dissent in Germany, Dempf adopted the pseudonym Michael Schäffler, and voiced his criticism in his book *Die Glaubensnot der deutschen Katholiken* [The Faith Need of German Catholics], which he published in Switzerland.

Carl Schmitt, as noted above, had influenced Eschweiler. After studying jurisprudence at the universities of Berlin, Munich, and Strasbourg, Schmitt served as a professor of law in Greifswald (1921), Bonn (1922–28), and Berlin (1928–45). During the 1920s, he had become a friend of the Catholic politician Franz von Papen.

Schmitt maintained in his early writings *Politische Romantik* (1919) and *Politische Theologie* (1922) that Western society was degenerating because of the individualism that had produced parliamentary democracy with its representative decision making and "government by discussion."[37] In order for Germany to regain its political and moral health, it needed to restore civil authority, the sovereignty of the state, and strong political leadership. While at Bonn, Schmitt emerged as a nationally respected constitutional theorist, presenting his conservative legal and political ideas in his book *Verfassungslehre* [Constitutional Theory] (1928), which had its sixth printing in 1983. The original work, dedicated to his Jewish friend Fritz Eisler, included praise of Hugo Preuss, the Jewish creator of the Weimar Constitution. In the editions printed after Hitler became chancellor, Schmitt removed the references to both Eisler and Preuss.

Although Schmitt had publicly criticized political extremism during the Weimar Republic, he changed his stance after the Reichstag passed the Enabling Act on March 23, 1933. He joined the Nazi party on May 1 and, being appointed the government's *Kronjurist*, devoted himself to giving legal support to the National Socialist state. In this capacity he described the Enabling Act as the "provisional constitution of the German revolution."[38] He held that Hitler was leading the German people into a new kind of polity, one that restored respect for the state and its leader. In his *Staat, Bewegung, Volk* [State, Movement, and People] (1933), he argued that Hitler's government rested on a new notion of leadership that presupposed the ethnic-racial identity of the leader and the people. He also insisted that the Nuremberg race laws of 1935 were a necessary component of the "constitution of freedom."[39] He called for the elimination of the "Jewish spirit" from German laws in 1936, and, insisting that good governance rests not on laws but on leadership, held that the law is "what the Führer wills."[40] Schmitt judged that the "Röhm blood purge" from June 30 to July 2, 1934, during which Nazis murdered hundreds of Hitler's political opponents, was required for the good of the state and its leader. In his book *Land und Meer* (1940), Schmitt gave a theoretical justification for Germany to expand its geographical space (*Lebensraum*) by means of military force.

Schmitt was initially rewarded for his pro-Nazi legal theories, being named a Prussian State Councillor, the director of the University Teachers' Group of the Nazi League of German Jurists, and the editor of the leading law review, *Deutsche Juristen-Zeitung*. He lost his influence in Nazi circles after 1936, however, attributable to the fact that he had remained a Catholic and that he was considered "tainted" by his participation in the government of the Weimar Republic and by his earlier friendships with Jews.

Schmitt was imprisoned by the Allied powers in the autumn 1945, brought to trial at Nüremberg, and exonerated in April 1947. He retired to his birthplace of Plettenberg, and died on April 7, 1985.

In Support of Hitler

Karl Eschweiler was serving as the dean of Braunsberg's Hochschule when Hitler became chancellor on January 30, 1933. At that time, the Staatliche Akademie comprised eleven regular professors who taught philosophy and theology to approximately 127 seminarians, most of whom belonged to the Diocese of Ermland, though some were affiliated with neighboring dioceses. During the winter and spring of 1933, the professors disagreed among themselves concerning the appropriate relationship between the church and the Nazi government. While Hermann Hefele (d. 1936), professor of church history, vehemently opposed Hitler, at least five professors called for the church's cooperation with the new state. The outspoken proponents of the National Socialist regime included Eschweiler in fundamental theology, Hans Barion in canon law, and Joseph Lortz in church history. Braunsberg's pro-Hitler scholars found themselves not only at odds with their colleague Hefele but also with the ordinary of the Diocese of Ermland, Bishop Maximilian Kaller, to whom they were accountable in ecclesiastical matters.[41] Kaller brought to his pastoral office his trust in Catholic Action and in the lay apostolate, programs on which he had relied when he was the pastor of St. Michael's Church in Berlin from 1917 to

1926, and when he was the apostolic administrator of the region of Tütz from 1926 to 1930. Convinced that the laity should share in the church's mission of assisting the poor and promoting social justice, Kaller established Catholic Action groups in the Diocese of Ermland. Moreover, he publicly supported the Catholic Center party in the region and sharply criticized Nazism, even after Hitler became chancellor. For this reason, he was called to Berlin in the spring of 1933 by Germany's papal nuncio, Archbishop Cesare Orsenigo, and told that the Vatican's secretary of state, Cardinal Eugenio Pacelli, and Orsenigo himself were ordering Kaller not to speak against the Nazi regime because it was complicating the Holy See's negotiations for a concordat. Returning to his diocese, Kaller temporarily remained silent on National Socialism, and even sent a letter of congratulations to East Prussia's Nazi leader, Erich Koch, after the concordat was adopted.

Bishop Kaller persisted, however, in his opposition to Hitler. He preached against Nazi ideology in September 1934 at a mass of Polish-speaking Catholics. He frequently visited those whom the regime had imprisoned as political dissidents, and urged Catholic Action groups to help people who had lost jobs because they refused to join the Nazi party. In the face of criticism from state officials, Kaller defended Catholic Action in a pastoral letter in May 1935. Seeing in 1937 that laborers in need of work were leaving their homes, he established a diocesan office to serve the "pilgrim church." Although he was labeled an enemy of the state by 1938, he was not deterred. He often went to the concentration camp at Theresianstadt to assist the incarcerated Jews and to administer the sacraments to Jewish Catholics. Beginning in 1939, he helped the war's refugees and grieved as one-third of the diocese's priests died at the hands of Nazis or in the war. Kaller was forced to leave Ermland in February 1945 as the Russian army advanced. He eventually moved to western Germany, and, in June 1946, was appointed by Pope Pius XII to assist displaced persons. Kaller died on July 7, 1947, in Frankfurt am Main.

While Bishop Kaller worked against the Nazi regime, Karl Eschweiler promoted it. When he learned that Carl Schmitt would be giving a public lecture against American imperialism at the University of Königsberg, he invited him also to speak at the Staatliche Akademie. After Hans Barion published his essay "Kirche oder Partei?," arguing that the bishops should withdraw their support for the Catholic Center party and collaborate with Hitler, Eschweiler voiced his agreement with Barion.[42] He also publicly backed Joseph Lortz, who urged in a public lecture that the church should cooperate with the Nazi state. Eschweiler officially joined the Nazi party on May 1, the same day on which Barion, Lortz, and Schmitt also became party members. Henceforth, Eschweiler frequently wore the Nazi uniform.[43] In June 1933, he published his essay "Die Kirche im neuen Reich," arguing that the church should become reconciled with Hitler. According to Eschweiler, the new chancellor had brought about a "genuine revolution" in Germany. In a few months, Hitler had transformed the nation's way of life by reversing the economic and moral decline of the Weimar Republic. In Eschweiler's view, the chancellor had won the respect of the German people with these accomplishments.[44]

Eschweiler asserted that the state and the Protestant and Catholic churches could attain a working relationship if each side were to remove needless obstacles. For its part, the government should recognize that the churches strengthen the German people. It would lose the good will of Protestants and Catholics if it tried to control the churches. Furthermore, the state must disregard those Nazis who insist that the government should make German Catholicism "free from Rome." For its part, the church should distance itself from the Catholic Center party and the Bavarian People's party, thereby acknowledging that it no longer needs them to defend the church's rights; the Nazi revolution has brought about a new national unity that transcends political parties. Forty-four percent of the German voters called for the unity of the state and the National Socialist party in the elections on March 5, and now the entire nation has accepted a state with only one political party. The bishops made the right decision when they decided on March 28 to drop their bans against membership in the National Socialist party. Further, the Bavarian bishops were correct when on May 4 they called for a national reconciliation among all Germans, regardless of their previous political stances.

According to Eschweiler, Catholicism and National Socialism have compatible worldviews. There is a close resemblance between Pius XI's vision of the corporate state in his encyclical *Quadragesimo Anno* (1931) and the Nazi party program. The bishops' prohibitions against membership in the Nazi party were based on a misunderstanding, which Hitler had corrected in his address to the Reichstag on March 23, 1933. Declaring the party's respect for the churches, the Führer had elaborated on article 24 of the Nazi party's program: "We demand the freedom of every religious confession in the state, so long as it does not offend the ethical and moral sentiments of the German race."[45] In Eschweiler's judgment, this principle has a strong basis in Catholicism. At the same time, article 24's view of human life stands in opposition to the anthropological dualism that operates in the thought of Plato, Augustine, Descartes, and "the human-rights ideology of the French revolution." Furthermore, it coincides with the philosophical and theological anthropology of Thomas Aquinas. Aquinas rightly saw that the soul animates the body with which it is intimately united, that it "operates as the personal, that is, inner principle in and through its body and only in and through its body." This idea is concretely expressed in article 24's assertion that the nation's soul, viz., the Protestant and Catholic churches, must respect the nation's body, which includes "the ethical and moral sentiments of the German race."

The phrase "the ethical and moral sentiments of the German race" can be restated in theological terms; it means that creation, including race, is "the natural or first act in which the Creator preserves us and our ancestors." This principle is an affirmation of nature and natural law; nature exists in relation to grace, and vice versa. According to Eschweiler, Catholicism affirms "that the grace of divine faith does not destroy the properly God-given natural abilities of those who are born German but presupposes —indeed includes—the most sacred obligation to preserve and develop these natural abilities in the face of evil inclinations which are the consequence of original sin." This Scholastic theological principle can be recast into a political theory: "[T]he mystery of the grace of the children of God presupposes the natural ethnic-racial community, not as an accidental and unimportant preamble, but as its elevation and fulfillment."[46] The Bavarian bishops reiterated this Catholic truth in their pastoral letter, stating "the conviction that just as the renewal of the German people comes only out of the source of our sacred faith, so also the Christian faith can grow interiorly with the living depths of the German people." In light of Thomism, the swastika should not scandalize Catholics but should be seen as an expression of Aquinas's understanding of the union of the natural and supernatural orders. If the swastika offends some Christians, it likely does so because they hold an Augustinian dualistic view of the relationship between creation and grace. They wrongly see National Socialism and Catholicism standing in "an unreconcilable contradiction"—a contradiction that produces "only hate and animosity" between state and church.

Inspired by Aquinas's theology, Catholics should strengthen the healthy elements in Hitler's movement so that the movement is not corrupted by the anti-Christian Nazis, who espouse the "disbelief" of Friedrich Nietzsche. If this neopagan group were to dominate the Nazi party, then the church would have to oppose the party's influence on the state. To prevent an anti-Christian takeover of National Socialism, the church should build bridges to the Nazi movement. Opposing the "unbelieving hero cult of Nietzsche," it must affirm people's desire "to make the natural order of creation effective in the life of families, the economy, the culture, and the state." This desire for life has originated in Germans' "genuine faith in God," and, if nurtured by the church, it will produce a religiously strong state. "The new Reich will pray." Moreover, the church should show that the way to international peace is by means of Pius XI's vision in *Ubi Arcano Dei* of "the peace of Christ in the reign of Christ." This reign is found in Catholicism, which is led by the pope "because he is the father of the Christian church." Church leaders must claim the church's inalienable right to hold "indirect power in the temporal realm." That is, they should insist not upon the church's "political power"—for example, the Catholic Center party—but upon "its purely spiritual mission" in the world.

In this article, Eschweiler condemned democracy and a liberal or secular society, accusing them of alienating people from one another, the church, and God. He conveyed the conviction that Germany was right to abandon the Weimar Republic. Employing the notion of the "natural human being" that he wrote about in 1925, he argued that Hitler's state will nurture the whole person, thereby disposing men and women to God's grace. In addition, he implicitly made use of the idea of the church's formal public status, for which he argued in his book of 1930 on Möhler's thought. He reiterated that the ideal church–state relationship, which he explained in his essay of 1931 on political theology, can be attained if the church and the Reich would work together. Eschweiler regarded Hitler's state as the polity that would benefit all Germans. While the Weimar Republic permitted individual Germans to thrive at the expense of other Germans, the new Reich will provide a good life for all Germans as they work for the common good.

After the publication of "Kirche im neuen Reich," Eschweiler looked for concrete ways to promote the church's cooperation with the state. On July 14, 1933, the Reich issued a law that permitted the government to sterilize Germans whom it judged unfit to become parents. Although Pius XI's encyclical *Casti Connubii* (1930) did not explicitly speak about sterilization, it insisted that a person's right over his or her sexual faculties is superior to the interests of the state, and that contraception is wrong. Nevertheless, Eschweiler and his colleague Hans Barion publicly backed the sterilization law. Eschweiler voiced his support in an address to the Hochschule's faculty and students at the start of the autumn semester of 1933. Appealing to the theological axiom that grace perfects nature, he argued that since God's grace cannot make up for the natural deficiency of someone who is mentally deficient or insane, the state—which must protect society from its unhealthy members—can decide that some people are not suited to be parents.

Eschweiler's views were not well received either by the students at the Staatliche Akademie or by Bishop Kaller. The students pointed out that the members of the Nazi party were always instigating fights with Catholics. Given this behavior, it was hard to imagine common ground between Catholicism and

National Socialism. The students also pointed out that what Eschweiler meant by "Volk," "nature," and "community" was not what Nazis meant by these same words. Bishop Kaller too informed Eschweiler that he disagreed with the theologian's views as expressed in his essay and by his support for the sterilization law. Disregarding others' comments, Eschweiler, as the dean of the Hochschule, promoted the Nazi state by requiring that the school's athletic teams wear Nazi sport uniforms. He also proposed to the government that all of Germany's Catholic seminarians be sent for one semester to the Braunsberg academy in order to experience the spirit and thought of National Socialism.[47]

In late autumn 1933, Cardinal Pacelli initiated canonical proceedings against Eschweiler and Barion because of their position on sterilization, and the Holy Office suspended Eschweiler's and Barion's permission for priestly ministry on August 20, 1934. As a result, both professors also lost their ecclesiastical approval to teach seminarians. They retained their professorships at the Staatliche Akademie, however, because these positions were granted by the state. In any case, Eschweiler now found himself in a contradiction. Having argued since 1926 for a greater public recognition of ecclesiastical authority, he himself stood in 1934 at odds with the church. Eschweiler and Barion immediately engaged in discussions with church officials, and soon afterwards publicly withdrew their statements in favor of the sterilization law. They were granted permission to engage in priestly ministry in September 1935 and resumed teaching seminarians in October.[48]

Because of their public support for the Nazi state, Eschweiler and Barion, as well as Lortz, found themselves in good standing with the Reich's minister of education, Bernhard Rust. Hoping that they would influence other Catholic theologians, Rust reassigned each of them to high-profile universities. He sent Lortz to the University of Münster on April 1, 1935, and transferred Barion to the University of Munich in 1938. He would likely have moved Eschweiler to a prestigious university but could not do so when the theologian became ill. Eschweiler suffered kidney failure and died on September 30, 1936. At his request, he was buried in his Nazi uniform and with a Nazi service as well as with a funeral Mass. The obituary in Alfred Rosenberg's newsletter, *Mitteilungen zur Weltanschaulichen Lage,* declared that Eschweiler was "a martyr to the Roman system."[49]

The Reich ordered Bishop Kaller to move the Staatliche Akademie out of its building in July 1939. As soon as he did, Nazi officials converted the facility into a field hospital. The reason for this change became evident on September 1, 1939, when the Wehrmacht invaded Poland. During the war, the academy operated in the seminary residence, but the number of students increasingly dropped because of conscription into the army. In 1945, as Russian troops advanced, the Staatliche Akademie was closed.

Bonn's Theologians against Hitler

While Karl Eschweiler was promoting the Nazi state at Braunsberg, his former professors at Bonn were doing just the opposite.[50] In 1933 the faculty of Catholic theology at the University of Bonn consisted of twelve regular professors, three extraordinary professors, and five instructors. They were responsible for teaching approximately 539 seminarians, many of whom were affiliated with the Archdiocese of Cologne. All of these teachers, except one, opposed Nazism. The one supporter was Albert Koeniger (d. 1950), professor of canon law, who was pleased in 1939 when Minister Rust assigned the Nazi sympathizer Hans Barion to Bonn. An outspoken critic of Hitler was Albert Lauscher (d. 1945), professor of pastoral theology, who was forced by Rust to retire on November 1, 1934. Another was Arnold Rademacher (d. 1939), who in 1935 included a sharp critique of National Socialism in his book *Religion und Bildung* [Religion and Education]. Wilhelm Neuss, professor of history and chairman of the faculty of Catholic theology in 1933, stood out among Bonn's opponents of the Nazi state. On June 1, 1933, Neuss published an article, "Gedanken eines katholischen Theologen zur Judenfrage" [Thoughts of a Catholic Theologian on the Jewish Question], in which he argued that anti-Semitism violated Christian belief.[51] A few months later, Neuss orchestrated a public critique of Alfred Rosenberg's Nazi ideology, which, at the time, was being promoted by the Reich.

Hitler's appointment of Rosenberg as the state's official philosopher on January 24, 1934, had alarmed church officials.[52] It indicated that the chancellor was officially espousing the anti-Jewish, anti-Christian, and neopagan ideas presented in Rosenberg's *Myth of the Twentieth Century* (1930). In response, Pius XI and Cardinal Pacelli directed the Holy Office to place *The Myth of the Twentieth Century* on the *Index of Forbidden Books* on February 7, 1934.[53] On the same day, Cologne's Cardinal Schulte (d. 1941) met with Hitler and formally protested Rosenberg's role in the government. He found that Hitler simply dismissed his criticisms, especially since Schulte himself had opposed Nazism in his sermons and pastoral letters. (It was with Schulte's blessing that the Cologne Carmel had welcomed Edith Stein in October 1933.[54]) Soon after this meeting, the cardinal decided that the church needed to do something to refute Rosenberg's falsehoods about the church. He appointed the Reverend Josef Teusch to direct a "defense against National Socialism's anti-Christian propaganda." Teusch eventually produced twenty booklets against Nazism; his *Catechism Truths* alone sold seven million copies.[55]

Josef Teusch contacted Wilhelm Neuss in the spring of 1934 and proposed that Neuss and his colleagues contribute essays to a pamphlet showing the errors and misconceptions in Rosenberg's *Myth of the Twentieth Century*. Neuss immediately gathered a team of professors, each of whom wrote a short, readable refutation of the historical and theological errors in Rosenberg's book. Along with Neuss, the contributors were Bonn's professors Anton Antweiler, Josef Greven, Hermann Platz, Karl Theodore Schäfer, Werner Schöllgen, and Josef Steinberg, as well as Bernhard Lakebrink at the University of Cologne. These contributors remained anonymous in order that they might be protected from Nazi revenge. Because Schulte's public criticisms of Nazism had already resulted in the disruption of diocesan printing offices by Storm Troopers, Münster's Bishop Clemens von Galen issued the pamphlet in his name. Entitled *Studien zum Mythus des XX.*

Jahrhunderts [Studies on the Myth of the Twentieth Century], the pamphlet was released simultaneously in Cologne, Berlin, Breslau, Munich, and Würzburg in October 1934. It also appeared as a supplement in the Catholic newspapers for the dioceses of Cologne and Münster.[56] It was so well received that a second edition appeared in December 1934. In 1935 Rosenberg attacked the booklet in his book *Against the Obscurantists of Our Time.* Third, fourth, and fifth editions of *Studien* were published in 1935, the last of which included an epilogue by Neuss and Teusch in response to *Against the Obscurantists.*[57] It is noteworthy, however, that while Neuss's essay of 1933 was a defense of Jews, *Studien* was a defense of the church. A concern for the preservation of Catholicism had apparently eclipsed a commitment to the protection of human rights in general.

During the Third Reich, Bonn's faculty of Catholic theology struggled to find ways to resist the state's control of their department. When Bernhard Rust established in 1935 new restrictive regulations on the granting of doctorates, Wilhelm Schwer, the chairman of Bonn's faculty of Catholic theology, protested against these new regulations as did Franz Stepper, the chairman of Münster's faculty of Catholic theology. In doing so, they were supported by Archbishop Schulte and Bishop Galen.[58] Further, when Neuss learned that Hermann Göring was intent upon claiming a statue of the Madonna from Cologne's diocesan museum for his personal art collection, the church historian succeeded in having a German court rule that the statue belonged to the museum.[59] Bonn's theologians were stifled after 1939, however, because Rust appointed Hans Barion as their chairman. They could do nothing when Rust and Barion neglected to fill academic chairs as professors retired. By 1944 Bonn had only six regular professors of theology. This reduction by fifty percent in the number of theologians from 1933 showed that Rust was punishing them for their resistance to the Reich. On June 6, 1945, Wilhelm Neuss wrote in his official statement to Cologne's Archbishop Joseph Frings and the Allied powers that "[t]here is no faculty in Germany that so early and so successfully contested the errors of the National Socialist world view as Bonn's faculty of Catholic theology."[60]

A Rejection of Modernity

As we have seen, the bishops and theologians of Braunsberg, Cologne, and Bonn searched for the most appropriate response to Hitler. While Cardinal Schulte, the theologians at Bonn, and Bishop Kaller opposed the Führer, Karl Eschweiler along with some of his colleagues at Braunsberg sought to reconcile Catholicism and the National Socialism. This divergence among the church's leaders reflected differing assessments not only of Hitler and his movement but also of modernity. Schulte and Kaller immediately perceived that the new state was a major threat to the German people and to the church. By contrast, Eschweiler held that a dictatorship under Hitler was better than a parliamentary democracy in a pluralistic society. He believed that the new chancellor, as the leader of Germany's "conservative revolution," would cure the social and political ills brought on by the French Revolution, Napoleon's secularization of Germany's ecclesiastical institutions in 1804, the end of the Holy Roman Empire in 1806, the abdication of Emperor Wilhelm II in 1918, and the establishment of the Weimar Republic in 1919. While Eschweiler was progressive because he envisioned theology moving away from neo-Scholasticism, he was simultaneously reactionary because he perceived no common ground between Catholicism and modernity regarding the notion of freedom.

The above analysis of Eschweiler's theological and political views coincides with that of Thomas O'Meara and Thomas Ruster. According to O'Meara, Eschweiler anchored his theology in the work of Scheeben: "Scheeben's theology unfolded speculative mysteries, Trinitarian life, and ecclesiastical authoritarianism. . . . But the many analogies, metaphors, and images never introduced the thought-forms of modernity." As a result, while Scheeben's writings gave Eschweiler some access to Thomism, they also fueled Eschweiler's rejection of modern thought. In O'Meara's words, "What Eschweiler glimpsed [in Scheeben's work] was an ecclesiastical mysticism produced by a profound (though perhaps hardly perceived) fear of modern process and subjectivity."[61] According to Ruster, Eschweiler decisively turned away from modernity and hence toward authoritarianism when he came under Scheeben's influence in 1925:

> Up until this point Eschweiler had developed a normal and open, predominantly traditional theology orientated toward Thomas Aquinas. . . . It became something other than this so that Eschweiler later wore with conviction the uniform of the National Socialist party and drew on Thomistic theology to justify the party program of the National Socialists. The shift in his thought was caused by this: he went beyond a solely formal determination of theological inquiry and let himself receive from the venerated Scheeben not only the principles concerning the relationship between reason and faith but also the content of faith. It is evident that his thorough work with Scheeben, already occurring in *Die zwei Wege der neueren Theologie,* led to a revision of his earlier position and intention. In his last years, his work resulted in the exact opposite of what it had initially announced and promised.[62]

As we have noticed, Eschweiler did not stand alone at Braunsberg in rejecting democracy and turning toward an authoritarian state. Among those who shared his political views was the church historian Joseph Lortz.

3

Joseph Lortz
Renewing Western Civilization

JOSEPH LORTZ (1887–1975) WAS ONE OF THE FOREMOST GERMAN Catholic proponents of ecumenism during the first half of the twentieth century.[1] A scholar in church history, he argued that although Martin Luther wrongly left the church, the reformer was deeply committed to the Christian faith and made justifiable criticisms of the late-medieval church's practices. Beginning in the 1940s, Lortz made his view of Luther available to general readers as well as to scholars in order to promote a reconciliation between Catholics and Protestants. For the next three decades, his writings played a significant role in the spiritual and theological renewal that eventually manifested itself in the Second Vatican Council's Decree on Ecumenism, *Unitatis Redintegratio* (November 21, 1964). What was not widely known, however, was Lortz's involvement with Nazism from 1933 until 1937.[2]

Joseph Lortz was born on December 13, 1887, in Grevenmacher, Luxembourg, not far from Trier, Germany. After graduating from the Gymnasium of the Benedictine Abbey of Echternach, he studied philosophy at Rome's Gregorian University. He was awarded a doctorate in philosophy from the Gregorian University in 1910 and, for the next three years, studied theology at Switzerland's University of Freiburg. Of his Dominican professors there, he was most influenced by the patristics scholar Johann Peter Kirsch, who advised Lortz to study the patristic apologist Tertullian, and the church historian Pierre Mandonnet, who introduced the young scholar to the study of the history of ideas.

After his ordination as a priest in 1913 for the Diocese of Luxembourg, Lortz pursued doctoral studies in theology at the University of Bonn, working closely with the church historians Heinrich Schrörs and Joseph Greving, as well as with the moral theologian Fritz Tillmann. At this time, Karl Eschweiler and Romano Guardini were also studying at Bonn. Lortz completed his doctorate in theology in 1920, writing his dissertation on the apologetics of Tertullian.[3] He had intended to remain at Bonn and write his Habilitationsschrift under the direction of the patristic scholar Albert Ehrhard.[4] However, while Ehrhard judged that the church had nothing to fear from the modern age and should recast its teachings in contemporary categories, Lortz was a sharp critic of modernity, praising Pope Pius X for his condemnation of modernism in 1907. Given these differences, Lortz went to the University of Würzburg for his further studies in 1923. Ehrhard eventually criticized Lortz's work for its view that modernity is the story of the West's cultural, moral, and religious decline.

At Würzburg, Lortz studied with the church historian Sebastian Merkle, who specialized in the history of ideas. Lortz, drawing on his study of Tertullian, envisioned historiography as a form of apologetics. He found, however, that Merkle, like Ehrhard, took a positive stance toward contemporary thought and methods. While Lortz used the historical-critical approach in limited ways, Merkle consistently employed it, even in his analysis of church history. Further, while the younger scholar was ultramontane, the older held that the church had become too centralized in Rome. Nevertheless, Lortz completed his Habilitationsschrift, a two-volume monograph on Tertullian's theology.[5]

Lortz was appointed professor of church history at Braunsberg's Staatliche Akademie in 1929. Among his courses was one on the history of the church in the West. Over three years, he arranged these lectures into his *Geschichte der Kirche* (1932), which appeared as *History of the Church* in 1938.[6] In this work, which eventually went through twenty-one printings, Lortz conveyed a broad theological view of the church's history, determined in large part by papal teachings, especially those of Pius X. In short, he portrayed the church of the 1800s and 1900s as the bastion of divine truth and moral values amid the decay of Western society.

History of the Church narrates the unfolding of the relationship between Christian faith and culture in the West. In Lortz's judgment, this relationship should be complementary, reflecting the harmony between grace and nature. The early church adapted itself to the Jewish, Greek, and Roman worlds, and it has continued to adjust to the societies into which it has moved. This Catholic idea of faith and culture, and also of grace and nature, stands apart from the Protestant view, which sees the two in greater tension. Furthermore, Western history has unfolded in three ages or epochs, each separated by a time of transition, a "boundary zone." According to Lortz, the first age, "Christian antiquity," began with the post-Easter communities and ended with the fall of the Roman Empire. Although Christian belief initially existed on the margins of society, it gradually shaped Greco-Roman culture until the church was the dominant influence on society and the state. The migration of the German peoples brought the end of Christian antiquity and produced the church's second epoch, the "German-Roman" age, which developed from the sixth century through the fourteenth century. During the medieval time, the West enjoyed an integration of faith and culture. The rise of humanism during the Renaissance led, however, to the breakdown of this synthesis, from which emerged the third epoch, "the age of nationalism," also known as "modernity."[7] This period began in the 1400s and moved into its last phase in the early 1900s.

In Lortz's reading of Western history, modernity, or "the age of nationalism," came about because of the subjectivism that began with the Renaissance. Since the fourteenth century, the idea had spread that each human being is an autonomous self so that it is now taken for granted that a person is a knowing subject who possesses the capability and freedom to shape his or her world and future. According to Lortz, this mistaken belief generated other erroneous ideas and attitudes. One of these is "liberalism," which calls into question every authority beyond the individual and which has manifested itself in the revolutions that produced the West's parliamentary democracies. The roots of individualism and democracy are found in the late medieval world when the faithful rebelled against clerical abuses.[8] A further manifestation of this political autonomy was the French Revolution of 1789, which led to the reorganization and secularization of European nation-states in the early 1800s. Liberalism's insistence on the separation of church and state has produced a "secular" society, which split apart faith and culture. Thus, a culture emerged "that is in the main mundane and autonomous, following its course of development largely outside the church and even in opposition to her." Subjectivism has also produced "relativism," the outlook that rejects absolute moral norms. If the knowing subject is the primary reality, then each self should determine his or her own ethical values and religious beliefs. Assuming this, people no longer embraced the values that formerly gave direction to the West. Further, subjectivism fueled "atheism." Since the turn to the self promoted ego-centrism among men and women, it has also legitimated society's rebellion against God. Descartes's meditations led to a "grandiose declaration of the sovereignty of the individual," and Kant's analysis of faith and reason left no conceptual room for divine revelation.[9] In short, personal autonomy required the rejection of God, or at least skepticism about God and the church.

Lortz's *History of the Church* was written in the shadow of Oswald Spengler's two-volume *Decline of the West* (1919–22). Like Spengler's work, it tells of the West's degeneration during the modern period. Subjectivism led not only to anthropocentrism and atheism but also to parliamentary democracy, which entails governance not in relation to God's will as known through the church but in relation to the will of the people. Since human consensus can be manipulated by self-interested individuals, democracy has resulted in the tyranny of the few in the name of the many. The Peace of Augsburg in 1555 empowered the state to control people's consciences, and the French Revolution allowed the victors to deny their opponents' human rights and political freedom. For Lortz the lesson is obvious: when human beings make themselves the standard of right and wrong, they become self-serving and arbitrary. The irony is that modernity came about because of Christian faith and the church. "In the modern age, the life which is both Christian and ecclesiastical suffers a partial defeat from the forces of the very culture which the Church had created. Culture breaks away from the Church and becomes increasingly non-Catholic, non-Christian, and nonreligious."[10] This view of the opposition between Catholicism and modernity disposed Lortz to the Nazi state.

According to Lortz, modernity has jeopardized the essence and form of Catholicism because it values subjectivism at the expense of objective reality. Again, in Lortz's words, "Catholicity means the unconditioned preponderance of the objective over the subjective, of order over impulse, of community over the individual."[11] Similarly, insofar as modern thought has influenced the church, it has produced "particularism"—the emphasis on the autonomy of the local church in relation to the universal church. The Councils of Constance (1414–18) and Basle (1431–49) wrongly favored a conciliarism that threatened the unity of Catholicism. "Episcopalism," which was promoted during the 1700s, called for the governance of local churches by their respective bishops. Subjectivism also fueled the desire for national churches, evident in Gallicanism and Febronianism, and it infected the church with rationalism, the Enlightenment's distorted view of the capability and authority of the human mind. This turn to the knowing subject also gave birth to the secular humanism that has "wrought havoc in the church."[12]

The church has, however, persistently defended itself against modernity. It rightly responded to subjectivism by deliberately strengthening the ecclesiastical centralization that St. Peter symbolized. The Council of Trent (1545–63) reasserted papal authority, thereby neutralizing the particularism of the Councils of Constance and Basle, and it opposed the individualism, nationalism, and democratic tendencies of the Protestant Reformation. In the late 1800s and early 1900s, the ecclesiastical authorities took decisive steps against modernity: Pius IX issued his *Syllabus of Errors* in 1864; the Vatican Council approved in 1870 both *Dei Filius* on faith and reason, and *Pastor Aeternus* on authority; Pius X condemned modernism in 1907; and Benedict XV instituted the Code of Canon Law in 1917.

During its struggle against modernity, the church actually gained strength, Lortz said, in at least two ways. First, it improved its governance through greater centralization, and, as a result, it remained strong even in democratic societies.[13] Second, the church enriched its spiritual life as it struggled against the contemporary world's corrosive forces. It manifested its holiness in the many saints since the 1400s and in the flourishing of new devotions. Finally, church officials learned that they could not use juridical or political means to force people to accept the church and its teachings. For example, it erred in its condemnation of Galileo. The popes now knew that they must nurture among people an interior assent to Catholicism.

Writing in 1930 and 1931, Lortz judged that the West was entering a cultural, political, and social transition that would lead to "a new universal epoch of church history." While the end of the age of nationalism was anticipated in Pius IX's *Syllabus of Errors* and the teachings of the (First) Vatican Council, it was clearly marked when Pius XI and Benito Mussolini signed the Lateran Treaty in 1929. This agreement resolved the political tensions between the Holy See and the Italian government, thereby inaugurating a new kind of collaboration between church and state based on a recognition of the church's mission as religious, not political. This acknowledgment sprang in large part from the fact that the papacy had earned a "mystic halo" for itself during its struggle with modernity. As the popes were stripped of their political power, they manifested their spiritual power. "The loss of political power became the strongest assurance of the development of the pope's religious authority (infallibility) and deeply impressed it on men's minds."[14] It also brought about an "epochal change" in the church–state relationship. Relinquishing its demand for political control, the church became intent on pursuing its spiritual mission by means of concordats that could juridically safeguard the concrete ways in which the church enriches a society's spiritual, intellectual, and cultural life.

This clarification of the church's mission has in principle freed the state to respect the church's authority and its contribution to the common good. Assuming a high degree of centralization for Catholicism, Pope Leo XIII correctly declared in *Immortale Dei* that the church respects various forms of civil governance and expects that its organizational structure and mission will also be respected by different forms of civil government. In other words, the church does not in principle favor monarchical governance. But the optimum form of government remains unclear. On the one hand, Bolshevism cannot respect the church because it avows atheism, and, on the other hand, parliamentary democracy is also deficient because, assuming that religious belief is a private or subjective matter, it refuses to acknowledge that its authority comes from God and that it should grant the churches a unique civil status so that they can properly pursue their spiritual mission in society. Since neither Bolshevism nor parliamentary democracy is the ideal polity, a third way must eventually emerge. It must be a state that possesses the authority to affirm objective reality, including God and the church. The Lateran Treaty is significant not only because it established the proper relationship between church and state but also because it indirectly supported a state that was an alternative to Bolshevism and democracy.

According to Lortz, the German people will play a key role in the coming of the epoch beyond modernity. They played this role in the fifth century when they initiated the medieval world; they must once again play a unifying role in the West. To assume this role they must overcome their attraction to the particularism of the Protestant Reformation. Since Martin Luther was influenced by subjectivism, he fueled the rise of secularism. Nevertheless, particularism and its offshoot, secular humanism, are "not native to German soil." Germans possess an innate orientation toward objectivity and community, an orientation that Peter Canisius perceived and affirmed in the 1500s. Thus, the German people would lead the West into its fourth age as they themselves turn away from the subjectivism embodied in the Weimar Republic. In this regard, Germans must also renounce the particularism of the neopagan German Faith Movement, which wrongly substituted German mythology for God's revelation in Jesus Christ.

History of the Church presented a coherent, engaging story of the church and the decline of the West. It was an apologia for the church. But was it true to history, to objective reality? Tragic events would show that Lortz had forced historical data into his theological view of history.

A *Positive View of National Socialism*

Joseph Lortz judged in 1933 that Hitler was moving the nation into the new epoch of Western civilization that he foresaw in *History of the Church*. He joined the Nazi party on May 1 and promoted the two associations Kreuz und Hakenkreuz and Arbeitsgemeinschaft katholischer Deutscher [Active Community of Catholic Germans], which Vice Chancellor Papen had formed to bring together influential Catholics and Nazi leaders. Aware that on June 3 the German bishops had approved a draft of the concordat with the Reich, Lortz lectured soon afterwards at the University of Königsberg on the common ground between Catholicism and National Socialism. During the discussion after the lecture, he told students that the conduct of the Hitler Youth group was an aberration from the ideals of the Nazi state. Lortz felt that he was confirmed in his view of Hitler when Cardinal Pacelli and Vice Chancellor Papen signed the concordat on July 20 and Pius XI ratified it on September 10. In October he published his pamphlet *Katholischer Zugang zum Nationalsozialismus, kirchengeschichtlich gesehen* [A Catholic Approach to National Socialism from the Perspective of Church History], contending that Catholics should seek a better understanding of Nazism and should explain their religious and moral convictions to Hitler's supporters.[15]

In this pamphlet, Lortz asserted that Catholics needed to revise their view of National Socialism in light of recent events. Hitler had in fact brought political order to Germany, thereby stopping the spread of Bolshevism to Germany and hence to all of western Europe. The Catholic Center party had dissolved itself on July 5 in order to facilitate the Holy See's negotiations with Hitler's government, and National Socialism was emerging as "a purely political movement" that respected the church's autonomy. Although Hitler was establishing a totalitarian state, he had acknowledged the validity of "positive Christianity" in his speeches on March 21 and March 23. He had also expressed his desire to work for "an acceptable and worthwhile solution" of his differences with the church. At the same time, ecclesiastical officials were untangling the confusion of "political Catholicism with Catholicism as a religious and spiritual idea." The bishops had done this by lifting their bans against membership in the Nazi party; political and religious lines were being reconfigured. According to Lortz, "National Socialism is not only the legitimate possessor of civil authority in Germany, it is—hardly a few short months after assuming power—the German state itself." In this new situation, the church was beginning to "de-politicize [itself] and return to its pure spiritual idea."[16]

Furthermore, said Lortz, "the basic kinship between National Socialism and Catholicism" was becoming evident in five concrete ways. (1) Like the church, "National Socialism is essentially an opponent of Bolshevism, liberalism, [and] relativism." It affirms what popes Gregory XVI, Pius IX, and Leo XIII explicitly taught: authentic civil authority is much more than the will of "the majority." (2) Like the church, "National Socialism is the declared opponent of the atheist movement and also of the lack of ethics in society." Building on this healthy formation, the church can address "the great task of the present age: the creation of a new 'Catholic human being' who will replace the Sunday Catholic." As Lortz saw it, this kind of cooperation between church and state occurred in Italy, where Pius XI and Mussolini initiated in 1931 collaboration between the Catholic youth organization and the state. (3) National Socialism and Catholicism affirm "the natural order of creation." National Socialism is intent upon leading Germans back to their cultural and ethnic origins so that they may once again flourish as a people. Since Catholicism believes in the complementarity of nature and grace, it can endorse Nazi efforts in this regard and simultaneously build on this foundation while it focuses on the spiritual realm. (4) National Socialism and Catholicism hold that a society is not merely an association of individuals but rather a social unity in which individuals participate. Pius XI himself called for a corporatist society in his encyclical *Quadragesimo Anno*. (5) National Socialism and Catholicism aim at overcoming modernity's "spiritless intellectualism." Both emphasize the "spiritual life" that undergirds intellectual inquiry. Finally, these five points indicate that National Socialism and Catholicism share a "kinship of essence." For this reason, in relating to the Nazi state, the church should "work for the fulfillment of the genuine essence of National Socialism."[17]

According to Lortz, the Nazi movement initiated changes in German society that are part of an epochal change in society and are creating "a new type of human being." This change is the "precondition" of the church's fruitfulness among the German people. National Socialism has produced a political unity that could join the Protestant and Catholic churches. A new cooperation is already under way among Protestants, and it could include Catholics, especially as the Catholic church ends its political activities (e.g., support for the Catholic Center party) and solely pursues its spiritual mission. Hitler surprised some of his followers when he improved the state's relations with the church; he saw that his improvement "prepared the way for a living faith and hope, and it also enlivened the idea of the church." Finally, this new unity among Germans is the "mother earth of the church's growth." Indeed, "[t]he history of the church demonstrates that nature is not only an external point of contact for grace"; there exists "an inner interaction of nature and grace that belongs to the essence of reality. . . ." While the popes have rightly moved to greater centralization, they have simultaneously affirmed the distinctiveness of the local churches. They have recognized that the church is "a super-national community," embracing national and ethnic groups into its spiritual unity. Thus the church in Germany is experiencing a new "national-ecclesial unity."[18]

The church must nurture the good qualities in National Socialism, linking it to Christian belief. As history teaches, there are risks and dangers during a period of transition. The present is such a time because National Socialism is "a primary wave of life, . . . the breaking in of [new] life in its whole breadth." Although Hitler's movement has produced excesses by some of its members, Vice Chancellor Papen rightly noted that "[o]n the margin of this historic happening much occurs that is immature and worthy of censure." The movement is affected by "the tragic law of the created order: to attain the harmony of all rights, much damage must occur." History also shows however that a mistake can become a "happy fault" (*felix culpa*). These aberrations in Hitler's movement are highlighted by Germany's critics—the same critics who have remained silent while Catholics have been punished by the ruling groups of Mexico, Russia, and Spain. In any case, Germans must now make sacrifices for the common good. In Lortz's judgment, "National Socialism is today not only the legal power in Germany, it is to a great extent Germany itself. . . . Either we follow this movement in rescuing Germany, or we land in chaos. No one denies this unwanted alternative. Chaos would bring about the destruction of the nation and the ruin of the German church. This thought concludes the discussion."[19]

Soon after the appearance of *Katholischer Zugang zum Nationalsozialismus*, Lortz published three additional essays, each arguing for a reconciliation between Catholicism and National Socialism.[20] Then in June 1934 he authorized a third printing of *Katholischer Zugang zum Nationalsozialismus* that included a critique of Rosenberg's *Myth of the Twentieth Century*—a critique consonant with the Holy Office's decision on February 7, 1934, to place this text on the *Index of Forbidden Books*. Lortz argued that the Führer himself could not agree with Rosenberg's presentation of Catholicism, since Hitler had expressed ideas in *Mein Kampf* that have much in common with Christian belief.[21]

Lortz reiterated his critique of Rosenberg's thought in paragraphs that he added to the third German edition of *History of the Church* in 1935. The second German edition of the book, which appeared in late 1933, included an appendix entitled "Nationalsozialismus und die Kirche." It paraphrased Lortz's ideas that were expressed in *Katholischer Zugang zum Nationalsozialismus*. But by 1935 Lortz saw that the anti-Christian voices in Hitler's movement were determining the Führer's decisions. Hence, he modified the 1933 appendix with paragraphs arguing that if the Nazi state were to succeed, it had to reject Rosenberg's ideology and strengthen its ties with the church. He judged that Germany stood at a crossroads: "The question of destiny is placed before us: in the breakthrough of the German people into a [new] nation —the breakthrough willed by God and finally attained by Adolf Hitler—will Christian faith remain the [nation's] foundation, or will non-Christian and anti-Christian [forces] take over [national] leadership?"[22] After writing these words, Lortz continued to have doubts about Hitler's direction. Although he included his modified appendix in the fourth German edition of *History of the Church* in 1936, he eliminated it from the fifth German edition in 1937 and from all subsequent printings.

Lortz was transferred from Braunsberg's Staatliche Akademie to the University of Münster on April 1, 1935. He was not invited to Münster by the university's faculty but simply assigned there by the Reich's minister of education. Bernhard Rust made this appointment both to reward Lortz for supporting Hitler and to punish the scholar whom Lortz replaced at Münster, Georg Schreiber, who had been a leader in the Catholic Center party. Lortz had grown restless at Braunsberg and had expressed an interest in returning to Würzburg to succeed Sebastian Merkle. But since he was not offered a position there, he had to settle for Münster. Thus, it is necessary to review the political stance of the bishops as well as of the Catholic theologians at Würzburg and Münster.

Bishop Ehrenfried
and Würzburg's Theologians

In 1933 the University of Würzburg's faculty of Catholic theology comprised eight regular professors, two extraordinary professors, and four instructors.[23] These scholars prized the creative spirit of Hermann Schell (d. 1906), Würzburg's professor of apologetics who had tried to reconcile neo-Scholasticism and modern philosophy but was frustrated in his efforts when in 1898 the Holy Office placed four of his works on the *Index of Forbidden Books*. Because Würzburg's theologians retained the respect of the German bishops, they were responsible in 1933 for teaching approximately 360 seminarians, and they worked closely with the Diocese of Würzburg's bishop.

Bishop Matthias Ehrenfried (d. 1948) was an outspoken critic of the National Socialism. From the outset, he consistently challenged the Nazi regime's policies and tried to protect Catholic opponents of Hitler. Bishop Ehrenfried's clergy shared his views; by the summer of 1933, the government had incarcerated thirty priests of the Diocese of Würzburg.[24] In the autumn of 1935, Ehrenfried stopped a Nazi student, Otto Krepel, from speaking on National Socialism at the seminary, and, in retaliation, the Reich suspended classes for ten days. Further, Storm Troopers broke into the bishop's residence on two occasions, physically abusing those in the building and destroying property. On more than one occasion, they threatened Bishop Ehrenfried's life. Because of his leadership, the Diocese of Würzburg remained a place of conflict between the church and the Nazi regime.

Most of Würzburg's Catholic theologians covertly resisted the Nazi state and paid a price for doing so. In February 1933, police conducted a disruptive search of each scholar's residence. Not intimidated by this action, Andreas Bigelmair, professor of patrology and pastoral theology, continued to criticize the new government throughout the winter and spring of 1933 and was therefore listed as an enemy of the state. Three Storm Troopers came to his residence at 3:00 A.M., on June 29, 1933, and searched in vain for seditious literature. Four years later, the Gestapo accused Bigelmair of helping students write a public letter of protest against the Third Reich. They detained Bigelmair and his niece, who was a student at the university, and interrogated each of them at length. Bigelmair and his niece were released after the Gestapo failed to substantiate the allegations against them.

Other members of the faculty of Catholic theology also opposed the Nazi state. Georg Wunderle, professor of apologetics and comparative religions, was the University of Würzburg's rector in January 1933 and resisted the Nazi effort to take control of the university's governance. As a result, Bernhard Rust forced Wunderle to resign as rector in the summer of 1933. Another public critic of Nazism was Franz Gillmann, emeritus professor of canon law. After learning of the political pressures on the Wehrmacht's Catholic chaplains, he wrote an article on the ethical obligations of priests in the military. Amazingly, in 1937, Gillmann managed to have it published in the SS's newspaper, *Schwarzen Korps*. Rust immediately informed Gillmann that he would eliminate Gillmann's emeritus status with its financial benefits if the retired professor made any further public statements about the Wehrmacht. Further, Rust denied academic advancement to the professors Joseph Zahn and Karl Staab, and to instructors Joseph Pascher and Joseph Ranft, because of their resistance to Nazism.

Würzburg's faculty of Catholic theology included one member of the Nazi party: Ludwig Ruland, professor of moral and pastoral theology since 1913. In early November 1933, he published an article in the Munich edition of the Nazi party's newspaper *Völkische Beobachter*, urging people to vote in favor of Nazi candidates in the Reichstag elections on November 12. He argued that Hitler was ending the threat of Marxism in Germany, improving employment, and restoring the nation's self-confidence. In Ruland's words, "Adolf Hitler's essential characteristics are a clear grasp of his goals and an unswerving iron will. His will is so strong that it directs not only his own actions, but also gives the nation the steely power again to believe in itself and to trust not in foreign help but in its own ability to create its future."[25]

The last professor of importance to this account is Sebastian Merkle, who approved Joseph Lortz's Habilitationsschrift. Along with Hermann Schell, Merkle stands out as a brilliant and controversial scholar in the history of Würzburg's faculty of Catholic theology.[26] He held Würzburg's chair in church history, the history of dogma, and Christian archaeology from 1898 until his retirement in 1935. Specializing in the history of the Council of Trent, he dedicated forty years to editing three thousand pages of documentation from the council, along with a commentary. He also wrote on Savonarola, Luther, and Hermes; his study on Luther in 1929 set the direction for Lortz's work on the Reformation.[27] Merkle judged that the church needed to take a more positive view of modernity and also permit greater intellectual freedom among Catholic scholars in the use of historical-critical methods in biblical studies and church history. In 1912 he promoted this view and criticized Ultramontanism in his book *Vergangenheit und Gegenwart der katholischen, theologischen Fakultäten* [The Past and Present of Catholic Theological Faculties], which the Holy Office placed on the *Index of Forbidden Books* in 1913.

Merkle initially supported Hitler in 1933, for he believed that greater national unity would strengthen German Catholicism against the Vatican's centralization of ecclesiastical governance. By 1935, however, he had become a sharp critic of National Socialism and also of his Nazi colleague Ludwig Ruland. Soon afterward, Rust rejected Merkle's recommendation concerning his successor at Würzburg and appointed a member of the Nazi party, Münster's Ludwig Mohler, to Merkle's chair. Six years later, the minister of education denied Merkle a prestigious scholarly award, the Reich's *Adlerschildes* [Eagle's Shield], for which Würzburg's professors had nominated him. There was one occasion, however, when Merkle supported the government's action: since he was a long-standing critic of the Jesuits, he agreed with Rust's decision in 1938 to close the faculty of Catholic theology at Innsbruck, which was composed of Jesuits, including Karl Rahner (d. 1984). In March 1945, Allied bombs destroyed Merkle's home, including his library of twenty-five thousand books and many personal manuscripts. Merkle died a month later.

Between 1933 and 1939, the minister of education diluted the political resistance of Würzburg's theologians by assigning to the faculty professors who supported National Socialism. After appointing Ludwig Mohler to Würzburg, he also moved two other party members to Würzburg's faculty, Johannes Fischer in 1936 and Anton Stonner in 1939. He assigned Thomas (Phillip) Ohm, O.S.B., to Würzburg in 1933, but removed him in 1938 because of his covert resistance to Nazism.

Bishop Galen and Münster's Theologians

In January 1933, the University of Münster's faculty of Catholic theology included twelve regular professors, eight extraordinary professors, and six instructors who taught approximately 530 seminarians.[28] Among these professors, Josef Mausbach, S.J., in moral theology and Georg Schreiber in church history were nationally prominent leaders in the Catholic Center party. They and the other theologians at Münster were committed to the Weimar Republic, as were the people of the State of Westphalia to which Münster belongs. These scholars and the people of Westphalia were dismayed, therefore, when President Hindenberg appointed Hitler as the nation's chancellor on January 30, 1933. Although they found ways to resist Hitler in the years that followed, they could not stop what Hindenberg had unleashed.

After three years of teaching at the German University of Prague, Michael Schmaus (d. 1994), at the age of thirty-five, became a professor of dogmatic theology at Münster on May 4, 1933.[29] Having done his theological studies with the medievalist Martin Grabmann at the University of Munich, he presented the history of dogma so that neo-Scholastic ideas would come to expression in a form of thought accessible to contemporary Catholics. As Schmaus was finishing his first semester at Münster, some professors and students asked him to give a public lecture on Catholicism and National Socialism in order to lessen the conflict between the church and the Reich. Speaking on July 11, 1933, he read an essay entitled "Begegnung zwischen katholischem Christentum und nationalsozialisticher Weltanschauung" [The Encounter between Catholic Christianity and the National Socialist Worldview] and then permitted it to be published as a pamphlet on August 15, 1933. Schmaus participated in Vice Chancellor Papen's professional association, Kreuz und Hakenkreuz, during the summer of 1933, but otherwise had little to do with the Nazi movement.[30] He published his three-volume *Katholische Dogmatik* in 1937 and repeatedly revised it so that its sixth edition, consisting of eight volumes, appeared from 1960 to 1964.[31] After Hitler's defeat, he taught at the University of Munich until 1963.

Schmaus's essay of 1933 highlights potentially fruitful "contact points between the Catholic faith and the National Socialist world view."[32] The Nazi movement emerged as an alternative to modernity's "spirit of freedom, of disconnectedness, of autonomy"—in short, its "spirit of liberalism." Nazism rests on three "basic pillars": "order," "community," and "life as an organic whole," and it promotes these three elements as it forms Germans into one ethnic-racial people. This national community cherishes the ideas of "community, ethnic-racial people, connectedness, [and] authority." In Schmaus's view, the Nazi opposition to liberalism and its emphasis on social order, community, and life as an organic whole are similar to Catholic teachings such as Pius IX's *Syllabus of Errors* and Pius XI's *Quadragesimo Anno.* "Catholic means connectedness—surely out of religious motives—to the given, to the objective, reverence for the becoming, the growing, above all the natural order." The church appreciates the idea of a national community because the church itself is a spiritual community whose unity is anchored in the papacy. "As the church itself is a community, so it recognizes and affirms naturally growing communities. Everything natural is indeed a transparency of the supernatural."[33] Since the values of Catholicism and National Socialism are congruent, Schamus said, the church and state should work together. Schmaus noted that "[a]ccording to Chancellor Hitler's clarification, the rights of the church will not be diminished; Christianity should be the necessary foundation of the new Reich." Further, since the church recognizes the value of strong ecclesiastical authority, it can appreciate the new regime's emphasis on civil authority, which "is necessary for the maintenance of the order willed by God."[34] In light of his analysis, the essay concludes that the church and state could combine their efforts for Germany's well-being.

Joseph Schmidlin began to teach at the University of Münster as an instructor of medieval and modern church history in 1907.[35] He had lectured at the University of Strasbourg in 1906 after working in Rome for four years with Ludwig von Pastor on his *History of the Popes.* At Münster, Schmidlin immediately won the respect of his associates for his creativity and high ideals but was also regarded by them as an emotionally complex colleague. Appointed Münster's professor of missiology in 1910, he founded the *Zeitschrift für Missionswissenschaft* in 1911 and wrote the ground-breaking texts, *Einführung in die Missionswissenschaft* (1917), *Katholische Missionslehre im Grundriss* (1919), and *Katholische Missionsgeschichte* (1925). From the outset of Hitler's regime, Schmidlin refused to give the Nazi salutation, "Heil Hitler!" As a result, he came into conflict with the University of Münster's administration and agreed at the age of fifty-eight to become a professor emeritus on April 30, 1934; three months later, he was forced into complete retirement. Between 1933 and 1939, Schmidlin completed his four-volume *Papstgeschichte der neuesten Zeit* [The History of the Papacy in the Modern Period], which received positive reviews from scholars around the world. Increasingly angered by Hitler's policies, he criticized his colleagues and Bishop Galen for not taking a stronger stand against the state. After denouncing Nazi officials in a letter, he was arrested by the Gestapo on October 23, 1943, and imprisoned in the concentration camp at Struthof bei Schirmeck, where he died on January 10, 1944. Although the official death notice said that he had collapsed of a heart attack, prisoners subsequently reported that he was brutally murdered by the camp's guards.

Georg Schreiber (d. 1963) joined Münster's faculty of Catholic theology in 1917 as professor of church history.[36] Having earned a doctorate in philosophy at the University of Berlin and doctorates in theology at the University of Freiburg, he had taught at Regenburg's Hochschule from 1915 to 1917. At Münster, Schreiber specialized in the history of folk culture. Among his many books were *Mutter und Kind in der Kultur der Kirche* (1918), *Die deutsche Kulturpolitik und der Katholizismus* (1922), *Auslandsdeutschtum und Katholizismus* (1927, 1932), *Das Auslandsdeutschtum als Kulturfrage* (1930), and *Brüning, Hitler, Schleicher* (1932). After the First World War, Schreiber emerged as a leader in the Catholic Center party and the Reichstag. Named a papal prelate in 1923, he was active in the Görres Gesellschaft, a Catholic professional society that promoted Catholic involvement in Germany's political, cultural, and intellectual life. This "political Catholicism" stood in contrast to the "religious Catholicism" advocated by the Katholische Akademische Verband to which Joseph Lortz belonged.[37]

After the Reichstag passed the Enabling Act on March 23, 1933, replacing the Weimar Republic with Hitler as the nation's dictator, Schreiber was immediately excluded from Germany's political life. As noted earlier, he was assigned by the Reich's minister of education from the University of Münster to Braunsberg's Staatliche Akademie on April 2, 1935. This was the day after Joseph Lortz was transferred from Braunsberg to Münster.[38] Schrieber did not, however, move to Braunsberg. Citing reasons of health, he remained in Münster and petitioned for early retirement. It was granted in 1936.

For the next two years, Schreiber pursued his scholarship at both Münster's German Institute for Foreign Studies (Deutsches Institut für Auslandskunde), which he had established in 1927, and the German Institute for Folklore (Deutsches Institut für Volkskunde), which he had founded in 1933. When the Reich closed both institutes in 1938, Schreiber continued his research at home for the next six years. After the assassination attempt against Hitler on July 20, 1944, he went into hiding at the Abbey of Beuron because the Gestapo had listed him among the former leaders of the Catholic Center party who were to be punished for the plot against the Führer. In 1945 Schreiber was reinstated as professor of church history at the University of Münster, and was elected by the faculty as the university's rector. He became a professor emeritus in 1951 and was named to the Max Planck Institute in 1960. His postwar writings included *Zwischen Demokratie und Diktatur* (1949) and *Deutsche Wissenschaftspolitik* (1954).

Bishop Clemens August von Galen was a critic of the Weimar Republic who later became an outspoken opponent of the Third Reich.[39] After serving in parishes in Berlin from 1906 until 1929, he became the pastor of Münster's St. Lamberti Church, where he initially upset some parishioners because of his political conservatism. He expressed his opposition to modernity in his book *Die "Pest des Laizismus" und ihre Erscheinungsformen* [The "Plague of Laicism" and Its Forms of Expression] (1932). At a meeting in Münster of the Association of Catholic Academicians in June 1933, Galen chastised the scholars for their criticism of the Nazi government and called for "a just and objective evaluation of '[Hitler's] new political movement.'" In response, the scholars sat "in icy silence."[40] Although Galen was not the popular candidate to succeed Münster's bishop, Johannes Poggenburg (d. January 5, 1933), he was chosen for the office by Pope Pius XI on September 5, 1933. On October 28, he was consecrated as bishop in Münster's cathedral. Storm Troopers attended, standing in formation with swastika flags.[41]

Bishop Galen began to criticize Hitler's movement in 1934.[42]

He condemned the Nazi "worship of race" in a pastoral letter on January 29 that subsequently circulated throughout Germany. As noted in chapter 2, he assumed responsibility for the publication of *Studien zum Mythus des XX. Jahrhundert,* the pamphlet of essays criticizing the ideology of Alfred Rosenberg and defending the teachings of the Catholic church. Rosenberg himself attacked Bishop Galen in a speech in Münster in July 1935. The next day, nineteen thousand Germans showed their support for Galen by joining in Münster's annual procession for the feast of Corpus Christi; in previous years, the procession had numbered seven thousand. Along with Munich's Cardinal Faulhaber and Berlin's Bishop Preysing, Bishop Galen drafted Pius XI's encyclical *Mit brennender Sorge* (March 14, 1937). Despite his criticism of Hitler's domestic policies, Bishop Galen supported the Führer's foreign policy; he judged that the Treaty of Versailles was unjust and that Bolshevism was a threat to Germany and the church. He approved of German troops entering the demilitarized Rhineland in 1936 and encouraged Catholics in 1939 to join in Germany's defense after the Wehrmacht invaded Poland, though he condemned the killing of civilians and unarmed prisoners of war.

Bishop Galen emerged in 1941 as one of the church's most outspoken critics of the Third Reich. On July 13, July 20, and August 3, he preached a series of sermons in Münster's cathedral against the state's seizure of church buildings, its expelling of members of religious orders, and its program of euthanasia for approximately fifty thousand disabled men, women, and children. (Thousands of copies of Galen's sermons were eventually dropped throughout Germany from Allied airplanes.) Curtailing the euthanasia, Hitler eventually retaliated against the bishop by imprisoning twenty-nine priests of the Diocese of Münster. He also incarcerated the bishop's brother, Franz Galen, who was a government official, after the unsuccessful attempt to assassinate the Führer on July 20, 1944. Further, Hitler secretly listed Bishop Galen for execution as soon as the Reich won the war. Because of his courageous preaching, Galen came to be called "the Lion of Münster." As Allied bombs killed Westphalian civilians in 1943 and destroyed homes and businesses, he preached on July 4, 1943, that Germans must forgive their enemies. (The British bombed Münster on October 10, 1943.) After the war, Bishop Galen spoke out against what he perceived to be the unjust policies of the Allied powers, including their assumption of the collective guilt of the German people. Named a cardinal by Pius XII on February 17, 1946, he died one month later on March 22.

The Unfolding of a Scholarly Career, 1935–1975

Joseph Lortz developed his views on Martin Luther and the Protestant Reformation during his years at the University of Münster. At the time, German Catholic treatments of Luther were dominated by the polemical works of Heinrich Denifle, O.P., and Hartman Grisar, S.J., both of whom characterized the reformer as malicious and emotionally ill. Building on the revisionist work of Joseph Greving in 1905, Hermann Mauert in 1906, Franz Xavier Kiefl in 1917, and Sebastian Merkle in 1929, Lortz produced in 1939 his two-volume *The Reformation in Germany*. (At the insistence of Pope Pius XII, the original German text was not immediately published in other languages.) Among the book's dominant ideas, Lortz stressed that the church itself was in turmoil in the 1500s because of the disintegration of the medieval worldview, clerical abuses, and the disarray of theology. "The schism in the Christian Church, which we call the Reformation, could not have happened if the state and Church of the west had still possessed the strength of its medieval, universal unity."[43] Further, according to Lortz, Martin Luther was a genuinely religious man who rightly perceived the church's need for reform. "In his search for the God of grace he found himself outside the Church before he knew that he was outside. His breach with the Church was in no way motivated by any preconceived revolutionary program or any base impulse or desire."[44] But Luther pursued his good intentions in the wrong way, Lortz maintained, because of his disregard of the church's magisterium. "For him the realm of the objective event of the Church lies completely on the periphery of [his] interest. All attention is focused on one's private experience of salvation. . . . That is to say, in addition to his psychological make-up there were also basic theological attitudes which characterized Luther as a radical subjectivist."[45] In stressing these ideas, Lortz brought about a radical shift in the Catholic approach to Luther, a shift from a polemic against him to an appreciation of him and his ideas in their historical context.[46]

While succeeding in his scholarship at Münster, Lortz did not fit in well with the faculty of Catholic theology. He was a member of the Nazi party and was assigned to teach the courses that had belonged to the highly respected Georg Schreiber. It was clear to everyone that Rust had sent Lortz from Braunsberg to Münster in order to reward him for his pro-Nazi statements. Soon after arriving at Münster in 1935, Lortz received a manuscript by three pro-Hitler Catholics in order to support the new Reich. It was entitled *Sendschreiben katholischer Deutscher an ihre Volks- und Glaubensgenossen* [An Open Letter from Catholic Germans to Their Associates Who are German and Catholic]. Initially enthusiastic about this work, Lortz presented it to Bishop Galen, who approved of its publication but refused to write a foreword. The bishop also advised Lortz not to serve as the text's editor. Since the pamphlet appeared in 1936 without Lortz's name, the omission probably signaled that Lortz was having second thoughts about the Nazi regime. As noted earlier, Lortz had already added a critique of Rosenberg's ideology to the 1935 edition of *History of the Church*. In 1937, perhaps influenced by Pius XI's *Mit brennender Sorge* and conversations with Bishop Galen, Lortz eliminated from *History of the Church* the appendix in which he regarded Hitler favorably. Also in 1937, he tried to cancel his membership in the Nazi party but was told that no one was allowed to withdraw from the party; Lortz continued to pay his membership dues until July 1944.[47]

After Hitler's defeat, Lortz was required by the British Military government to undergo de-Nazification—an official inquiry into his activities in the Third Reich and an educational program concerning democracy. In his formal statement of 1945 to the Allied powers, Lortz clarified his relationship to National Socialism:

> I found in the National-Socialist idea [in 1933] . . . elements that I, without knowledge of National Socialism, had characterized in 1930 as decisive for the [nation's] imminent, spiritual-religious

development . . . namely: an epochal turn to objective reality . . . to authority, to community, and to faith. Such ideas were expressed, for example, in the encyclical *Mirari* of Pope Gregory XVI and in the *Syllabus* of Pius IX. . . . These were the elements that were necessary for the strengthening of a spiritual-religious rebirth [of Germany] if they were developed in the right way.[48]

On November 25, 1946, the provisional German government granted Lortz a temporary teaching license while it decided whether he could permanently remain in higher education. While awaiting the government's decision, Lortz anguished over his future. His turmoil has been described by Josef Pieper:

> After the war, Joseph Lortz would have a few difficult years. His early statements in favor of the [Nazi] regime would be held against him. An embittered clerical colleague of his used his not inconsiderable influence to stop him from getting any other academic post. Once again his natural susceptibility for immediate impressions thwarted the defenseless man. Uncomprehending, he watched the perpetration of what had long been simply naked injustice. In vain I tried to get him simply to turn his back on all that and sit down to work; but that was just what he could not do. It took a sinister "de-Nazification process"—the only one in which I have ever testified—to give him at the age of more than sixty, the possibility of a new start.[49]

Lortz received permission in 1948 from the provisional German government to retain a professorship at a German university. He immediately encountered difficulties at the University of Münster, however, since he was required to relinquish his courses to Georg Schreiber, who had taught them prior to 1935 and who was once again a professor at Münster. Lortz lost his academic position at the University of Münster on April 1, 1949, fourteen years to the day after Rust had assigned him to Münster. On December 1, 1949, he was appointed to the faculty of philosophy at the University of Mainz.

Lortz had inadvertently planted the seeds for his postwar career during the early 1940s by participating in the ecumenical group Una Sancta, which had been founded in 1939 by Max Metzger and Matthias Laros.[50] Metzger had earned a doctorate in theology in 1910, had served as a military chaplain in the German army during the First World War, and afterward had devoted himself to ecumenism and pacifism. Metzger proposed to Lortz in 1940 that he recast the ideas in *The Reformation in Germany* into a booklet for use in parish discussions, and, in 1941, Lortz published "The Reformation: Theses Put Forward as a Friendly Approach for Oecumenical Conversation."[51] While promoting ecumenism, Metzger also pursued his commitment to pacifism by clandestinely organizing in 1939 an international coalition of religious leaders dedicated to stopping the war. After building a secret network of communications among these leaders, he was arrested by the Gestapo on June 29, 1943, brought to trial as a traitor, and executed at the age of fifty-seven in Berlin on April 17, 1944.[52]

After Metzger's death, Matthias Laros (d. 1965) assumed leadership of Una Sancta.[53] After earning a doctorate in theology in 1913, he worked in parochial ministry while writing essays on the thought of Blaise Pascal and John Henry Newman. From 1922 to 1940, he edited a ten-volume German edition of selected writings by Cardinal Newman. Although he lost his library of seven thousand books in an Allied bombing raid in 1945, he did not lose his desire to renew the church. In late 1945, Laros initiated a second printing of Lortz's "Reformation: Theses" and eventually arranged for Lortz to give four public lectures in 1946 and 1947, which were published in 1948 under the title *The Reformation: A Problem for Today.*[54] In 1949 Laros urged the German government to establish an ecumenical institute at Mainz directed by Joseph Lortz, who in Laros's judgment was the only individual capable of promoting "the unity of the confessions and internal peace among Germans."[55]

After his appointment to Mainz's faculty in late 1949, Lortz was named in 1950 Mainz's professor of the history of Western religions and also codirector with Fritz Kern of Mainz's new Institute for European History.[56] Kern died in 1950, and Lortz continued as the Institute's sole director, committed to its goal of eliminating religious and national prejudice, especially between Germany and France. Over the next twenty-five years, he published some fifty articles and two books, *Einheit der Christenheit:*

Unfehlbarkeit und lebendige Aussage [The Unity of Christendom: Infallibility and the Living Testimonies] (1959) and *Tradition im Umbruch* [Tradition in Upheaval] (1959).[57] Lortz also contributed to the effort of Germans to acknowledge their failure in protecting Jews from Nazi persecution. In a postwar German edition of *History of the Church* he observed, "The horrific mass crimes of recent times are the most grave single evil in current history. These were committed in Hitler's Third Reich against Jews (six million were put to death) without the Christian conscience being moved to prevent the harm or at least to protest sufficiently against it." He also highlighted the challenge to Christians in general: "In relation to that unprecedented crime the question about our Jewish brethren is posed to every Christian. The church as a whole must ask itself whether it did enough and does enough to retrieve the elements of divine revelation contained in Judaism in order to make them fruitful for both Christians and Jews."[58]

While Lortz never publicly acknowledged his own failure to discern the true character of Nazism, he came close to doing so on October 10, 1959, in a lecture he gave at Echternach in Luxembourg on his career as a historian. He stated, "Whoever has never been scalded in the service of truth and righteousness has not grasped life properly."[59] In 1964 Lortz saw the Second Vatican Council adopt the ecumenical orientation that he had pursued. He had misgivings, however, about the church in the postconciliar period. In the last months of his life, he wrote *Ökumenismus ohne Wahrheit?* [Ecumenism without Truth?] (1974) in which he argued that dialogue between Catholics and Protestants had gone astray because it had failed to challenge secularization. Lortz died on February 21, 1975, in Luxembourg.

A Rejection of Modernity

Joseph Lortz claimed that he had demonstrated in his *History of the Church* what popes Gregory XVI, Pius IX, Pius X, and Pius XI had declared time and again, namely, that modernity was destroying Western culture, along with the church and belief in God, and that the modern era needed to yield to a new age characterized by a fresh respect for ecclesiastical and civil authority.

In Hubert Wolf's words, Lortz "understood history since the twelfth century as above all a process of liberal and subjective degeneration, against which there began in 1900 an epochal turn to objective reality, authority, political leadership by a Führer, and to religious reality." In light of his "critique of liberalism," Lortz saw "National Socialism as a spiritual cousin [of the church] and a conqueror of 'liberalism.'"[60] Michael Lukens has also observed that Lortz was attracted to Nazism because he rejected modernity's atheistic communism, individualism, and secularism: "On the basis of these concerns, Lortz saw not just a compatibility between Catholicism and National Socialism but the possibility therein of religious renewal and mutual reinforcement."[61] Victor Conzemius has made the same point: "The anti-liberalism of National Socialism was for [Lortz] the contemporary manifestation of the church's anti-liberalism: Liberal theology, liberal church politics, liberalism as a spiritual movement were always for him the gravedigger of ecclesial-religious unity, the outstanding enemy of dogmatically anchored religiosity."[62]

Lortz was not the only Catholic historian to misjudge Hitler in 1933. He was joined by others like Johannes Hollnsteiner and Andreas Veit, who were members of the Katholische Akademiker Verband. These scholars agreed that the magisterium should influence the study of church history. In taking this position, they accused other historians such as Heinrich Finke, Sebastian Merkle, and Georg Schreiber—who were members of the Görres Gesellschaft—of succumbing to liberalism by engaging in historical inquiry about the church apart from papal teachings. According to Lortz, church history "follows its own principles drawn from revelation—it is theology."[63] Guided by his early study of Tertullian, Lortz held that history is a form of apologetics. Explaining this view, Erwin Iserloh has written, "According to Lortz, the 'manner of seeing' distinguishes the church historian from the profane historian. The church historian sees the process of history through the eyes of faith: I believe in the church."[64] Yet, as we have seen, this commitment to a specific theological outlook or to a theory of history initially blinded Lortz and others to the actual state of affairs in Hitler's new Germany. As Michael Lukens noted, "The key to Lortz's approach to Nazism is that he developed his historical scholarship within a theological vision."[65]

Lortz was motivated in his study of Martin Luther by the theological conviction that there was one true church. Because Lortz took seriously Christ's prayer "that they may be one" (John 17:11), he judged that Catholic scholars needed to take a fresh look at Luther's life and thought, thereby questioning the prevailing Catholic view that the reformer was filled with rancor and was unstable. Lortz believed that if the Protestant and Catholic churches were united, they would help to bring about a new epoch in the West—an epoch characterized by the overcoming of secularism and the flourishing of a Christian society. Guided by these religious commitments, Lortz emerged as a Catholic pioneer in ecumenism. Indeed, his *Reformation in Germany* (which appeared in its sixth German edition in 1982) was, according to Hans Küng, "epoch-making."[66] Nevertheless, as subsequent studies have shown, Lortz misrepresented Martin Luther's life and ideas. Concerned with stressing Luther's common ground with the Roman church, Lortz made too little of the reformer's distinct theological orientation and of his deliberate decision to break away from Rome.[67] Thus Lortz's theological conviction about a single church led him to minimize significant aspects of Luther's life and thought. Similar to his mistaken view of National Socialism, Lortz forced historical data into a preconceived theory. For this reason, Victor Conzemius has described Lortz's view of church history in general and of National Socialism in particular as "idealism separated from reality."[68]

An analysis of Joseph Lortz's attraction to Hitler has brought us to a conclusion that we reached in our study of Karl Eschweiler's support for the Nazi state. Because they judged that modernity was a form of rebellion against God and the church, some theologians rejected democracy and favored an authoritarian state that would formally recognize the church. Some Catholic scholars who were progressive in their efforts to move beyond neo-Scholasticism were simultaneously reactionary in their view of the political and social forms that they associated with the Enlightenment and the modern age. A similar theological and political orientation manifested itself in the theologian Karl Adam.

4

Karl Adam

Searching for a National Community

IN 1924 THE THEOLOGIAN KARL ADAM (1876–1966) PUBLISHED A BOOK
that became one of the most important studies in Catholic theology during the period between the First Vatican Council (1869–
70) and the Second Vatican Council (1962–65). In this relatively
short work *The Spirit of Catholicism,* Adam argued that, while the
church is an institution, it is primarily a community of believers
united in Jesus Christ by the Holy Spirit.[1] Although Adam was
not the first modern theologian to present this understanding of
the church, he explained it with a clarity and coherence that made
it appeal to general readers as well as to scholars. This book went
through at least fourteen printings in German over a period of
forty years and was translated into thirteen languages, including
Chinese and Japanese. The Italian text made an exceedingly positive impression on Monsignor Giovanni Battista Montini who
gave out copies of it to his colleagues at the Vatican in 1930 and
who, after being elected Pope Paul VI in 1963, implicitly drew on
The Spirit of Catholicism in his first encyclical, *Ecclesiam Suam*
(1964). Moreover, *The Spirit of Catholicism* shaped the ideas of
English-speaking religious thinkers such as Robert McAfee
Brown, Dorothy Day, Thomas Merton, Flannery O'Connor, Alec
Vidler, and Evelyn Underhill. Because of *The Spirit of Catholicism,*
Karl Adam stands out as one of the most creative theologians of
the early twentieth century. But he was also one of the most naive
scholars in his attempt to find a common ground between
Catholicism and National Socialism. In the summer of 1933, he
spoke of Hitler in messianic terms and of his new state as the start
of a national community that could bring about a renewal of
Catholicism.

Born in Pursruck (Oberpfalz) on October 22, 1876, Karl Adam was ordained a priest of the Diocese of Regensburg in 1900. Soon afterward, he matriculated at the University of Munich in historical and systematic theology. Earning his doctorate in 1904 and his Habilitation in 1908, he was influenced by the legacy of J. J. Ignaz von Döllinger (d. 1890) and the historical studies of Albert Ehrhard as well as by the works of Joseph Schnitzer (d. 1940), who was excommunicated in 1908 because of his alleged modernism. From 1908 until 1917, Adam taught at Munich's Wilhelm Gymnasium, tutored the sons of Crown Prince Rupprecht of the royal family, and lectured at the Bavarian Cadet Corps. He accepted a call in 1917 to the University of Strasbourg but was required to leave there in December 1918 because the Treaty of Versailles prohibited German citizens from holding civil service positions in France. After teaching during the spring of 1919 at the Regensburg seminary, he moved to the University of Tübingen, where he assumed a professorship in systematic theology that Wilhelm Koch had vacated because his use of the historical-critical method had led to allegations of modernism. Adam remained at Tübingen for the next thirty years, developing his thought in relation to three coordinates: a critique of the church, a critique of modernity, and the development of a contemporary theology.

Beginning in the late 1800s, numerous German Catholic scholars and pastoral leaders, working for the renewal of the church, promoted what came to be called "reform Catholicism."[2] Distancing themselves from neo-Scholasticism, they looked for fresh forms of thought in which to express the Christian tradition while striving to avoid what they perceived to be the mistakes of the Enlightenment and of Kant.[3] Inspired by the writings of J. M. Sailer, I. H. von Wessenberg, J. A. Möhler, and J. B. Hirscher, they envisioned the elimination of what they saw to be the church's outdated practices and structures, such as the requirement of priestly celibacy and the *Index of Forbidden Books.* They also called for more intellectual freedom for theologians, historians, and biblical scholars as well as a greater recognition by the papacy of the authority of bishops and local churches. The first generation of scholars in this renewal movement included F. X. Kraus, Josef

Müller, and Hermann Schell, while the outstanding members of the second generation were Albert Ehrhard and Sebastian Merkle. Prominent in reform Catholicism's third generation were Karl Adam and Joseph Wittig. Finally, the fourth generation gave rise to the "Rhine Circle," led by Oskar Schroeder and Josef Thomé.[4]

Karl Adam was dedicated to the renewal of the church and theology throughout his entire scholarly life. During his career's first phase (1900–1918), he inquired into the history of doctrine. Working at the University of Munich on the Latin Fathers, in his doctoral dissertation (1904) he examined Tertullian's ecclesiology and, in his Habilitationsschrift (1908), studied Augustine's theology of the Eucharist. In 1917 he completed one monograph on Pope Callistus's instruction on penance, and a second on Augustine's understanding of the forgiveness of sins. He would have likely produced other historical studies while teaching at Munich if he had not publicly criticized Pius X's instruction *Sacrorum Antistitum* (1910), which required all priests to take the Oath Against Modernism.[5] Although only thirty-four years old, Adam published an article arguing that if the Oath were required of professors of Catholic theology, it would function in Germany as "the official death notice regarding Catholic scholarship." In expressing this view, Adam stood not far from Albert Ehrhard and Joseph Schnitzer, each of whom had written against Pius X's condemnation of modernism in 1907. Shortly after his essay appeared, Adam learned that the Holy Office was examining his publications. For many months, he thought that he would be required to stop teaching theology, but he was eventually told that the Holy Office had suspended its investigation because Bavaria's Crown Prince Rupprecht had intervened in his behalf.[6]

During the second phase of his career (1919–54), Adam wrote about Christian faith, the church, and Jesus Christ in numerous books and articles, including "Glaube und Glaubenswissenschaft im Katholizismus" [Faith and the Scholarly Study of Faith in Catholicism] (1920), *The Spirit of Catholicism* (1924), *Christ our Brother* (1927), *The Son of God* (1933), and *The Christ of Faith* (1954). Avoiding neo-Scholasticism, he employed ideas found in *Lebensphilosophie*, "philosophy of life," which flourished in Germany from the late 1800s into the 1930s. *Lebensphilosophie*—a form of existentialism that was promoted by such diverse thinkers as Friedrich Nietzsche, Henri Bergson, Stefan George, Rainer Maria Rilke, and Max Scheler—was rooted in German Romanticism, that is, in the mode of thought "meant to identify subject and object, to reconcile man and nature, consciousness and unconsciousness."[7] In contrast to the empirical thought of the natural and social sciences, *Lebensphilosophie* highlighted the interconnectedness or organic character of all life. After the First World War, many Germans yearned for a sense of life as a whole, for a return to nature, and for a recognition of objective reality. They were attracted to Nietzsche's exhortation "Stay loyal to the earth," and to Stefan George's monitory verse "The worst . . . is that your mind . . . may rend apart the bond with clod and creature."[8] Along with this emphasis on feeling, there was a stress on the intuitive grasp of reality, expressed particularly in the philosophical writings of Wilhelm Dilthey, Edmund Husserl, Max Scheler, and Martin Heidegger.

Karl Adam's reliance on *Lebensphilosophie* in his theological writings eventually prompted the Holy Office to resume its scrutiny of his books. Bishop Michael Buchberger of Regensburg informed Adam on August 1, 1932, that the Holy Office might place *The Spirit of Catholicism* on the *Index*. For almost a year, Adam was burdened by anxiety about the Vatican's decision. On June 10, 1933, Archbishop Gröber of Freiburg told Adam that the Holy Office would not condemn *The Spirit of Catholicism* if it were revised to remedy the doctrinal ambiguities that the Holy Office listed; in addition, the Holy Office would not condemn *Christ Our Brother* if it, too, were modified to the Vatican's satisfaction. That the Holy Office was not condemning his books came as good news to Adam, who wept for joy when he spoke about it with his students.[9] He edited both books during the summer of 1933 while also writing an essay in support of Hitler, and he submitted the revised texts to the Holy Office in the autumn of 1933. As he did so, he learned that Rome also wanted revisions in his recently published *The Son of God* (in German, *Jesus Christus*). He immediately made these changes and submitted his text. In December 1933, Adam received word that the Holy Office had approved his clarifications for all three books.

Adam's commitment to the renewal of the church and theology meant that he wrote a truly contemporary theology.[10] Unlike the theological manuals, his books and essays appealed to general readers as well as to scholars and took seriously such issues as the widespread longing for community. His writings awakened in readers like Edward Schillebeeckx, O.P., a desire to undertake innovative forms of theological inquiry.[11] The theologian Heinrich Fries has recalled that "Adam was the shining star of Catholic theology in Tübingen and far beyond; he documented and exemplified how good and fruitful some vitalization from outside could be like a burst of fresh air."[12]

While calling for changes in the church and theology, Karl Adam was also critical of modernity. He held that rationalism had disconnected people from themselves, from their neighbors, and ultimately from God. The Enlightenment had introduced an imbalance into contemporary life by valuing the intellect at the expense of feelings and interpersonal relationships. Finding support for his views in Max Scheler's work, Adam expressed his critique of modernity in *The Spirit of Catholicism* and in *Christ and the Western Mind*.

Max Scheler provided the language to move beyond what Adam perceived to be the limitations of the Enlightenment, including the neo-Kantianism, which dominated the German academy in the late 1800s and early 1900s. Building on the phenomenology of Edmund Husserl, Scheler developed an intuitive method for illuminating "objective realities."[13] He inquired into human feelings, commitments, and values in such books as *Ressentiment* (1912), *The Nature of Sympathy* (1913), and the two-volume *Formalism in Ethics and Non-Formal Ethics of Values* (1913–16). He maintained that persons are not solely objects that are apprehended by empirical methods; they are also "relations" that are known as they interact with other persons and the world. A community is much more, therefore, than an assembly of discrete persons held together by a social contract; it is an interpersonal reality, a whole that is greater than its parts. Moreover, the interpersonal character of human beings opens them to sensing a reality greater than themselves—God. In his book *On the Eternal in Man* (1921), Scheler argued that human beings' religious sentiments and practices arise in response to an irreducible, transcendent reality. This reality is "a realm of being and value which is in basis and origin utterly different from the empirical world."[14] Belief in this transcendent reality involves more than ethics; it includes a relationship to and an apprehension of a higher being. Scheler's work, which had similarities to Rudolf Otto's *Idea of the Holy* (1917), spoke to many theologians, including Karl Adam.[15]

In *The Spirit of Catholicism* Adam highlighted what he perceived to be the illness afflicting the modern world. Along with Joseph Lortz and Oswald Spengler, he held that the West was experiencing a spiritual and cultural decline that had begun in the late Middle Ages, had spread during the Reformation, and had culminated in the Enlightenment. In the twentieth century, this degeneration showed itself in atheism, individualism, liberalism, moral relativism, and secularism—mentalities that erode interpersonal life as well as Christian faith. These trends pulled people apart from one another and from Christ and the church. As a result, they had brought the West to a spiritual and cultural breakdown. But these corrosive forces could be reversed, Adam judged, by a rebirth of belief in Christ and the church: "Just as the church by the compact unity and strength of its Christian faith gave the Middle Ages their inward unity and their strength of soul, . . . so it alone is able in our modern day to introduce again amid the conflicting currents, the solvent forces and growing exhaustion of the West, a single lofty purpose, a constructive and effective religious power, a positive moral energy and a vitalizing enthusiasm."[16] Although Adam had argued in 1910 that the Vatican should exempt German theologians from the Oath Against Modernism, he stated in 1924 that Pius X's condemnation of modernism in 1907 had spared the church from the destructive ideas of liberalism.[17]

In *Christ and the Western Mind* (1928), Adam elaborated his critique of the Enlightenment and modernity. In the late Middle Ages, the West began to separate human learning from belief in Jesus Christ and the church, thereby initiating the secularization of society and culture. Subsequently, the Reformation fueled this process of separation; Luther and Calvin eroded the church's authority when they broke away from the papacy. The Enlightenment added to the West's malaise because it established human authority against God's authority as realized in the church. During the post-Enlightenment, Kant, Hegel, and Freud posited criteria that negated the validity of divine revelation and church teachings. The people of the West now faced a choice: either they could experience the degeneration of their society, or they could move beyond individualism, rationalism, and subjectivism to a new sense of community, to a fresh understanding of personal existence, and to the recovery of objective reality. This breakthrough could occur by a return to Christ as known in the church: "In the midst of our western civilization there is still an authority, older than all the states, firmer than all the thrones, more powerful than all dictatorships, more sacred than the law of nations. But this authority in our midst lives by the eternal will of Christ, spirit of his spirit, power of his power. It will forever proclaim this authority of Christ, forever be ready as our guide, in order to help us find our way out of chaos. And on this rock rests the western church."[18] A new trust in the church would depend in part on a clear presentation of the truths of Christian belief.

Karl Adam offered engaging insights on the nature of faith, the church, and Jesus Christ. In his "Glauben und Glaubenswissenschaft im Katholizismus," he elucidated a notion of faith that stood apart from a neo-Scholastic understanding of belief as intellectual assent and also from a rationalist view of faith as knowledge of a universal idea. According to Adam, Christian belief involves the assent of the whole person, who makes a commitment not in private but in the church. Faith is self-involving and possesses a communal character; it is not solely intellectual or notional as construed by Scholasticism, but springs out of a person's encounters with the living Christ, encounters that occur in the church. Against the Enlightenment's stress upon the autonomous self, the church recognizes the "organic" or interconnected essence of personal existence. Although faith requires an individual decision, it happens only in the mystical or spiritual body of Christ. "The early Christian community of faith was the result of an elementary experience of the Spirit. And the community itself expressed the early Christian community of faith. It was the visible embodiment of the effect of the Spirit, the body, in which the Spirit revealed itself. . . . Not the 'I,' but the 'we' is the bearer of the Spirit."[19]

In *The Spirit of Catholicism* Adam described the church as the community of the living Christ. In doing so, he differed from both the neo-Scholastic and the Protestant understandings of the church. According to the first, the church is an institution, indeed a perfect society; according to the second, the church is an assembly of discrete individuals, a notion that Adam perceived in Friedrich Heiler's presentation of the church as a conjunction of opposites.[20] Drawing on the work of Möhler, Adam retrieved St. Paul's metaphor of the church as body of Christ (1 Corinthians 10:17–18; 12:27; Romans 12:5). As a community, the church makes the living Christ present in the world so that all people might become united with the one true head of the human family. Indeed, as Möhler said, the church is the ongoing incarnation of Christ. In Adam's words, "[T]he divine is incarnated in the community, and precisely and only insofar as it is a community." He added that "[t]he incarnation is for Christians the foundation and planting of that new communion which we call the Church." As body of Christ, the church shares in the mediation which Jesus Christ has accomplished between God and creation. "The church as a whole, as a community, an an organic unity is a divine creation."[21]

Christ Our Brother and *The Son of God* accentuated the humanity of Jesus Christ that neo-Scholastic theology had neglected. An emphasis on the divinity of Christ had fueled, Adam maintained, a misrepresentation of him in contemporary thought as in Nietzsche's writings, where Christ is presented as a passive and weak figure. In fact, as the one true mediator between God and creation, Jesus Christ is the new Adam (Romans 5) who embodies the best qualities of humanity and brings them to their full realization. Jesus Christ is the perfect human being who has fully united the divine word and human nature. Therefore, the central event in the drama of creation and history is the incarnation, which is remarkable not so much because God raised human nature to share in the divine life as because the divine Word descended or emptied himself (Philippians 2) to become a whole human being. According to Adam, "The Christian gospel announces primarily not an ascent of humanity to the heights of the divine in a transfiguration, an apotheosis, a deification of human nature, but a descent of the Godhead, of the divine word, to the state of bondage of the purely human."[22] As St. Athanasius insisted, Jesus Christ brought about the salvation of the world by becoming completely human. As a result, Christ meets and redeems women and men in their very humanity, that is, in their deepest yearnings, in their marriages, friendships, and daily work, and also in their history and culture.[23]

Bishop Sproll
and Tübingen's Catholic Theologians

Karl Adam's desire to find a common ground between Catholicism and National Socialism sprang in part from his relationship to the Tübingen School. Since its founding in 1817, the faculty of Catholic theology at the University of Tübingen had committed itself to bringing about a fresh synthesis of the Christian faith and contemporary thought.[24] After the consolidation of the German states in 1804, the king of Baden moved the Catholic theologians from the seminary in Ellwangen to the University of Tübingen. Housed in a building with the university's Protestant theologians, Tübingen's first generation of Catholic theologians, led by J. S. Drey and Möhler, employed the prevailing categories of Romanticism as they engaged in their respective inquiries. The next generation of scholars, led by J. E. Kuhn, relied on the concepts of Idealism, especially of Hegel, as they undertook their theological investigations. In the third generation, J. B. Hirscher used the ideas of neo-Kantianism, and his successor, Paul Schanz, brought Christian faith into dialogue with the natural sciences. As already noted, Wilhelm Koch had been forced to resign from Tübingen's faculty in 1918 because of his historical approach to church teachings. Since 1919, Karl Adam had set out—in the spirit of the Catholic Tübingen School—to create a new synthesis of faith and culture. But was it appropriate to pursue this ideal when the dominant ethos was National Socialism?

The proponents of National Socialism at Tübingen maintained that this worldview was the foundation of a new German polity. They echoed the pro-Nazi ideas of Martin Heidegger at the University of Freiburg as they argued that Hitler was leading the German people beyond the individualism of the West, and also beyond the collectivism of the Soviet Union. The pro-Hitler scholars included some of the most respected members of the university's faculty of Protestant theology: Gustav Bebermeyer, Karl Fezer, Friedrich Focke, Wilhelm Geiseler, Gerhard Kittel, Ernst Stracke, and Arthur Weiser.[25] These professors endorsed anti-Semitic and nationalistic ideas that were embraced both by the "German Christians," who tried to synthesize Christian faith and National Socialism, and by the proponents of the German Faith Movement, who were intent on replacing Christian belief with ancient Aryan beliefs. In 1933, Jakob Wilhelm Hauer, Tübingen's professor of Indology and the scientific study of religion, emerged as a national spokesman for the German Faith Movement. The widespread support for Hitler among Tübingen's professors meant that the Reich's minister of education, Bernhard Rust, dismissed very few professors from the university.

The Catholic professors in all faculties at the University of Tübingen found themselves in a complex situation beginning in 1933. As a distinct minority at the university, they were viewed with suspicion by the Protestants and were always looking for ways to strengthen their ties with their non-Catholic colleagues. Prior to the Weimar Republic, Catholic instructors and Catholic students were underrepresented in higher education throughout Germany. They increased at the universities during the Weimar Republic because the Catholic Center party had lobbied the state and national governments for greater educational opportunities for Catholics. The Catholic professors were, therefore, indebted to the Weimar Republic, but at the same time they—like the Protestant professors—favored a monarchy, or an authoritarian government, over a parliamentary democracy. Most of the Catholics remained distant, however, from the National Socialist movement because of its neopaganism, racism, and anti-Catholicism, and they opted to remain silent in public on political issues.[26]

Bishop Johannes Baptist Sproll of the Diocese of Rottenburg

took, however, a strong public stand against Hitler.[27] Sproll opposed the Nazi state from the outset and did not waver in his opposition to Nazism even after the Catholic bishops dropped their bans on membership in the Nazi party. He wrote articles against it in the diocesan newspaper and held meetings throughout the diocese at which he explained his criticism of National Socialism. At Ulm on May 27 and 28, 1933, he gathered twenty thousand Catholics to show their solidarity against the Nazi party. On December 28, 1933, he sent a confidential letter to Cardinal Bertram in which he pointed out that "[t]he Concordat will not put the government on notice; it will not even contain it. This is obvious."[28] In January 1934, after Karl Adam came into conflict with the Nazi party, Sproll again wrote to Bertram: "The struggle between faith and unbelief appears to be beginning."[29]

Sproll's opposition to the Reich came to a dramatic head on April 10, 1938, when he refused to vote in the so-called national referendum concerning the Reich's annexation of Austria. Incensed by the bishop's action, Nazis demonstrated outside the diocesan chancery and made threats on the bishop's life. Arrested by the Gestapo on August 24, 1938, and banished from his diocese, Sproll went into hiding in Bavaria. In 1943, as the war was turning against Germany, he held a secret meeting at Heil Krumbad with the former president of the State of Württemburg, Eugen Bolz. Soon after, Bolz was arrested for treason and executed at Berlin's Plötzensee prison. Sproll went back into hiding until Hitler's defeat. On June 12, 1945, he resumed his pastoral leadership of the Diocese of Rottenburg, working until his death at the age of seventy-nine on March 4, 1949.

In 1933 Tübingen's faculty of Catholic theology consisted of approximately seven professors who, along with their assistants, were responsible for teaching 233 students.[30] As priests, these scholars were loyal to Bishop Sproll. At the same time, as professors they participated in an academic tradition dedicated to bringing about a synthesis between Catholicism and contemporary ideas. In the Nazi state, most of Tübingen's theologians opted for silence, even when in 1934 one of their colleagues, Paul Simon, was dismissed because of his Jewish ancestry. Among Tübingen's Catholic theologians, Karl Adam stood out because of his public effort to mediate between the church and the state. Although he maintained a cordial relationship with Bishop Sproll, he did not support the bishop's hard line against Hitler. Because of his years in Munich, Adam was also aware of the effort of Munich's Cardinal Faulhaber to work with Hitler.

Cardinal Faulhaber
and Munich's Catholic Theologians

Munich was a center both of support and of resistance to Hitler. On the one hand, it was the birthplace of National Socialism, the site of Hitler's failed *Putsch* on November 8, 1923, and the national headquarters of the Nazi party. It also allowed one of Hitler's first concentration camps to be opened in its suburb of Dachau, and hosted in 1937 the exhibit of what Hitler called "degenerate art." On the other hand, Munich nurtured strong Catholic resistance against Hitler. Erich Przywara preached against Nazism until 1935.[31] Rupert Mayer, S.J., was such an outspoken critic of the Nazi regime that he was imprisoned and slated for execution. He eventually was released on the condition that he remain in seclusion in a monastery. The student resistant group, the White Rose, emerged at the University of Munich in the early 1940s and, inspired by the writings of Theodor Haecker and Romano Guardini, distributed fliers condemning Nazi atrocities on the war's eastern front and calling for peace. The students were eventually captured, immediately tried, and then executed in February 1943. Another opponent of Hitler was Alfred Delp, S.J., who helped Jews flee to Switzerland, participated in the Kreisau Circle (which drafted a democratic constitution for postwar Germany), and was executed on February 2, 1945.[32] The conflicts in Munich between pro-Hitler and anti-Hitler groups did not escape the notice of the city's ecclesiastical leader, Cardinal Faulhaber.

Michael Faulhaber (d. 1952) was made the archbishop of Munich-Freising in September 1917 and named a cardinal on March 7, 1921.[33] Prior to this appointment, he had taught the Old Testament at the University of Strasbourg and served as the bishop of Speyer. As Munich's ordinary, he was also the president of Bavaria's conference of Catholic bishops. Since he held that the church's mission was best accomplished in a state with a constitutional monarchy, he was troubled when the Wittelsbachs abdicated the throne in 1918.[34] He abhorred Bolshevism and had witnessed its bloody effects in Munich during the spring of 1919 when a "soviet" government had briefly ruled Bavaria. At the same time, he did not accept parliamentary democracy with its principle of religious freedom. As noted in chapter 1, Faulhaber had expressed his concerns about democracy in a public address that he gave in 1922 at the Katholikentag in Munich. Nevertheless, Faulhaber held no illusions about National Socialism and publicly condemned Nazi ideology, most strikingly in his Advent sermons of 1933.[35]

In 1933 and 1934, Cardinal Faulhaber tried to affirm the ideals that the church held in common with Hitler while also calling attention to significant differences between the church and the Nazi regime. Influenced by his German patriotism, Faulhaber wanted Germany to reassert its leadership among the nations and thereby to overcome the injustices of the Treaty of Versailles. Hence, he supported Hitler's seizing of the Saarland, his annexation of Austria, and his takeover of the Sudeten region, and he did not publicly protest Germany's invasion of Poland. At the same time, he labored to protect the church's autonomy. Working with Bishop Preysing and Bishop Galen, he assisted in drafting Pius XI's encyclical *Mit brennender Sorge* and condemned the state's disregard of the concordat. Further, beginning in 1938 he secretly sought ways to assist Jews. In the 1940s, he joined Bishops Preysing and Galen in advising Cardinal Bertram to take a more confrontational stance against the Reich and labored unsuccessfully to have the bishops issue a pastoral letter in March 1942 against the Reich's violations of human rights. Faulhaber's opposition to the Third Reich had a direct impact on Munich's faculty of Catholic theology.

The University of Munich accommodated itself to Hitler's demands. The majority of professors remained silent as the University's Nazi administration dismissed professors because they were Jews or "political dissidents."[36] As a result, there was a 50-percent turnover of professors at the University of Munich from 1933 through 1939. In 1933 Munich's faculty of Catholic theology was composed of approximately fifteen professors who, with their assistants, were responsible for teaching 252 students, most of whom were seminarians. While none of these professors publicly supported National Socialism, each tolerated it. They did not protest in 1937 when Bernhard Rust gave one of their professorships to Ludwig Mohler, a member of the Nazi party.

The apparent tranquility ended in 1938. The minister of education informed Cardinal Faulhaber on August 16, 1937, that he was sending from Braunsberg to Munich the canon lawyer Hans Barion, who was a member of the Nazi party and who had temporarily supported the sterilization law. But Faulhaber informed Rust on January 5, 1938, that he would not approve of this appointment. According to the Reich Concordat, the state could not appoint a theology professor to a faculty without the appropriate bishop's conferral of a *missio canonica* (ecclesiastical permission) on the candidate. Disregarding Faulhaber's veto, Rust assigned Barion to Munich's faculty in the spring of 1938, and, on June 15, 1938, appointed the instructor Sebastian Schröcker, also in canon law, to Munich's faculty without Faulhaber's approval. Cardinal Faulhaber lodged official protests with the government and the Vatican and refused to give Barion and Schröcker ecclesiastical permission to teach theology, which in effect meant that no seminarians could enroll in their courses. Bavaria's minister of education, Adolf Wagner, retaliated against Faulhaber on November 12, 1938, by sending a Nazi mob to the diocesan chancery. Some protesters broke into the building and rampaged through each office, while others remained outside and chanted "Drag [Faulhaber] out," "To Dachau," and "Prison for the traitor." A few days later, the Reich incarcerated Faulhaber's advisor, Johannes Neuhäuser, at Dachau.[37]

Having informed the University of Munich on December 23, 1938, that the Reich would soon close its faculty of Catholic theology, Adolf Wagner implemented this decision on February 16, 1939, as the university ended its autumn-winter semester.[38] Two weeks later, Cardinal Faulhaber went to Rome and told the newly elected Pope Pius XII about his conflict with Rust and Wagner. (Pius XI had died on February 10, 1939, and Cardinal Pacelli was elected pope on March 2.) Soon after Faulhaber returned to Munich, the government sent Ludwig Mohler to Rome in order to defend the actions of Rust and Wagner. Next, Faulhaber received word from the Holy See that he should negotiate a settlement with the state. Complying with this directive, the cardinal proposed to Rust on March 24, 1939, that if Rust and Wagner reopened Munich's faculty of Catholic theology, Faulhaber would grant Barion the *missio canonica,* though he would not confer it on Schröcker. Rust rejected the cardinal's proposal and ordered that Munich's faculty of Catholic theology remain closed; he gradually assigned Munich's theologians to other universities.

Karl Adam's Dream of a New Germany

Karl Adam saw himself as a mediator between the church and the Nazi state.[39] Not belonging to the Nazi party, he criticized National Socialism. In March 1932, after Nazi students manipulated the University of Tübingen's senate to approve changes in voting procedures that would favor the advocates of National Socialism, Adam observed, "It is a scandal the way the student body has been beaten down by the National Socialists."[40] He refused to give the salutation, "Heil Hitler." Nevertheless, Adam judged that the church could find a common ground with Germany's Nazi leader.

In the summer of 1933, Adam called for a reconciliation between the church and the new government in his essay "Deutsches Volkstum und katholisches Christentum" [German Nationality and Catholic Christianity].[41] At the outset, he posed the question "What does the German race give to Catholicism, and what does Catholicism give to the German race, so that each develops and fulfills itself?" In response, he proposed that the answer to this question depended on one's view of the relationship between nature and grace. Following the path taken by Karl Eschweiler, he observed that, in the Protestant perspective, the church and the state stand apart from each other because grace and nature are opposed. In contrast, in the Catholic perspective, the church and the state should assist each other because grace completes nature. Since human nature is "wounded" but not "ruined" by original sin, it possesses a point of contact for God's supernatural activity. The inherent, good qualities of human nature serve as the place for grace. Using the ethnic-racial vocabulary of the day, Adam insisted that "redemption in its full sense is God's act and at the same time the work of humankind, a divine and human act—blood and spirit in one."[42]

The distinct theological anthropologies of Protestantism and Catholicism manifest themselves in ecclesiology. In the Protestant view, since the church is primarily concerned about Christians' relationship with God, its ministry is limited to the divine word and sacrament. In the Catholic view, since the church directs its attention to Christians' life in the world as well as before God, it must be engaged in the entire life of the person, including education. This outlook was evident, Adam noted, in the German Catholic bishops' announcement on March 28, 1933, in which while withdrawing their bans against membership in the Nazi party, the bishops claimed primary responsibility for their schools, youth groups, and adult organizations. Through these associations, the church assumes its duty of educating the "whole living human being." It presumes a stable civic order, maintained by the state, and it contributes to this order through its various programs. The church's work for the spiritual well-being of people builds on and supports the state's work of keeping good order in this world; in other words, the church and the state are "organically linked." "Without the church's work of education, the state's education remains fragmentary. Conversely, it is on the basis of the state's education that the church's education starts. The state's education produces the natural material and basis for the church's supernatural effects."[43]

While the church presupposes a people's specific culture, even its ethnic and racial identity, according to Adam, it also enhances every culture in which it is present. "The sacramental and educational activity of the church can be fruitful only when the church carefully observes the blood-given determinations of a race or people." The church has in fact demonstrated this respect. Pope

Pius XI encouraged missionaries to increase the indigenous clergy in Africa and Asia, just as his predecessors encouraged local churches throughout Europe to adapt to their respective ethnic groups and their cultures. As a result, German Catholicism and Italian Catholicism are distinct; each has its own saints, pilgrimages, and religious customs. While German spirituality possesses a philosophical orientation, Italian spirituality displays an aesthetic expression of Christian belief. These examples indicate that the church is "the true mother of all ethnic-racial identity." Insofar as the Nazi state wants to strengthen the ethnic and racial character of Germans, it can depend on cooperation from the church. "Nationalism and Catholicism possess no intrinsic opposition. They belong together as the natural and supernatural orders."

The prospect of new cooperation between the state and the church raised, however, a question about the civil status of Jews in Germany. "How do we as Catholic Germans stand in relation to Judaism?"[44] The new laws that restrict the involvement of Jews in German society are valid, said Adam, because Germans have a duty to strengthen their racial identity just as Jews are obliged to foster theirs. This racial obligation stems from the Old Testament's laws prohibiting Jews from intermarrying with their non-Jewish neighbors. Nevertheless, Germans must relate to Jews with justice and love. They are required by their Christian faith to help all people, regardless of religious belief and race. "As a trans-national community, embracing all races and heritages the Catholic church is no less obligated to respect the *natura individua* of Jews than to respect the racial character of other races." Further, the church's respect for Judaism springs from the fact that Jesus was a Jew. It is wrong to deny that Jesus was a Jew. Since Jesus was surely Jewish, Catholics should acknowledge their bonds with all Jews.

Adam ended his essay at this point with the parenthetical note: "To be continued." He eventually chose, however, not to publish the essay's second part, perhaps because he came into conflict with the Nazi regime.

During the autumn of 1933, Adam became alarmed by the neo-pagan German Faith Movement, whose leaders included Alfred

Rosenberg, General Erich Ludendorff, Count Ernst Reventlow, and Tübingen's Jakob Wilhelm Hauer, who wanted the state to give formal recognition to the worship of Wotan and the other gods of German mythology.[45] Adam criticized the state's support for the German Faith Movement at an assembly of Catholic youth in Stuttgart on Sunday, January 21, 1934. Speaking after Bishop Sproll, he gave an address entitled "Vom gottmenschlichen Erlöser" [On the Divine-Human Savior], arguing that if Germans wanted their nation to grow strong, they needed to maintain Christian belief as their nation's dominant religion. The proponents of neopaganism erred in holding that Germans would once again become a strong nation if they would throw aside Christian belief and retrieve their ancient Aryan rituals, symbols, and myths. Christianity had in fact continually strengthened the German people since the 800s, when St. Boniface evangelized the Teutonic tribes; and, similar to a noble oak tree, Germany would thrive again as a mighty nation when its roots draw on the spirit of Jesus Christ who is the world's true savior. Adam stated:

> If the German Faith Movement basically denies the divine revelation revealed in Jesus Christ in its particularity and uniqueness, it does so only because its god is a god enslaved to this world, a truncated god, not the living, personal, infinite God who created heaven and earth. . . . We would all like to search for and to find again that one and singular person, who—since he is the cornerstone for the whole world—determines the world's destiny and thus will remain for us Germans the only ground of life, from which blossoms the true German life.[46]

After Adam's speech, Nazi officials immediately took steps to silence the highly respected theologian.[47] On Monday, January 22, the Nazi newspaper *N. S. Kurier* accused Adam of provoking political unrest. On Tuesday, Storm Troopers sat in Tübingen's large lecture hall and disrupted Adam's lecture with catcalls and loud talking among themselves. Adam eventually stopped speaking, gathered up his notes, and left the hall. Later that day and throughout the night, Storm Troopers boisterously walked through Adam's neighborhood and shot their pistols at his home. On Wednesday, the government revoked Adam's teaching license and canceled his courses until further notice. In support of

Adam, his colleagues in the faculty of Catholic theology refused to give their lectures. On Thursday and Friday, Bishop Sproll, Cardinal Bertram, and Cardinal Faulhaber pressured Vice Chancellor Papen into intervening on Adam's behalf with Bernhard Rust. On Monday, January 29, it was agreed that the government would restore Adam's license to teach on the condition that he would not criticize National Socialism. Although Adam kept his promise, he indirectly touched on politics in his lecture "Jesus Christ und der Geist unserer Zeit" [Jesus Christ and the Spirit of Our Time], which he gave on February 5, 1935. Aware that the Nazis stressed heroism inspired by Nietzsche and Teutonic mythology, Adam argued that true heroism required faithfulness to Jesus Christ.[48]

Karl Adam reentered the political realm in 1939 after the Wehrmacht invaded Poland. He judged that the war was Germany's effort to correct the injustice of the Treaty of Versailles and to reassert Germany's rightful leadership in the world. It was important, therefore, that German Catholics show their patriotism. Adam conveyed his positive view of the war in a public lecture, "Die geistige Lage des deutschen Katholizismus" [The Spiritual Situation of German Catholicism], which he delivered before more than a thousand people in Aachen on December 10, 1939.[49] Arguing that Catholics should enter more fully into the mainstream of German life, he proposed three concrete ways in which to nurture Christian belief on German soil, ways that would simultaneously strengthen Germany. First, the German bishops should permit the state to conscript future priests into the Wehrmacht. Why? "It can be only a rich experiential success for our seminarians—for their personal development as well as for their future effectiveness among the German people—if they are accepted in this school of manliness after the hothouse atmosphere of their seminary years." Further, the Vatican should permit the use of German instead of Latin in the celebration of the mass by German-speaking people. This change in the liturgy would allow the meaning of the Eucharist to become clearer to the faithful. Finally, the pope should canonize more of Germany's holy men and women, thereby acknowledging the richness of

German Catholicism. These three actions, he judged, would bring about a greater blending of Catholicism and German culture. Adam concluded, "We must be Catholic to the last fiber of our hearts, however we must also be German to our very marrow, thereby being Catholic. Only then will our Christian faith blossom in this particular soil."

Adam soon regretted having given this lecture. It sparked a controversy.[50] Judging that his ideas were being misunderstood, he insisted that this lecture not be published. He could not retract his words, however, which had pleased Catholic supporters of Hitler while angering Hitler's Catholic opponents. Cologne's lay leader, Joseph Joos, and Berlin's pastor, Bernhard Lichtenberg, accused Adam of watering down the Catholic faith and failing to clarify the significant differences between Catholicism and National Socialism. Joos, a sharp critic of the Third Reich, was incarcerated in a concentration camp; Lichtenberg was imprisoned in 1941 and died on November 5, 1943, while being transported to the Dachau concentration camp.[51] Adam's lecture in Aachen also displeased the German bishops.[52] Bishop Josef Krumpfmüller of Augsburg, who was the administrator of the Diocese of Rottenburg in the absence of Bishop Sproll, called Adam to his office and told him that his lecture had harmed the church. He demanded that Adam no longer speak in public about the war. At the same time, the dioceses of Aachen, Augsburg, and Cologne instructed their seminarians at the University of Tübingen not to attend Adam's lectures.

Karl Adam's anti-Jewish sentiments showed themselves in 1943 in an essay entitled "Jesus, der Christus, und wir Deutsche" [Jesus, the Christ, and We Germans], written to refute three neopagan allegations against Christian belief: that it is mythological, that it is essentially a Jewish cult, and that it fosters passivity among its adherents. In response, Adam argued that Christian belief is not mythological, since it concerns an actual historical figure, Jesus of Nazareth. Houston Stuart Chamberlain (who was the son-in-law of Richard Wagner) erred when he asserted in *The Foundations of the Nineteenth Century* (1899) that Jesus was not Jewish. Christian faith surely originated with a Jewish man and with Jewish belief. At the same time, Jesus was not a pure Jew, because he came from Galilee, a region with a history of inter-racial marriages. Further, because of Mary's immaculate concep-tion, Jesus did not possess the negative traits usually associated with being Jewish: "Jesus' mother Mary had no physical or moral connection with those ugly dispositions and forces which we condemn in full blooded Jews. Through the miracle of the grace of God, she is beyond these Jewish hereditary traits, a figure who transcends Judaism. And, what had occurred in Mary took place too in the human nature of her son."[53] Further, since Jesus ful-filled the Jewish law and moved beyond it, he separated his fol-lowers from Judaism and called them to the fullness of life. Hence, belief in Jesus Christ as the redeemer should lead not to passivity but to a zeal for life: "Christian faith is not an escape from the world but an illumination of the world."[54] When rightly understood, it generates "energy and courage." In conclusion, the Nazi critics of Christian faith should recognize that "the Christian spirit and the German spirit are not essentially foreign to each other. They are not essentially opposed to each other, as the anti-Christian movement would like us to say. Rather, they are essentially related to each other. Thus they must always search for and fulfill themselves. The Christian realm is broad and bright enough so that the German genius can again be at home there."

The French army occupied Tübingen in the summer of 1945. As part of de-Nazification, a military tribunal reviewed the writ-ings and activities of the university's professors during the Third Reich. Although the tribunal temporarily imprisoned pro-Nazi professors and subsequently prohibited some of them from returning to the lecture hall, it detained none of the professors of Catholic theology and ruled that none of them had promoted either Nazism or the Reich's violation of human rights. Karl Adam and his colleagues continued their teaching in the autumn of 1945 and found that their students included priests like Bernard Häring, who had survived the war on Germany's front lines.[55]

During the postwar years, Adam—along with Matthias Laros and Joseph Lortz—contributed to the ecumenical movement, Una Sancta, which promised to unite in Christian faith Catholics and Protestants who had helped one another as neighbors during Hitler's reign of terror and the war. Speaking in churches filled to overflowing, Adam stressed that since Catholics and Protestants agree on the same basic truths of Christian belief, they should work together for the good of the church and the rebuilding of Germany. He edited these lectures into his book One and Holy (1948). He also wrote a privately circulated essay in 1947 observing that the German people bore a collective guilt for Nazi atrocities and the extermination of millions of Jews, and that they needed to repent of unwittingly cooperating with "the anti-Christian satanism."[56] It is not clear, however, that Adam himself ever acknowledged his own misjudgment about and complicity with the Third Reich.

In 1949, at the age of seventy-three, Karl Adam retired from the University of Tübingen with the academic rank of professor emeritus and devoted himself to fashioning his lectures of thirty years into The Christ of Faith (1954), which gave a balanced, comprehensive history of Christology. He also published an essay sharply criticizing Rudolf Bultmann (d. 1976) for "demythologizing" the New Testament. He argued that the Christian faith depends not on a historical reconstruction of Jesus' life but on an encounter with the living Christ as known in the church, scripture, and tradition.[57] Having withdrawn from public life in the 1950s, Adam died in Tübingen on April 1, 1966.[58]

A Rejection of Modernity

Karl Adam was a leader in the renewal of Catholic theology during the first half of the twentieth century. Working outside of neo-Scholasticism, he brought together Christian belief and human experience in his theology of life. At the same time, however, he weakened the church's resistance to Hitler by naively stressing what he perceived to be the common ground between Catholicism and National Socialism. How could a man so talented in theology have been so wrong in his politics? One source of his theological success and his political failure was his reliance on Romanticism, on the ideas and categories that had originated in the early 1800s with J. W. Goethe and Friedrich Schlegel, and that had contributed to the creative work of Möhler and eventually developed into *Lebensphilosophie,* the diverse existentialist ideas of Nietzsche, Dilthey, and Scheler. Adam fashioned an engaging theology for his day as he employed rich notions of life, interpersonal existence, and community. But he simultaneously misjudged the social and political forces of the Weimar Republic and the Third Reich because he dreamed of a polity that would overcome the individualism of parliamentary democracy and thereby form a national community in harmony with the church. Enthralled by this vision, he failed to see that Hitler used terms such as "community," "blood," and "people" in ways irreconcilable with the Christian faith.[59] In other words, Romanticism was both a blessing and a curse for Karl Adam. According to Klaus Schatz, Adam stood among the "representatives of the liturgical movement and its corresponding theological tradition who became in 1933 the bridge builders to National Socialism out of their community mysticism (I. Herwegen, K. Adam, R. Grosche). The predilection for the 'vital' and 'organic', the rejection of liberalism and rationalism could lead to illusions."[60] Bishop Hans Kreidler has made a similar point: "It is his theology of life that brought Karl Adam's thought into the neighborhood of the world view of National Socialism. The organic thought of Romanticism comes to bear on his notion of 'life.'"[61] Referring to Adam, T. Mark Schoof has observed that "there were certainly in church circles ideas which were related to particular points in the Nazi program, one of these being, for example, the notion that the national community ought to form the basis of the saving community of the church."[62]

While Adam was drawn to Hitler's rhetoric because of his Romanticism, he gave specific theological reasons for his political stance—reasons similar to those of Karl Eschweiler and Joseph Lortz. He held that modernity was destroying Germany because of its individualism, secularization, and democracy. The modern notion of freedom was distancing people from one another, the church, and God as it promoted cultural, ethnic, and racial diversity in Germany. The situation required a new social and political reality that would restore order to society and foster community and German tradition. In doing so, this new polity would nurture Germans to become more whole human beings who as such would be more responsive to God's grace. In other words, the church would flourish within a vibrant national community, held together by cultural, ethnic, and racial ties. Conversely, the church would strengthen the new Germany as it embraced the nation's language, saints, and distinct customs. In holding these ideas, Adam stood beside both Eschweiler and Lortz, who were also critics of modernity and proponents of a new, though vague, social and political order. In their efforts to reconcile Catholicism and National Socialism, Adam, Eschweiler, and Lortz did not, however, represent all progressive German Catholic theologians of their day. As chapters 5 and 6 show, Romano Guardini and Engelbert Krebs gave theological rationales to undergird the church's opposition to the Third Reich.

5

Romano Guardini

Respecting the Human Person

ROMANO GUARDINI (1885–1968) WAS A PROFESSOR AT THE UNIVERSITY of Berlin when Hitler became Germany's chancellor in 1933.[1] Born in Italy, Guardini grew up in Germany and attained national prominence for his writings on the liturgy, prayer, and the church, as well as for his pastoral leadership of Catholic youth. Having taught at the University of Berlin since 1923, he was attracting to his lectures not only hundreds of students but also Berlin's intellectuals and cultural elites. Guardini was regarded as a progressive thinker because, avoiding neo-Scholasticism, he used the language of existentialism as he shed light on such aspects of personal existence as loneliness, depression, and the search for life's meaning. He usually steered clear of political topics, saying that he had always relied on the judgment of his close friend, Karl Neundörfer, who tragically died while hiking in 1926. But after Hitler assumed leadership of Germany, Guardini decided to comment on what was occurring around him. In 1935 he published an article, "Der Heiland" [The Savior], accusing Hitler of promoting idolatry, of putting himself where only Jesus Christ should stand in people's lives. Henceforth, Guardini was stalked by Nazi informers.

Romano Guardini was born on February 17, 1885, into a relatively wealthy family of Verona. During his first year, he moved with his parents to Mainz, Germany, where his father established an import business and eventually served in the Italian consulate. An intelligent child, he became fluent in Italian and German and also read English, French, Greek, and Latin. He delighted in the writings of Dante, Shakespeare, and Stendahl in their original

107

languages. After graduating from Mainz's Humanistisches Gymnasium in 1903, he matriculated at the University of Tübingen, where he studied chemistry during the 1903–4 academic year, but he did so poorly in it that he turned to economics during the fall of 1904 at the University of Munich and during the spring of 1905 at the University of Berlin. Realizing that he had little interest in economics, he endured a summer of self-doubt and of religious questioning that climaxed in his conversion. Struck by Jesus' teaching that "Whoever finds his life will lose it, and whoever loses his life for my sake will find it" (Matthew 10:39), he recommitted himself to Christ as known in the church and decided to become a priest. In the spring of 1906, Guardini moved to Freiburg, where he studied theology at the University of Freiburg while residing in the seminary. As a result of conversations with his classmates, he wrote his first book, *Michelangelo: Gedichte und Briefe* [Michelangelo: Poems and Letters] (1907). He entered the seminary for the Diocese of Mainz in 1908, and was ordained a priest on May 28, 1910. He was held in suspicion by diocesan officials, however, because he made known his views that neo-Scholasticism was intellectually deadening, and that the seminary administration was too authoritarian.[2]

Guardini served in parishes for two years, during which time he became a German citizen. He resumed theological studies at the University of Freiburg in the fall of 1912, and, working with the systematic theologian Engelbert Krebs, completed his doctoral dissertation on St. Bonaventure's theological method in May 1915.[3] Bonaventure's Neoplatonism shaped Guardini's theology for the remainder of his life and simultaneously brought him close to the late dialectical thought of Friedrich Schelling (d. 1854) and the phenomenology of Max Scheler.[4] Returning to parish ministry, Guardini wrote *The Spirit of the Liturgy* in 1918, a book that immediately won him national recognition and brought him into conversation with Scheler and the Jewish religious thinker Martin Buber (d. 1965). Studying at the University of Bonn from October 1920 until December 1922, Guardini completed his Habilitationsschrift concerning St. Bonaventure's teaching on the illumination of the mind.[5] During this time, too, he gave a series of public lectures on the church that were published in 1923 as *The Church and the Catholic*. He received a "call" to the University of Berlin in the spring of 1923.

From 1923 until 1945 Guardini had his permanent residence in Berlin, though he also kept a room at Burg Rothenfels, a medieval castle near Würzburg, where Catholic youth from all parts of Germany gathered for retreats and conferences. At the University of Berlin, he was the professor for the Catholic *Weltanschauung* (worldview). Although this academic chair was located at the University of Berlin, it was officially affiliated with the University of Breslau's faculty of Catholic theology, since Berlin lacked such a faculty. Guardini taught courses in systematic theology, New Testament, and religion and literature. On the basis of these lectures, which filled the university's largest lecture halls to capacity, he wrote his books on Anselm of Canterbury (1923), the coincidence of opposites in theology (1925), Pascal (1935), Augustine (1935), Dostoevski (1939), and Rainer Maria Rilke (1953). Wanting to meet students outside the academy, he became the spiritual leader of Quickborn, a national Catholic youth association, and edited the association's journal, *Die Schildgenossen* [The Fellowship of the Shield]. Whenever time permitted, Guardini resided with young men and women at Burg Rothenfels, leading them in discussions of the Bible and of world literature, and in the performance of plays and puppet shows. In Burg Rothenfels's chapel, he led youth in meditation, prayer, and worship. Presiding at masses with scripture readings, hymns, and congregational responses in German, he faced the assembly instead of a wall. Out of this involvement, he wrote such books as *Sacred Signs* (1929), *The Living God* (1930), and *The Life of Faith* (1935). For sixteen years, he delighted in being both a professor and a charismatic religious leader. He was upset, therefore, when in 1939 the Third Reich dismissed him from his academic chair and barred him from Burg Rothenfels.

In order to appreciate Guardini's role in the church's confrontation with the Third Reich, we must see him in relation both to Cardinal Bertram and to the faculty of Catholic theology at the University of Breslau, with whom he was formally associated because of his academic chair. We must also view him in relation to Bishop Preysing and the pastoral leaders of Berlin, with whom he was affiliated because of his teaching at the University of Berlin.

Cardinal Bertram
and Breslau's Catholic Theologians

Cardinal Adolf von Bertram was the official leader of the German bishops throughout the twelve years of Hitler's dictatorship.[6] Born into nobility and gifted in leadership, in 1914 he became the ordinary of the Archdiocese of Breslau, which included Berlin until 1930. (The former Archdiocese of Breslau is today divided into Poland's Archdiocese of Wroclaw and Germany's Diocese of Gorlitz.) Standing in the heart of Prussia, this archdiocese contained some of Germany's most powerful interest groups. Although Bertram disdained National Socialism, he wanted to avoid another Kulturkampf and hoped to use the Nazi state as an ally in opposing Bolshevism on the one hand and liberalism on the other. In his judgment, the church needed to remain neutral in relation to the Third Reich. Hence, he directed his priests to adhere strictly to the Reich Concordat by devoting their energies to the sacraments and religious education, and to refrain from any activities that could be construed as forms of political or social activism. When a disagreement between the church and the state arose, Bertram negotiated in secret for a resolution that would satisfy both parties. This readiness to make accommodations meant the avoidance of conflict at almost any cost. Thus, when the Reich declared in 1941 that all Jews must wear a star of David, Bertram instructed his priests to advise Jews who had become Catholics to attend mass in the early morning hours so as to avoid contact with large groups of parishioners.[7] Also, when the state began to deport Jews to concentration camps, the cardinal insisted that the bishops remain publicly silent, since this action did not directly relate to the church's spiritual mission.

Cardinal Bertram maintained his ties with Catholic theologians at the University of Breslau. Although most professors at the university were pro-Hitler, the Catholics were wary of the Führer.[8] The fifteen professors in the faculty of Catholic theology, along with their assistants, taught approximately four hundred seminarians in 1933.[9] Similar to the Catholic theologians at other universities and academies, Breslau's theologians worked within neo-Scholasticism while also cautiously introducing a phenomenological approach to theology. Moreover, recognizing the value of historical studies, they published a series of books entitled *Breslauer Studien zur historischen Theologie*, which generated twenty-four volumes from 1922 to 1933 and yielded a new edition of nine volumes after 1933. They steered clear, however, of topics or conclusions that might alarm the Holy Office. They did not want to repeat the mistakes of their predecessor, Anton Günther (d. 1863), whose books in speculative theology were placed on the *Index* in 1857. Nor did they want to follow the path of their colleague Joseph Wittig, whose article "Die Erlösten" [The Redeemed] sparked a controversy in 1922 and whose historical study of Jesus, *Leben Jesu in Palästina* (1925), was placed on the *Index* soon after its publication.[10] Wittig himself was excommunicated in 1926 but was reconciled with the church before his death in 1949.

The Reich's minister of education took control of Breslau's faculty of Catholic theology in 1933 by appointing Felix Haase, a member of the Nazi party, the faculty's chairman. Bernhard Rust also gave Haase the professorship that had belonged to Berthold Altaner (d. 1946), a historian, whom Rust had dismissed because of his participation in the Catholic peace movement. Since Rust made these changes without Cardinal Bertram's approval, as required by the concordat, Bertram charged the seminarians not to take Haase's courses in church history. This conflict was resolved when Rust and Bertram quietly agreed that the seminarians would take their history courses from an instructor at the seminary, but would be examined by Haase at the university. In 1937 Bertram assigned Hubert Jedin to teach church history at the seminary; Jedin had been dismissed from the University of Breslau in 1933 because his mother was Jewish. Jedin fled to Rome in 1939 in order to avoid incarceration in a concentration camp. (Residing at the Vatican from 1939 to 1949, Jedin undertook the research on the Council of Trent that led to his monumental, four-volume *History of the Church* [1949–75].)[11] The teaching of theology at the University of Breslau and at the seminary came to an abrupt halt on January 25, 1945, when the Reich ordered all citizens to vacate Breslau. Breslau's theologians fled west, leaving behind their manuscripts and personal libraries. Cardinal Bertram died on July 6, 1945.

Bishop Preysing's Opposition to National Socialism

Konrad von Preysing became a bishop only five months before Hitler was named Germany's chancellor.[12] Born into nobility, he had earned a degree in law at the University of Munich, passing the bar examination in 1905. As noted in chapter 1, he was the only German bishop in the Third Reich with a diploma in civil jurisprudence. After working in the Bavarian government, Preysing entered the seminary and was ordained for the Archdiocese of Munich in 1912. He subsequently served as the secretary to Munich's Cardinal Franciscus von Bettinger (d. 1917), as the pastor of Munich's cathedral, and as the director of the archdiocesan office of communications. While serving in the last role, he met the apostolic nuncio Monsignor Eugenio Pacelli in 1920. In 1932, on Pacelli's recommendation, Pope Pius XI named Preysing the bishop of Eichstätt.

Bishop Preysing attended his first meeting of the Fulda conference of bishops in April 1933. Having already lifted their prohibitions against membership in the Nazi party on March 28, the bishops, aware that Cardinal Pacelli and Vice Chancellor Papen were negotiating a concordat, wanted to clarify their relationship to the new government. Speaking as a civil lawyer, Preysing explained to the bishops that a legal agreement between Rome and Berlin would be unenforceable because Germany no longer had either a civil constitution or a code of civil law. Disagreeing with those who saw the Nazi persecution of the church as an aberration that Hitler would eventually correct, he cautioned against compromising with the new regime and urged that the bishops clearly differentiate the church's teachings from Nazi ideology.

Preysing was elected the bishop of Berlin by the diocesan canons in the summer of 1935 and was installed on August 31 in ceremonies that Nazi officials boycotted because of Preysing's public criticisms of National Socialism. The bishop immediately faced a formidable challenge in the capital. Because it was only five years old, the Diocese of Berlin, which included 548,000 Catholics and 427 priests, needed a religious education program, social agencies, and ecclesiastical infrastructure. By 1940 Preysing had established thirty-six new churches and several services for the poor, the homeless, and the victims of Nazi persecution. While overseeing the Diocese of Berlin, Preysing emerged as a leader in the episcopacy. In January 1935, he urged the bishops not to issue a public statement approving the deployment of German troops in the Saarland, and in 1936 he argued that the bishops should not publicly sanction the presence of German troops in the Rhineland. Elected by the bishops as their press secretary, Preysing vigorously tried to protect the freedom of Catholic newspapers, journals, and publishing houses, and urged the bishops to take common public stands against specific policies and actions by the Reich. In this effort, he contributed to the drafting of Pius XI's encyclical *Mit brennender Sorge*. When Bertram blocked the release of a pastoral letter in August 1937 from the German bishops in support of *Mit brennender Sorge*, Preysing wrote a memorandum to the cardinal insisting on the need for public statements against the Reich's abuses.

During the Second World War, Bishop Preysing prohibited Berlin's churches from ringing their bells for Wehrmacht victories.[13] Disapproving of Cardinal Bertram's birthday greetings to Hitler in April 1940, he submitted his resignation to Pope Pius XII, but remained in office upon the pope's insistence. He preached in support of human rights in November 1942, and in March 1943 he wrote to Pius XII urging him to publicly defend the "many unfortunate and innocent people" being persecuted by Hitler. This letter was one of many that Preysing wrote to the pope during the war. During 1943 and 1944, he sent thirteen letters to the pope informing him of the death camps and imploring him to speak out. Further, Preysing established a diocesan agency to assist everyone, including Jews, who sought to emigrate or who were in need of work, food, and shelter. After the agency's director, Bernhard Lichtenberg, died during imprisonment in 1943, Preysing appointed Margarete Sommer as the new director and personally supported her efforts to inform the bishops, especially Cardinal Bertram, of the Reich's deportation and extermination of the Jews.[14] Although Preysing had contact with Helmuth James Count von Moltke and the Kreisau Circle, he had no direct involvement in the attempt to assassinate Hitler on July 20, 1944.

Russian troops entered Berlin in April 1945, destroying the cathedral, the chancery, and the bishop's residence. When the fighting ended, Bishop Preysing was disconsolate at the death and the destruction. A third of the diocese was incorporated into Poland, and Berlin was divided into four military zones. Bishop Preysing was named a cardinal by Pius XII in late 1945, and during 1947 he traveled throughout the United States raising money for the victims of Nazism. He died on December 21, 1950.

National Socialism as Idolatry

Residing in Berlin and teaching at the University of Berlin, Romano Guardini saw the emergence of the Nazi state and had no illusions about its character. When he went to the university in spring 1933, he walked near the ashes that remained at Franz-Josephs-Platz after Storm Troopers and Nazi students had burned books on the night of May 10. These texts included the writings of German authors such as Albert Einstein, Thomas and Heinrich Mann, Hugo Preuss, Walther Rathenau, Erich Maria Remarque, and Arnold and Stefan Zweig, and also books by foreign writers such as Sigmund Freud, Andre Gidé, Helen Keller, Jack London, Marcel Proust, Upton Sinclair, H. G. Wells, and Émile Zola. Having loved world literature since his youth, Guardini was horrified by what Hitler's followers had done to approximately twenty thousand books. A few months later, on November 13, he heard about the gathering of twenty thousand "German Christians" in Berlin's *Sportspalast,* at which Reinhold Krause, a Protestant minister and Nazi official, proclaimed that the church would become "Nazified" by discarding "all things not German in its services and confessions, especially [beliefs and customs] from the Old Testament with its Jewish system of quid pro quo morality."[15] The rally at the Sportspalast gave national prominence not only to the German Christians who wanted a Nazi church but also to the neopagans of the German Faith Movement, such as Alfred Rosenberg, who wanted to replace Christian belief with the worship of Wotan and the other gods of Teutonic or "Aryan" mythology.

The Nazi rally, Krause's speech, and the book burning all showed Guardini that Hitler's movement was "barbarian."[16] The theologian initially opted, however, for silence. He was able to avoid conversations about politics with his colleagues at the university because he had rarely associated with them and served on no faculty committees.[17] But by 1935 he could remain silent no longer. Alarmed by Hitler's mesmerizing effect on Germans, he published an essay on idolatry, entitled "Der Heiland" [The Savior]. In order to understand the essay, one must appreciate that both *der Heiland* and *der Heilbringer* signify "the bringer of health and blessings," "the savior," and "the redeemer."[18] The root of both terms is *das Heil*, which means "prosperity," "happiness," and "salvation." *Das ewige Heil* is "eternal salvation." As a greeting, *"Heil"* means "Good health to you!" *"Heil dem König!"* conveys a twofold sense of "Long live the king!" and "Health to you through the king!" Similarly, *"Heil* Hitler!" meant "Long live Hitler!" and "Health to you through Hitler!" Perceiving that Hitler was exploiting the ambiguities of *das Heil* in the Nazi salutation and propaganda, Romano Guardini wrote "Der Heiland" in order to explain that, while Hitler may be a bearer of blessings, he is not the savior; there is only one true savior—Jesus Christ.[19]

The need for linguistic clarity led Guardini to reflect on the difference between Jesus Christ and the savior figures in pagan mythologies by drawing on Gerardus van der Leeuw's *Phenomenology of Religion* (1933). There is an experience, Guardini noted, that is common to people regardless of their religion. All human beings have moments when they sense a numinous or transcendent power in ordinary occurrences, such as the rising of the sun, the changing of the seasons, and the birth of a child. On these occasions, people may feel a healing and health-giving power, a sacred dynamism, *das Heil*. At other times—in a storm, for example—they may experience a threatening force, a destructive energy, *das Unheil*. Ancient peoples expressed their perceptions of beneficial and harmful power in myths and other imaginative forms. They associated healing energy, *das Heil*, with light, spring, and savior figures, and they spoke of destructive forces, *das Unheil*, in terms of darkness, winter, snakes, dragons, and witches. Further, they told stories about *Heil*-bearers who struggled with *das Unheil* and overcame it, sometimes by first having to endure hardship or undergo death, which in turn brought about new life for themselves and others. Ancient peoples recounted myths about Dionysius, Baldur, Osiris, and Mithras. They also applied the imagery of a savior figure to their rulers. For many peoples, "[t]he king is the bearer of sacred (*heiliger*) power." For instance, at one time people in the orient held that when a new emperor or empress assumed the throne, he or she brought *das Heil* to everyone in the kingdom. At times, people have attributed their well-being to the ruler's positive or negative relationship to a numinous power. When a harvest was poor, they judged that the emperor had become a bearer of *das Unheil*, and they put him to death, either in fact or in a ceremonial drama.

In light of this mythology, Guardini raises the question whether Jesus Christ was merely one savior figure among others like Osiris and Mithras. Answering this question, he asserts that Jesus Christ was not a mythic figure but a historical individual: he lived, suffered, died, was raised to new life, and appeared to his followers, who then bore witness to him. In other words, "Jesus Christ is historical. To be sure, he exists in relation to eternity: by means of his preexistent origin, his departure from eternity and singular return to it. However, he exists at the same time in history and, indeed, in an essential manner." Myths about savior figures like Dionysius convey a cyclical sense of time, while biblical narratives present a linear sense of time. In myths, what is important happens time and time again in the circle of being born, maturing, dying, and then coming to life again. By contrast, the Gospels portray Jesus Christ in a drama of events that occur only once, thereby conveying that Jesus Christ has broken the grip of death once and for all. For this reason, he is not one savior figure among many others but the savior, *der Heiland*.

Implicitly referring to Hitler and his followers, Guardini added that when twentieth-century people regard the Gospels as no different from pagan myths, they revert to a cyclical view of the world and open themselves to life's destructive forces. In other words, they dismiss God's singular revelation in Jesus Christ and what this revelation communicates about the sanctity of human life. When modern men and women come under the influence of neopagan symbols and legends, they are disposed to treat other human beings as nonpersons, as objects having value not in themselves but in their usefulness. Further, the return to a mythic consciousness destroys respect for human beings as persons because it leaves people vulnerable to the dark forces in the human psyche. Jesus Christ has saved people from the demonic or evil powers by entering this world from outside it and revealing God and the character of human life. "When human beings accept what comes to them in Christ, their eyes open to who God is and who they are."

The relationship between ancient myths concerning a savior figure and the Gospels is one of opposition, not contradiction. The Gospels affirm, overturn, and complete ancient stories of a savior. Christian belief accepts the potential worth of non-Christian images, symbols, and myths of savior figures, regarding these as anticipations of the genuine savior. But it also rejects these imaginative constructs, because they are the product of human projection. Further, it fulfills these myths because Jesus Christ is the one person who was free to act responsibly and uniquely in history. Moreover, Christian belief attests that those people who truly commit themselves to Jesus Christ are freed from life's destructive forces and become genuine persons. The confrontation between Jesus and Pilate in John's Gospel (18:33–19:11) highlights the human tendency to reject the genuine savior: Jesus, the bearer of the truth, is brought before Pilate, the legitimate civil ruler who condemns Jesus to death. This world's leaders are disposed to reject Jesus Christ and the salvation that he offers to all people.

In his essay "Der Heiland," Guardini opposed Rosenberg's and Hauer's contention that Teutonic myths and Nazi neopaganism should replace Christian faith. Further, he undercut the view of Hitler as Germany's savior, implicitly condemning the salutation, "*Heil* Hitler." Ultimately, Guardini indicated that something demonic was at work in Germany, something attacking the very character of personal existence.[20]

Soon after the publication of "Der Heiland" in 1935, Nazi party members attended Romano Guardini's university lectures in order to note possible criticisms of the Führer and the Third Reich. They heard, however, nothing of interest to them since the theologian discussed only theology.[21] In 1937 Guardini followed through on "Der Heiland" by publishing his book *The Lord*, which identifies the world's true savior by means of eighty-six short, biblical meditations on the life, death, and resurrection of Jesus. While Nazi propaganda presented Hitler as the national savior, *The Lord* portrayed Jesus Christ as the transcendent savior. This book won the hearts of so many Germans that it underwent four printings in four years.[22] Guardini found other ways, too, to resist Nazism. As the editor of *Die Schildgenossen*, he published in it articles with an implicit critique of the Nazi state, and, as the national leader of Quickborn, he guided the organization so that it stood as an alternative to the state's "Hitler Youth." Moreover, Guardini continued to promote the renewal of the liturgy and religious devotions. These explicitly religious activities assumed political significance in the Third Reich, for they expressed people's rejection of the idolatry of Hitler and their faithfulness to the God of the Bible and to the church.[23] It is true, however, that Guardini could have perhaps done more to directly help Hitler's victims. For example, he could have worked with Berlin's Bishop Preysing, Bernhard Lichtenberg, and Margarete Sommer as they assisted Jews. This involvement would have probably led, however, to the theologian's imprisonment and death.

Bernhard Rust acted against Guardini after the Gestapo alleged that the theologian had criticized National Socialism at an informal gathering of friends and associates.[24] Guardini eventually recalled what transpired in January 1939 when Rust dismissed him from his professorship: "The official representing the government opened the meeting with words regarding its purpose, words which I remember well: when the state itself has a [Nazi] world view, there can be no room at a university for a chair of Catholic *Weltanschauung*. A discussion of this axiom was of course not possible, and I could do nothing other than indicate a nod of acceptance. Apart from this foundational principle, the conversation developed in a cordial manner."[25] Rust asked whether Guardini would be interested in an academic chair in dogmatic theology at Bonn, Freiburg, or Tübingen, but the theologian explained that he was no longer prepared to teach dogmatic theology in the strict sense and that he was currently doing research on Dante's *Divine Comedy*. Rust feigned an interest in this project, saying that it might strengthen the political ties between Hitler and Mussolini, and he ended by saying that he needed more time to consider Guardini's options. A few days later, Rust called the theologian and advised him to retire without financial benefits. Guardini said he would do this; he quietly withdrew from the University of Berlin.

The Reich was not satisfied to remove Romano Guardini from the lecture hall. It also stopped him from going to Burg Rothenfels when it took control of the castle and restricted it to the SS. Recalling these events, Guardini eventually wrote, "The life and work which now unfolded were truly different from previously, and even more so when six months later even Burg Rothenfels was seized, and I lost both of the great points of reference to which, until that time, my concern and work was related and which had fulfilled my life with a consciousness of fruitful activity and of profound human connectedness."[26]

Guardini soon lost even more. The Reich banned the publication of *Die Schildgenossen* in 1939 and, two years later, it prohibited Guardini from giving public lectures and threatened him with imprisonment.[27]

Remaining in Berlin from 1939 to 1943, Guardini directed his energies to writing such books as *The World and the Person* (1939), *The Rosary* (1940), and *Die Offenbarung* [Revelation] (1940). During the final years of the war, he had no idea what the future held for him. In 1943, exhausted from the incessant Allied bombing of Berlin, Guardini sought shelter with Pastor Josef Weiger at the rectory in Mooshausen, a rural village in southern Germany's Allgäu Alps, where he remained until 1946.[28] During his stay in Mooshausen, he wrote his memoirs, *Berichte über mein Leben* [Recollections About My Life].

Guardini became a professor at the University of Tübingen in 1946. Amid his lecturing, he expanded his article "Der Heiland" into a short book, *Der Heilbringer in Mythos, Offenbarung und Politik* [The Redeemer in Myth, Revelation and Politics], which made explicit what in the article was only implicit, namely, his ideas about Hitler's manipulation of the German people.[29] According to Guardini, the human subconscious reasons by means of images, symbols, and myths. Even when a person is not aware of it, the human psyche applies imaginative constructs to the everyday world so that a person perceives meaning in people, things, and situations. Drawing on the work of C. G. Jung, Guardini argued that the human psyche fashions a "kernel of meaning" by means of imaginative motifs and that this human search for life's meaning has persisted even after the Enlightenment. Although people will distance themselves from the natural world because of their critical consciousness, they will still invest their leaders with a religious or mythic significance that is determined by their unconscious, collective images of a savior figure.

Hitler gained absolute authority by engaging the imaginations of the German people in his ideology of "blood and race," coupling with it the myth of himself as the nation's *Heilbringer.* Giving himself the title "Führer," he claimed to bring *das Heil* to the entire *Volk* and hence to be the mediator between the *Volk* and God. As such, he claimed the ability to judge all aspects of life, including politics, military strategy, science, economics, family life, and even art. Caught up in this myth, some Germans spoke of sunny days as "Hitler weather," and Nazi officials insisted that new buildings include the inscription, "For everything, we thank our Führer." Further, Nazi propaganda deliberately transferred to Hitler images that Christians have applied to Jesus. Photographs showed Hitler standing among children and benignly looking down at them. Parks included altarlike tables on which were placed pictures of the Führer and a vase of flowers. "German Christians" on occasion put a photograph of Hitler on their church's altar. In schools, the state required that children say the Nazi prayer, "Small hands folded, small heads bowed, thinking within on the Führer who gives us work and bread, who delivers us from all need." The Nazi party instructed Germans to hang a photograph of Hitler in their homes in the place usually reserved for a cross or a portrait of Christ. This idolatry was expressed in the salutation *"Heil* Hitler," which—as required by the state—Germans uttered countless times each day instead of their conventional Christian greeting, "Gelobt sei Jesus Christus" ("Praised be Jesus Christ)." As already noted, to greet someone with *"Heil* Hitler" was to pray that God would continue to bestow divine favor on Hitler and through him to all Germans. In sum, said Guardini, "The new myth of the earthly savior was intended to eliminate Christ and his salvation and to bind human beings to this world. Whoever believed in this earthly savior [Hitler] no longer had the possibility of resisting the grip which seized them."

Der Heilbringer in Mythos, Offenbarung und Politik also stressed that Europe's future depended on its affirmation of the Christian tradition. "Either Europe becomes Christian, or Europe will no longer exist," wrote Guardini.[30] That which gives Europe its identity and orientation is its belief in Jesus Christ. "Christ's essence freed the heart of the European. His personality has given to the European the extraordinary ability to live in history and experience his destiny." Over the centuries, the risen Christ empowered the people of Europe to live in relation to the "personal, holy God" and therefore to attain "the freedom of the redeemed." Nazism hated this freedom, this personal existence, and attacked it with the aim of taking "a formless mass into its hands." If Europe is to flourish, it must renew its commitment to Jesus Christ.

Romano Guardini became a professor at the University of Munich in 1948, and developed further his ideas on the character of personal existence, writing such books as *Freedom, Grace and Destiny* (1948), *The End of the Modern Age* (1950), and *Power and Responsibility* (1951).[31] These books set the direction of the theologian's thought for the remainder of his life. In 1953 he completed his book *Rilke's Duino Elegies,* in which he compares the existentialist poet's anthropology to the Christian understanding of personal existence. He illumined human life's moral dimensions in

The Virtues (1963) as well as in his lectures at the University of Munich, which appeared posthumously in the two-volume work *Ethik* (1993). He shed light on the spiritual wellspring of the Christian faith in a series of meditations entitled *The Wisdom of the Psalms* (1963) and also in personal reflections on discipleship, *Die Existenz des Christen* (1976).

Although Guardini had not invested himself in the Weimar Republic, he deliberately contributed to the formation of the Federal Republic of Germany. While envisioning Germany and indeed Europe as a Christian society, he argued during the late 1940s and 1950s for the humanistic values and beliefs to which Germans could assent.[32] He developed, for instance, his ideas on personal freedom in two public lectures at the University of Tübingen. On November 4, 1945, he reflected on the witness of the martyrs of the White Rose in the essay "Die Waage des Daseins" [The Measure of Personal Existence], and then on May 23, 1952, he spoke on Germans' responsibility to Jews in the essay "Verantwortung: Gedanken zur Jüdischen Frage" [Responsibility: Thoughts on the Jewish Question]. He worked, too, at reknitting Germany's ties with the European nations. In 1948 he spoke in Paris on "the search for peace," thereby becoming one of the first German citizens to give a public lecture in postwar France. Moreover, in 1949 he published an article on Jean Pierre de Caussade in the prestigious French journal *Dieu Vivant*.[33] Remaining dedicated to the cultural and spiritual life of Europe, he was awarded the prestigious Erasmus Prize in 1962.

A Theology of Personal Existence

Romano Guardini retired in 1963 from the University of Munich and passed his academic chair on to Karl Rahner, who had known the senior theologian since 1920, when Rahner, age sixteen, made a retreat with him at Burg Rothenfels. The Jesuit had subsequently drawn on Guardini's writings in his own theological work. After Guardini's death on October 1, 1968, Rahner published a tribute to his mentor, stressing that Guardini's deepest desire was to illumine "that ineffable mystery which we call

God" and also human life "in its ultimately ineffable qualities."[34] As a result, Guardini's writings on being a human person in God's presence manifest "the really unique character of his work." Indeed, they were meant "to serve only the eternal in man, his original and authentic relationship to God, as it is lived and not merely talked about. All of this in countless pages telling of man and thus seeking to tell of God, who is the true mystery of man." This observation by Rahner has pinpointed the core of Guardini's many ideas, namely, his theology of personal existence.[35] Amid his confrontation with the Third Reich, Guardini presented his understanding of the human person in his book *The World and the Person*.

According to Guardini, as men and women become persons, they mature as individual subjects, as social beings, and as subjects in relation to God. A person is first of all a "knowing and acting subject." He or she is a subject who relates to himself or herself as an "I," as one who searches for the truth and knows the exhilaration and the burden of making decisions and bearing their consequences. At the same time, as Martin Buber explained in his book *I-Thou* (1922), a person is more than a discrete subject; he or she is also a human being in relation to other human beings. In other words, "a human being does not exist as a self-enclosed block of reality or a self-sufficient individual who takes shape solely out of inner resources; rather a human being exists also in relation to that which comes to him or her from without."[36] To be a person is therefore to enter into "I–thou" or "I–you" relationships. Personal existence requires that I respect another man or woman as an "I," not an "it." Simultaneously, it also requires that another man or woman respects me as an "I." Being a human person involves mutual respect and interpersonal communication. "When I regard another individual as an 'I,' I open up and 'disclose' myself [to him or her]. But the relation remains incomplete if the same movement does not proceed from the other side so that the other person permits me to become his or her 'you.'"[37]

Personal existence also involves living in relation to the transcendent, personal mystery called God. God is the only authentic person, and human persons are analogues of God. God is, in some sense, a knowing and acting subject and simultaneously a social being in the divine life itself; God is simultaneously the divine self and also the triune reality of Father, Son, and Spirit. Further, God has chosen to relate not only to the divine self but also to creation, especially to human persons. "From all eternity God is the prime reality and ultimate mystery, who also communicates this reality," says Guardini.[38] God freely chose to communicate God's self outwardly, and this divine word once fashioned, and now sustains, the created order. The "I–thou" relationship that exists between God and the Logos has opened itself in the Holy Spirit to include creation. In other words, creation possesses in itself, though in a derivative manner, the character of the "you" or "thou" to whom God speaks as an "I." In particular, God tries to awaken in each human being the awareness that "I exist only in relation to God." This dialogue between God and each man and woman is universal. "A human being is both one who is intended to hear the word that God speaks to the world and also one who answers this word."[39] This divine–human communication is mediated, however, through Jesus Christ. Christ is the mediator between God and creation; he is the divine word spoken to creation and simultaneously the human word spoken in response to God. Hence, all people—non-Christians as well as Christians—relate to God (either consciously or unconsciously) through Jesus Christ, the universal *Heiland.*

A human being does not, however, attain full personal existence at birth or at a single instant during life. A man or a woman becomes a person during life's journey. He or she must walk between the Scylla of heteronomy and the Charybdis of autonomy in order to move toward theonomy.

Heteronomy occurs when a man or woman relinquishes living as a knowing and acting subject by submitting to the control of another human being or an external authority such as a government, a set of laws, or even a religious institution. It involves a flight from oneself as an "I," a denial of being a person. "'Person' means that I can be possessed in my self-existence by no external authority, for I belong to myself."[40] The German people opted for heteronomy when they gave Hitler power over their lives, eventually permitting him to murder six million Jews. In relinquishing their moral and religious integrity from 1933 to 1945, they had weakened their personal existence. Relinquishing their conscience, they had allowed the Führer to combine in the Holocaust "the instincts of the animal directly with human calculations and technology."[41] As a result, there emerged a diabolical force that "eradicates the personal character of the human being."[42] After Hitler's defeat, Germans needed to take steps to regain their integrity, their personal existence. One such step, beginning in 1952, was for Germans to make financial restitution to Jews. Guardini himself made a monetary donation to the State of Israel, encouraged other Germans to do the same, and renewed his ties with Martin Buber.[43] This action was necessary not only to grant justice to Jews but also to restore the well-being of Germans, who needed to develop themselves once again as persons, as human beings committed to the good of other human beings.

Autonomy involves a false assertion of the "I." It accentuates the knowing and acting subject to the exclusion of the social self. Whereas heteronomy places authority completely outside of oneself, autonomy locates authority solely in oneself. As a result, a human being stands alone, alienated from others. A representative of the autonomous self was the poet Rainer Maria Rilke (d. 1926), who described in his *Duino Elegies* (1923) the futility of searching for interpersonal relationships: "Ah, who can we turn to, then? . . . Maybe what's left for us is some tree on a hillside we can look at day after day."[44] These poems express skepticism about the possibility of love, or even friendship, and convey self-isolation. This individualism is ultimately destructive of a society as well as of each of its members, for a human being yearns for full personal existence, which includes I–thou relationships. A man or woman cannot sustain a Promethean or isolated sense of self; he or she eventually grows tired of standing alone, and when this fatigue sets in, the individual is tempted to swing from the extreme of autonomy to the extreme of heteronomy, to domination by others. Such an abrupt shift occurred, Guardini averred, when Germans rejected the Weimar Republic and gave themselves over to Hitler's dictatorship. In his study of the *Duino Elegies,* the theologian asserted that "with the emergence of the modern world persons asserted their autonomy. . . . They declared themselves to be the lords of their lives and, as such, also the lords of life in general, and they eventually grew tired of this burden. But instead of returning to their authentic selves directed toward God, they abandoned themselves. That is, they renounced God and also the authority of God's representatives, and they gave themselves over to totalitarian rule."[45] The only orientation that brings a man or woman between the extremes of individualism and authoritarianism is theonomy.

Theonomy leads a human being toward union with God, self, and other human beings. It directs men and women to recognize God as the only absolute authority in human life. By committing oneself to live in relationship with God, a man or woman is set free to become a whole person, one who is an "I" in "I–thou" relationships. One experiences himself or herself as an "incommunicable being." He or she is "that uniqueness who comes to life not because of special talent and advantage of social circumstance but because he or she has been called forth by God."[46] Implicit in these statements are three distinct ideas: a person is a mystery, an irreducible reality, who is constituted by more than other human beings can ever know; a person's dignity rests not in an activity or accomplishment but in his or her very being; and a person exists in relation to God. The primary safeguard of the value of a person is the acknowledgment of the person's sacred relationship to God. This is the most important guarantee against the pressures of a totalitarian state or a utilitarian society to treat human beings as objects. From a Christian perspective there is only one appropriate answer to the question, What is the decisive element of a human being? The answer, said Guardini, lies in the fact that the decisive element in human life is "[t]o be a person. Called forth by God. Thus capable of being responsible for oneself and of entering into the real world by means of one's inner powers of initiative. . . . [A] person is one who exists in relation to God, one who is inviolate in dignity, one who is irreplaceable in the responsibility which is called forth with a spiritual decisiveness that was previously not possible."[47]

Theonomy was evident in the lives of the martyrs of the White Rose, who wrote and distributed leaflets condemning the Reich's abuse of human rights. On February 18, 1943, the siblings Sophie and Hans Scholl went to the University of Munich with the sixth issue of their leaflet—the issue in which Professor Kurt Huber criticized the Wehrmacht's atrocities in Russia—and were leaving stacks of the White Rose leaflet at the university when they were seized. Soon afterwards, the Gestapo also arrested Christoph Probst, Alexander Schmorell, Willi Graf, and Professor Huber. All six were tried, found guilty of "conspiracy to commit high treason," and executed in 1943.[48] Two years later, Guardini praised these martyrs for witnessing to the fact that true personal existence originates "in the heart of God."[49] Living human life with such intensity "was brought into the world by Christ. Its meaning is grounded in him, and it can be known only from him." It requires a commitment to the living God and a willingness to sacrifice oneself in imitation of Jesus Christ. The White Rose martyrs "struggled for the freedom of the Spirit and the honor of humankind, and their names will remain bound with this struggle. In essence they lived in the radiance of the sacrifice of Christ, which is not found in immediate human existence but freely proceeds out of the creative source of eternal love."[50] In relation to the martyrs, we see how "our muddled personal existence can be illuminated only in relation to the eternal."

According to Guardini, some social-political situations are more conducive to theonomy than others. While heteronomy was demanded in the Third Reich and autonomy was prized in the Weimar Republic, theonomy is encouraged in a Christian democracy. In contrast to a liberal democracy, which doubts objective values, a Christian democracy rests on a common respect for the truths of human life that have been illuminated by the Christian tradition. It acknowledges both the common good and the appropriate autonomy of each human being. In other words, a Christian democracy is "a fortunate unity of order and freedom."[51] In Guardini's judgment, it was this kind of polity that the members of Quickborn had experienced at Burg Rothenfels. Those who participated in this community had "the feeling of a personal, formed existence." On the basis of this experience, Guardini declared in 1946, "I am a proponent of democracy—but [I must] immediately add, [I am] a Catholic proponent who acknowledges absolute values and objective authorities as givens."[52] It was Guardini's hope that the Federal Republic of Germany would flourish as a Christian democracy.

A Critical Dialogue with Modernity

From 1923 to 1925, Romano Guardini wrote nine letters concerning modernity to Pastor Josef Weiger at Mooshausen. While adjusting to his new life as a professor at the University of Berlin, he was also struggling to clarify the appropriate Christian stance toward modern society—the society that confronted him each day on Berlin's streets. This urban world stood in sharp contrast to the bucolic life at Italy's Lake Como, where he vacationed with his family in the late summer. Como's organic or holistic world was symbolized by its sailboats, in which men and women moved in harmony with wind and water. By contrast, Berlin's industrial world was expressed in automotive garages, where hydraulic lifts allowed mechanics to do things far beyond their own strength and with little understanding of the technology on which they relied. The former society was humane while the latter was harsh, indeed at times "barbarian." How should someone, especially a Christian, proceed in this situation? By his last letter, Guardini had reached his answer; he had decided not to flee to the past but to live in the present, even though "we are homeless in the midst of barbarism." Since the new order had in fact come about in part because Christian faith set people free from mythologies that deify natural powers, one needed to trust that belief in Jesus Christ could continue to have a beneficial effect upon modernity. Guardini had come to his "decision": "We must first say yes to our age. We cannot solve the problem by retreating or simply seeking to alter or improve. Only a new initiative can bring a solution."[53] In light of this decision, Guardini adopted a positive yet critical stance toward contemporary society and culture.

The vision of bringing the wisdom of Christian faith into a critical dialogue with modernity persisted throughout Romano Guardini's life. In 1944 he wrote in his memoirs that since the start of his scholarship, he had tried "to bring into relationship the unconditionality of Christian faith and an unbiased view of everyday reality and culture."[54] In 1955, on his seventieth birthday, he commented that theologians should foster "a methodical encounter between faith and the world": "faith should speak and give answers," and "the world should pose questions to faith and be illumined by it."[55] In 1965 Guardini reiterated this idea when he said that "on the basis of Christian faith, there should open a view of the world, a glimpse of its essence, an assessment of its values, that is otherwise not possible." At the same time, contemporary culture should enrich our understanding of the Christian faith, for "from the world and its problems questions are posed to revelation which bring this otherwise silent content to speech. In this ever new, changing encounter, there is attained a fruitful illumination of Christian existence."[56]

Rejecting one-sided evaluations of the modern age as a period of degeneration in the West—evaluations offered by Karl Eschweiler, Joseph Lortz, and Karl Adam—Romano Guardini held a complex view of modernity. In his judgment, one of modernity's merits is its emphasis on the dignity of every human being. It recognizes in principle the sacred value of every human being, ordinary individuals as well as highly creative ones. It does not, however, consistently act on its conviction concerning human dignity with respect to the needy, for example, in its treatment of the elderly. Further, modernity rightly values honesty, a truthfulness brought about by secularization. By separating church and state and embracing religious freedom, modern society leaves people free to accept or reject belief in God. Men and women are now Christians because they have chosen the faith, not because society or family expect them to be Christian. The absence of Christian faith as society's cornerstone means, however, that there is no publicly agreed-upon system of moral values. In this pluralistic situation, people in positions of influence can abuse their power, and, as a result, "the effectiveness of democratic values for the new age is problematic."[57] In many ways, a parliamentary democracy presupposes the values that Christian faith has engendered in the West. Contemporary secular society refuses to admit that it rests on a foundation laid by

Christian belief. Given this dialectical stance toward the world, Guardini did not accept Hitler's state as the instant remedy for the ills of modernity in general and of the Weimar Republic in particular.

After the founding of the Federal Republic of Germany, Guardini worried that Germany and other European nations might eventually turn from democracy to totalitarianism. They would do so, he conjectured, if liberalism gained such dominance that it tried to exclude Christian values from society. In 1953 he wrote that "[d]emocracy is a utopia and at its depths unrealistic. . . . I believe that in twenty years we will again have authoritarian regimes. The difference [among them] will only be whether they respect or distrust the person."[58] In 1964, at the age of seventy-nine, he criticized the "blindness of liberalism" and lamented liberal democracy's loss of "absolute norms." Then he added, "German liberalism was the father of Nazism—and will be again in some kind of form."[59] According to Guardini, the emphasis on personal autonomy in the Weimar Republic had distanced Germans from the objective human values presented in the Christian tradition, thereby leaving people vulnerable to a dictator's persuasive rhetoric.[60] Despite these concerns, Guardini worked tirelessly to support the building up of Germany into a pluralistic society with a vibrant parliamentary democracy.

6

Engelbert Krebs

Witnessing to God's Kingdom

DISCUSSIONS ABOUT THE UNIVERSITY OF FREIBURG IN NAZI
Germany inevitably involve the philosopher Martin Heidegger
(1889–1976).[1] While teaching at the University of Marburg, he
won international recognition in 1927 for his book *Being and Time*.
In 1928 he moved to Freiburg, and in early 1933 he assured Nazi
leaders that if he became the university's rector, he would be
accountable not to the faculty senate but to the Reich's minister of
education. He served as the rector beginning in April 1933, joined
the Nazi party in May, and returned to full-time teaching in April
1934. A politically naive man, he judged that National Socialism
could bring about the renewal of Western society. As he explained
in the summer of 1935 in his lectures on metaphysics, Europe was
situated "between the pincers of Russia and America," between
communism and capitalism, both of which erode what is essential in human life. Europe needed to find a new way of being in
the world, and it could do so by means of the "inner truth"
grasped by Hitler.[2] In rejecting modernity and backing Hitler,
Heidegger stood apart from his colleague and former mentor, the
theologian Engelbert Krebs (1881–1950).[3]

Engelbert Krebs was born into an established banking family
in Freiburg on September 4, 1881. After graduating from the
Gymnasium in the summer of 1900, he matriculated at the University of Freiburg and also entered the seminary for the Diocese
of Freiburg. During his first year of studies, he took courses with
Heinrich Finke, a historian of the Middle Ages who was a leader
in the Görres Gesellschaft, and also with Adolf Dyroff, a philosopher of Idealism who also studied Christian spirituality. From

October 1901 into March 1902, Krebs attended lectures at the University of Munich by Odilo Rottmanner, O.S.B., a patristics scholars, and Georg Freiherr von Hertling, the political philosopher who had founded the Görres Gesellschaft in 1876. Active in the Catholic Center party, Hertling was a member of the Reichstag from 1875 to 1890 and again from 1896 to 1912. He served as Bavaria's president from 1912 to 1917 and then as Germany's chancellor from November 1, 1917, to October 3, 1918.[4] Hertling made a lasting impression on the twenty-year-old Engelbert Krebs, who, returning to the University of Freiburg in the spring of 1902, completed a doctorate in philosophy in 1903 by writing a dissertation on the medieval mystic Dietrich von Freiburg (in Saxony).[5]

Both Krebs and his role model, Hertling, were inspired by the life of Joseph von Görres (b. 1776), for whom the Görres Gesellschaft was named.[6] Görres gained international prominence in the 1800s for his defense of civil liberties and for his writing in literature, history, and politics. Teaching science at Coblenz from 1800 to 1806, he united the Idealism of J. G. Herder and F. W. J. Schelling with the values of Catholicism in his book *Glaube und Wissen* (1805). During the Napoleonic Wars, Görres promoted German independence. Seeing the need for a new kind of political journalism, he started an international newspaper, *Rheinische Merkur*, in 1814 and five years later published his book *Germany and the Revolution* (1819), calling for greater political freedom in society and a fuller role for the Catholic church in society. Because this work enraged the Prussian government, Görres fled to Strasbourg. Görres had distanced himself from the church during his early years, but formally returned to it in 1824 and, beginning in 1827, taught at the University of Munich along with Franz von Baader, Döllinger, and Schelling. At Munich, Görres wrote his four-volume study of the Christian mystics, *Christliche Mystik* (1836–42). After the Prussian government imprisoned Cologne's Archbishop Clemens August von Droste-Vischering in 1836, Görres came to the archbishop's defense. In his tract *Athanasius* (1837), Görres compared Droste-Vischering's defiance of the Prussian state with St. Athanasius's confrontations with the Roman emperors. (Görres drew on Johann Adam Möhler's book on St. Athanasius, which appeared in 1827.) Although he died in 1848, Görres remained an inspiration to Catholics like Krebs and Hertling, who were intent upon participating in the intellectual life, culture, and politics of the German states.

In 1903 Krebs moved to Rome, where he studied theology at the Camposanto Teutonico, taking courses with the medievalists Heinrich Seuse Denifle, O.P., and Franz Ehrle, S.J., the prefect of the Vatican Library. Ordained a priest for the Diocese of Freiburg in 1906, Krebs served in parishes for two years and then returned to Rome for three years, during which time he pursued doctoral studies under the direction of the church historian Franz Josef Dölger. In 1910 Krebs completed his dissertation on the understanding of the Logos as savior in first-century Christian literature and was awarded a doctorate in theology.[7] Two years later, he finished his Habilitationsschrift at the University of Freiburg, writing on the theologian Hervaeus Natalis, O.P. (d. 1323).[8]

Engelbert Krebs was an adjunct professor at Freiburg from 1911 to 1919, teaching courses in philosophy as well as in theology.[9] During that period, he studied neo-Kantianism, while publishing articles on the history-of-religions view of Christian faith, patristic notions of salvation, and the writings of Johann Baptist Hirscher (d. 1865).[10] He had been temporarily exempted from the Oath Against Modernism in 1910 when he successfully argued for academic freedom. In 1912, however, he reluctantly took the Oath after diocesan officials said that they would remove his ecclesiastical permission to hear confessions if he did not do so. This action prompted some of Freiburg's professors to question appointing him to the faculty, for they wondered whether Krebs had compromised his academic freedom in professing the oath. In any case, Krebs continued to devote himself to his scholarly writings, teaching, and academic advising, which included directing Romano Guardini's doctoral dissertation. He was appointed to a professorship at Freiburg in 1917 and on June 8, 1917, gave his inaugural lecture "The Problem of Moral Values in Catholic Dogmatic Theology."[11] In 1919 he succeeded Carl Braig (d. 1923) as Freiburg's professor of dogmatic theology.

During the First World War, Krebs linked Catholicism and German patriotism in weekly articles that appeared in the *Freiburger katholische Gemeindeblatt,* a newspaper of the Archdiocese of Freiburg. He believed that God intended the German people to renew the West during the twentieth century. Belonging to the Committee for the Defense of German and Catholic Interests, he visited the front lines and drove wounded soldiers to hospitals. At the same time, he called for improved conditions in Germany's prisoner-of-war camps and published essays reviewing international criticisms of Germany's conduct in the war, including that of Belgium's Cardinal Mercier, Archbishop of Mechelin.[12]

After the war, Krebs served as a part-time chaplain for local groups of workers and also for the young women studying at Freiburg's Hochschule. Drawing on his conversations with these young women, Krebs published articles calling for a greater respect for women in the church and the university.[13] Because of this public stance, Edith Stein sought Krebs's counsel in April 1930, probably concerning her possible future in the German academy. In the spirit of Görres, Krebs became increasingly involved in civic matters, and in late 1918 publicly called for the abdication of Baden's Grand Duke, Friedrich II. Valuing the new openness of the Weimar Republic, he became an advisor in the Catholic Center party and envisioned the emergence of a society that was both democratic and Catholic.

Amid his pastoral and political activities, Krebs also published articles in Christology, ecclesiology, and the Syrian and Russian Orthodox churches; he also wrote *Dogma und Leben* [Dogma and Life] (1921, 1925) and *A Little Book on Christian Charity* (1921).[14] His medieval research bore fruit in *Grundfragen der kirchlichen Mystik* [Basic Issues in Church Mysticism] (1921) and in a study of Dante. He inquired, too, into Catholicism's common ground with Protestantism and also with Judaism.[15] Yet he criticized Joseph Wittig at the University of Breslau for taking a historical-critical approach to the Bible in his study of Jesus.[16] Prior to the First World War, Krebs had advised the young Martin Heidegger in academic matters and even presided at his wedding; but he watched their collegial relationship cool during the 1920s as the philosopher distanced himself from Catholicism.[17] Interest in the church outside Germany prompted Krebs to visit parishes in the United States, Japan, China, Korea, Indonesia, Ceylon, Egypt, and the Holy Land during 1926. Upon his return to Freiburg, he wrote *Um die Erde* [Around the World] (1928), in which he reflected on Catholicism in non-European societies and on the church as a global community. He expressed amazement and respect for the church in the United States, where, he noted, the church was thriving in a secular society. On July 1, 1931, he celebrated his twenty-fifth anniversary of priestly ordination with no inkling that Hitler would soon stifle his creativity and his vision of Catholicism in society.

Theology in Life

In his theology, Engelbert Krebs deliberately drew on diverse theologians from the twelfth to the twentieth centuries, enriching their ideas with his own insights and synthesis of the Christian faith. He mined both the Neoplatonic and Aristotelian traditions, studying St. Bonaventure and St. Thomas Aquinas, and simultaneously moved beyond Scholasticism by recognizing the accomplishments of modern scholars, including Freiburg's neo-Kantian philosophers. This respect for post-Enlightenment thought brought him close to transcendental Thomists such as Pierre Rousselot and Joseph Maréchal, but it also distanced him from scholars like Karl Eschweiler, Joseph Lortz, and Karl Adam, who rejected the ideas of Kant. Moreover, appreciating the importance for theology of the notion of the coming of God's reign, he turned to the works of Bernhard Galura, Franz Anton Staudenmaier, and J. B. Hirscher. He also studied the writings of Hermann Schell and Wilhelm Koch.

Krebs's most comprehensive theological work was *Dogma und Leben*, which on the one hand implicitly challenged what the author saw to be subjective presentations by some theologians of the church's objective truths and, on the other hand, explained dogma's existential and ethical implications. In Krebs's words, the book examined "how the faith of our church, and indeed, how the salvation of our life is grounded in the context of dogmas . . . and how general human values or supernatural goals, blessings, empowerments, and mediations of salvation are contained in these truths."[18] To attain this twofold goal, the book's language is precise without being technical, making it readable by the laity as well as by theologians. Although it received little attention from scholars, it caught the eye of Karl Eschweiler, who praised the book's Catholic view of nature and grace.[19]

Dogma und Leben systematically presents the major tenets of Catholic doctrine. The first volume (457 pages) treats seven topics: faith and knowledge, God, the Trinity, creation, original sin, salvation in Jesus Christ, and Mary. The second volume (752 pages) discusses six aspects of Christ's saving work in the church: the church's teaching office, for example, papal infallibility; the church's priestly office, including the seven sacraments; the church's pastoral office such as the role of the bishops; the church as body of Christ; grace beyond this life, including in purgatory; and the advent of God's new reign. While it summarizes conciliar and papal teachings, it also addresses modern issues such as suffering and develops the ethical theme that love of God entails love of neighbor. Volume 1 begins by recalling Andrew's testimony to Peter: "'We have found the Messiah' (John 1:41). How much delight concerning life's deepest yearning . . . lies in these words. . . . We Catholic Christians share this delight, this inner security and joy, with those ordinary people at the Sea of Gennesaret through the fortunate possession of our dogmatic faith." Faith, and hence theology, must focus on the living Christ. The first volume concludes with a discussion of Christ as the new Adam, the initiator of the new kingdom. Volume 2 opens with a reiteration of the work's Christocentric orientation: "In all parts [of this volume] the theme is always the same; we are always speaking only of Christ, living and working in his mystical body, the church."[20] The second volume ends with the image of the coming Christ and the new Jerusalem (Revelation 21:1–5). This Christocentric perspective on life does not mean, however, that God loves only those who have formally professed Christian belief. Grace extends to all people, and, for this reason, love of neighbor includes respect and care for those outside the church, including Jews.[21] Christians should reject a triumphalist view of the church and should avoid speaking about the church as the ongoing incarnation of Jesus Christ, since this idea can be misunderstood to suggest a divinized church.[22] God's last judgment will be based on the degree to which men and women demonstrated their devotion to God through their generosity to those in need; Jesus Christ highlighted the primacy of love of neighbor in his parable of the last judgment (Matthew 25:31–46). "Love of God and Christian love of neighbor are in essence identical. Whoever loves God loves therefore everything that bears God's influences, loves the divine resemblances in other men and women. Deficient love of neighbor is a sign of deficient love of God."[23]

Approximately five hundred thousand Jews resided in Germany immediately after the First World War, constituting less than one percent of the nation's total population.[24] They moved into the public realm during the 1920s in part because of the influx of Jews into Germany from eastern Europe and Russia. Unlike German Jews, many of the newcomers wore distinctive attire and preferred to speak their own languages; as a result, they stood out in Germany. Jews also came to public attention because of the Weimar Republic's commitment to Germany becoming an open, democratic society. Leadership in the Republic included Jews such as the author of the Weimar Constitution, Hugo Preuss, and Weimar's foreign minister, Walther Rathenau, who was assassinated in 1922 by anti-Semitic nationalists. A higher percentage of Jews attended the universities during the Republic than had previously. The Jews' obvious presence in the universities irritated some Protestants and Catholics.

In 1926 Engelbert Krebs chose to address the racism of some Catholics. In his article "Katholische Studenten und Judentum" [Catholic Students and Judaism], he observed that "vulgar anti-Semitism" existed at the German universities and asked, "May a Catholic student participate in this?"[25] No, answered Krebs, because Catholics are called to follow the example of Jesus; that is, a Catholic should relate in love to a Jew. In particular, a Catholic student "should be concerned in prayer and action to draw the Jewish student nearer to the church." The Catholic must remember that St. Paul urged Gentile Christians in Rome to show respect to Jews, for "from them, according to the flesh, is the

Messiah" (Romans 9:5). Moreover, St. Paul taught that in Christ "[t]here is no distinction between Jew and Greek" (Romans 10:12). "As a Christian and disciple in the church I must never condemn Jews, for Christ in the flesh originated from them." The large number of Jews in the universities should inspire Catholics in their studies. Christians should not "relate to [Jews] with power, with derision and subjugation." "If our Catholic student groups show tendencies to crude German-racial anti-Semitism, our academic leaders should be conscious that this conduct conveys little genuine Catholicism and little rational German thought. Our obligation is not anti-Semitism but the intellectual engagement and realization of the valuable Jewish creative energies."

Krebs further elaborated his views in a pamphlet entitled *Urkirche und Judentum* [The Early Church and Judaism] (1926), which appeared as an article in English in 1927 and went into a second printing in German in 1929.[26] He insisted that Christians must regard Judaism as the home in which they were born and which they must continue to respect. He criticized the French diplomat Joseph Gobineau, who contended in *The Inequality of the Human Races* (1853–55) that Christianity's origins are not Jewish but Aryan, a view that won the support of the Assyrian scholar Friedrich Delitzsch. Similarly, Adolf von Harnack (d. 1930) spoke of the church's separation from Judaism in his book *Marcion* (1921). Krebs argued that these anti-Jewish views were wrong, that Christian belief cannot be separated from its Jewish origins. For Krebs, the positive influence of Judaism on Catholicism manifests itself in at least four ways. First, Judaism was the home of Jesus and the early church. This origin is clearly evident in Jesus' proclamation "The kingdom of God is at hand; repent, and believe in the gospel" (Mark 1:14). This message, which concerns God's immanence and transcendence in human life, springs out of the Old Testament, for example, from the *Shema*, "Hear O Israel, the Lord, your God is your only God" (Deuteronomy 6:4). Jesus' Jewish character was displayed also in his teaching as a rabbi of his day, as he stood in Nazareth's synagogue to explicate the prophecy of Isaiah (Luke 4:15). "Hence it is entirely certain that the content of Jesus' preaching, although containing something new, remains entirely in continuity with Jewish piety and the expectation of salvation." Further, the early church saw from the outset that it must locate its message in relation to Judaism; "it had to proclaim to Jews and pagans the fulfillment of the Jewish religious hope." On the road to Emmaus (Luke 24), the risen Christ explained his suffering and death to two followers on the basis of the "Scriptures." The Acts of the Apostles and the Pauline letters attest that St. Peter and St. Paul preached about Jesus Christ on the basis of the Old Testament and that Jesus' Jewish disciples worshiped at the temple in Jerusalem.

Krebs argued that even though Jewish faith and Christian faith became distinct as differences arose between Jews and Jesus' followers, Christians continued to acknowledge their Jewish origins. Paul accepted hospitality from Jews, and his close companions—Barnabas, John Mark, Silas, and Timothy—did not renounce their Jewish roots. Paul deliberately preached first to Jews before turning to Gentiles (Acts 13:46) and required that his associate Timothy, whose mother was Jewish, undergo circumcision so that he not scandalize Jews (Acts 16:3). In his letter to the Romans, Paul declared that God has not rejected the people of Israel; indeed, "all Israel will be saved" (Romans 11:26).

Being reminded of Paul's teaching, Krebs asked, what does Paul's instruction mean for today? The answer is clear: "Therefore, no despising of Jews! Therefore, no anti-Semitism in Rome!" Of course, Christians must pray for Jews "in the faith and in the sure hope that the Jewish community will come to the recognition of the truth and will participate in the salvation of the church." Finally, the church today has kept its essential ties with Jewish faith by upholding the Decalogue and respecting the Old Testament as a "divinely inspired text." The church cherishes in its celebration of the Eucharist those rituals and prayers that originated in Judaism. The inclusion at mass of readings from the Old Testament attests to the church's recognition of "the entire canon of the Old Testament as divinely given revelation." In light of Christian faith's roots in Judaism, Catholics cherish "on the one hand, a gratitude for that which we have received as heritage from the Jews and continue to hold sacred. On the other hand, because we are convinced that the fulfillment of the Jewish hopes exists in our savior, we say the intercessory prayer—as did Jesus, James, and Paul—for the people, the people of the Messiah and of his most holy mother Mary."

In 1933 Krebs published yet another article on Jewish belief. As Hitler was demanding the boycott of Jewish businesses and the removal of Jews from law, medicine, and education, Krebs reiterated his positive view of Judaism. In the article "Judentum und Christentum" in the prestigious *Lexikon für Theologie und Kirche* he clarified that "Judaism constitutes the preparation, the mother's lap, and ongoing witness for Christian faith."[27] Because of God's covenant with the people of Israel, Jews remain the "recipients and guardians of divine revelation." They are the people to whom Jesus belonged "according to the flesh" (Romans 9:5), whose scriptures are seen as sacred by the church, and in relation to whom a full understanding of Jesus is made possible. Today, without their temple in Jerusalem, they witness to the necessity of worshiping God "in spirit and truth" (John 4:23). Paul sought to extirpate anti-Semitism from among Gentile Christians by denouncing disrespect for Jews and also by incessantly praying for them (Romans 9–11). Over the centuries, the church "did not foster defamation against the [Jewish] race because the savior and his most holy mother belong to it." In the twentieth century, tensions exist between Catholicism and Judaism, for example, concerning "modern Jewish liberalism." Nevertheless, the two faiths remain connected in love. "The difference between Christian faith as fulfillment and Jewish faith which continually holds fast to [its belief in] unfulfilled preparation remains a difference in religious beliefs, but this difference should not bring about the opposite of love."

Krebs expressed a view of Judaism that was remarkable for its day. He challenged both Hitler's racial anti-Semitism and the church's religious anti-Semitism, which manifested itself, for example, in the prayer on Good Friday concerning the "perfidious Jews." But the theologian eventually paid a personal price for speaking the truth out of season.

Archbishop Gröber
and Freiburg's Catholic Theologians

Freiburg's Archbishop Conrad Gröber and its faculty of Catholic theology initially held opposing views of the Third Reich. The archbishop at first judged that the church and Hitler could work together in building up Germany's social, economic, and political life. In contrast, Freiburg's theologians stood at a distance from the Nazi regime throughout its twelve years.

Conrad Gröber was born on April 1, 1872, in Messkirch, where Martin Heidegger was born seventeen years later.[28] After studies in Constance, Gröber matriculated at the University of Freiburg in the autumn of 1891, studying theology and the history of art with the progressive theologian F. X. Kraus. After further studies in Rome, he was ordained a priest on October 28, 1897, and completed a doctorate in theology in 1898. After three years in parish ministry, Gröber was appointed the rector of the seminary in Constance. Among his students were Martin Heidegger, who became the University of Freiburg's first Nazi rector, and Max Metzger, who was martyred by the Reich on April 17, 1944. Gröber became the pastor of Constance's Holy Trinity Church in 1905, and, during the next seventeen years, restored the church's art while also strengthening Catholic organizations in the politically liberal Constance. Appointed the pastor of Freiburg's cathedral in 1922, Gröber gained public recognition because of his revision of the church's hymn book and his preaching on the radio. In 1929 he became friends with the papal nuncio Monsignor Eugenio Pacelli who soon afterward became the Vatican secretary of state. Gröber was named bishop of Meissen in the spring of 1931 and, one year later became archbishop of Freiburg, succeeding Archbishop Carl Fritz.

At the outset Gröber tried to find common ground between the church and the Nazi movement. He instructed his priests in late 1932 to take a conciliatory approach to National Socialism so that they might influence it. He reportedly even donated personal funds to Nazi organizations.[29] After the bishops dropped their bans on Nazi membership on March 28, 1933, he engaged in discussions with Vice Chancellor Papen and Monsignor Kaas, the president of the Catholic Center party, as they negotiated the concordat. When the bishops considered a draft of the concordat in late June, Gröber spoke on behalf of Pacelli and then conveyed the concerns of the bishops to Pacelli during July. After the signing of the concordat on July 10, 1933, he collaborated with Papen in bringing together influential Catholics and Nazi leaders to form the Arbeitsgemeinschaft katholischer Deutschen (AKD) in October 1933.[30]

Gröber began to have doubts about the Third Reich during 1935 as he saw that the state was permitting Nazis to act against Catholic organizations. Because he voiced some of his concerns in pastoral letters and radio sermons, he found himself at odds with Nazi officials. In the autumn of 1936, Julius Streicher, the Nazi leader in Franconia, publicly criticized the archbishop for lack of patriotism. Since Gröber held that the violence against Catholics was being done by extremists without the backing of Nazi officials, he remained willing to cooperate with the regime by editing in 1937 the *Handbuch der religiösen Gegenwartsfragen* [Handbook for the Religious Questions of the Day], which contained articles on the supposed congruity between Catholicism and National Socialism.

The archbishop eventually distanced himself from the Nazi movement while showing respect for the Reich's officials. On the one hand, he judged that in principle he had to affirm civil authority. In March 1942, Gröber explained in a letter to Bishop Heinrich Wienken, the secretary of the bishops' conference, that he wanted to respect the state without promoting Nazism: "I have never gone against the state or attacked the party as such. Yet I have never said the name 'National Socialism' from the pulpit."[31] He may have been influenced by this logic when he chose to remain silent in 1938 when the Gestapo banished Bishop Sproll from the Diocese of Rottenburg. On the other hand, Gröber criticized the Reich's abuse of power in a sermon on December 31, 1940; and again, two months later in his Lenten pastoral letter, he called upon the state to respect all German citizens. Beginning in 1941, he supported Gertrud Luckner of the Caritas Association in her efforts to help Jews escape from Germany, and he tried to aid her in 1943 when she was imprisoned in the Ravensbrück concentration camp.[32] In 1943 Gröber also sent a letter to Berlin in defense of Max Metzger. Although the archbishop's intervention did not change Metzger's fate, it heartened Metzger and his supporters. According to Gordon Zahn, "this letter represents the strongest and perhaps the *only* episcopal support given any German Catholic objector to Hitler's wars."[33] Despite his efforts to remain on good terms with the Reich, he was also ineffective in stopping the state's execution of two Freiburg priests, Heinrich Feuerstein and Josef Schmidlin.

In November 1944, Gröber watched Allied bombs destroy Freiburg, and, after the war, he worked closely with military officials to ensure that food and clothing reached the people in need. Gröber was appointed a papal counselor by Pius XII, but he was not named a cardinal along with bishops Frings, Galen, and Preysing, who were the most outspoken episcopal critics of Hitler. Gröber died on February 14, 1948.

Freiburg's professors publicly opposed Hitler in 1933. Many of them, including all of the theologians, signed a public petition on April 6, 1933, in support of retaining Freiburg's anti-Nazi mayor, Karl Bender, whom Hitler replaced. Under pressure from Bernhard Rust, the professors softened their resistance to Hitler by electing Heidegger the university's rector on April 21, 1933. The philosopher immediately gave two public lectures on the role of the university in the Nazi state. On May 27, 1933, he spoke on "Die Selbstbehauptung der deutschen Universität" (The Self-Assertion of the German University), and on June 6, 1933, he lectured on "Die Universität im neuen Reich" [The University in the New Reich]. Both lectures indicated Heidegger's total support of the regime, and, following Rust's directives, Heidegger dismissed professors from the university because they were Jewish or political dissidents.

The university's fifteen theologians and its instructors in theology taught approximately 320 seminarians in 1933.[34] No theologian was a member of the Nazi party, and none of them joined the AKD, despite Archbishop Gröber's support for it. A lone pro-Nazi voice was that of Ludwig Andreas Veit, professor of church history, who publicly supported National Socialism on the grounds that it was overcoming liberalism and restoring Germany's sense of tradition and community.[35] Bernhard Rust was intent on changing the political character of Freiburg's faculty of theology. He dismissed Franz Keller, a Christian pacifist and professor of moral theology, from the faculty on July 1, 1933. He appointed Johannes Beeking, but then removed him from his academic chair on July 10, 1935, because of his criticisms of the Reich. In the summer of 1935, Theodor Haecker, who had publicly criticized the Nazi regime, gave a public lecture entitled "Der Christ und die Geschichte" [Christ and History]. Nazis disrupted it with catcalls and loud talking. Soon afterward, Haecker was not allowed by the Reich to speak in public or to publish anything.[36] In Munich, Haecker became an advisor to the White Rose martyrs. The moral theologian Rupert Angermair had his residence searched by the Gestapo in April 1936 and was interrogated about an article that he published in 1932. Soon afterward, Angemair was dismissed from the faculty. In 1937 Bernhard Rust overturned the theology faculty's election of Nikolaus Hilling as their chairman because Hilling had publicly questioned some of the decisions and policies of the minister of education. On October 15, 1938, Rust closed the university's Institute for the Study of the Caritas Movement, an institute run by the theology faculty and the Diocese of Freiburg.

An Opponent of National Socialism

Soon after Hitler became chancellor, Engelbert Krebs saw that the Nazi government would abuse the power of the state. On March 22, 1933—the day before the Reichstag passed the Enabling Act, which established Hitler as the nation's dictator—he noted in his diary that Berlin's Nazis were bullying the parliament's elected representatives into rejecting the Weimar Constitution. He even jotted down a cynical comment circulating in the nation's capital: "Berlin wit: Why is spring coming so late this year? Because so many 'leaves' [anti-Nazi political leaders] were beaten down during the time that should have been spring. Why is the autumn coming so early? Because so many 'leaves' have already become brown [Nazi]."[37] Unwilling to remain silent, Krebs publicly took issue with the ideas that Heidegger had presented in his lectures on the university in the Nazi state. In May 1933, Krebs published the article "Die Aufgabe der Universität im neuen Reich" [The Task of the University in the New Reich], arguing that the University of Freiburg needed to include professors in its governance if it were to remain a true university.[38] Furthermore, on June 1, 1933, he explained in a public lecture entitled "Vom Wesen der Authorität im Lichte des christlichen Glaubens" [On the Essence of Authority in the Light of Christian Faith] that the state should respect the authority of God and the church.[39] Because of this lecture, he was formally reported to the rector's office by one of the university's Nazi professors. Nevertheless, a few weeks later, he published an article in the *Freiburger Tagespost* concerning the Reich Concordat. While acknowledging that the agreement was a legal framework for a working relationship between the church and the Reich, he warned Catholics to stay alert to new "dangers" as the concordat was implemented.[40]

As already noted, Krebs permitted in 1933 the publication of his article on Judaism in the *Lexikon für Theologie und Kirche*. Consonant with this article, he spoke out on April 21, 1933, against the Reich's dismissal of Jewish professors. He also did not shy away from asserting his political convictions when he answered questionnaires that Rust issued to all professors in 1933 and 1934 concerning their political and professional views. These forms gathered information so that the state could decide which professors should no longer teach at the universities because they held views incompatible with the Nazi *Weltanschauung*. Aware that truthfulness might have dire consequences for him, Krebs honestly answered that he had always voted for the Catholic Center party, in which he was an advisor, and also that he was a member of the Franciscan Third Order, a commitment that Nazi officials viewed with suspicion because of disdain for Catholic religious orders.[41]

Krebs came into more overt conflict with the regime in 1934. He gave a public lecture at Freiburg on February 15 in which he presented the traditional Christian view that a state derives its authority from God. Entitling the lecture "Jesuitischer und deutscher Geist" [The Jesuit and German Spirit], he observed that Nazi officials had rightly opposed atheism and Bolshevism but needed to work more closely with the churches. In this regard, they should follow the example of the Jesuits, whose institutions united German culture and Christian faith.[42] This lecture infuriated the Nazis because they hated the Jesuits. When the lecture's reprints were made available at the University of Freiburg, they were immediately destroyed by members of the Hitler Youth and the Nazi Student Association.

In August 1934, Krebs made a statement in private that would haunt him until the end of Hitler's rule. During a social gathering at his brother's house in the Black Forest village of St. Märgen, he spontaneously gave his negative assessment of the Third Reich, allegedly including the statement, "We are being governed by robbers, murderers, and criminals." He eventually learned that this comment was reported to Nazi officials by one of the guests.[43]

In October 1934, Krebs visited Austria's St. Ottilien Abbey, where he spoke with Bishop Boniface Sauer of Korea's Diocese of Wonsan. Krebs had previously met with Sauer at Wonsan in 1926; he and the bishop had enjoyed their days together and afterward had stayed in contact. Reunited at the Abbey of St. Ottilien, Krebs and Sauer discussed the theologian's conflict with the Reich. Aware that Krebs's future would be bleak so long as Hitler remained in power, Sauer invited the professor to move to the Diocese of Wonsan. Declining the invitation, Krebs returned to Freiburg.

Krebs published two provocative articles in 1935 on aspects of the relationship between church and state. In "Arteigenes Christentum" [Authentic Christianity], he criticized Alfred Rosenberg's *Myth of the Twentieth Century*, arguing that Catholicism could not become a nationalized church without betraying its very essence.[44] In the other essay on Möhler's book of 1827 on St. Athanasius, he stressed the importance of the church's autonomy in relation to the state.[45] Quoting at length from Möhler, he explained that Athanasius had fought not only against the false ideas of Arianism but also against the efforts of the Roman emperor Constantius to control the church. Without going into details, Krebs emphasized that Athanasius's defense of the church's freedom in relation to the state had significant implications for German Catholics.

Krebs's conflict with the Third Reich moved into the legal arena in November 1935, when he submitted a written request to the University of Freiburg for a visa to travel to Vienna in order to give an invited lecture on mysticism. Since he received no response from the university's administration after four weeks, he resubmitted his request in December and was soon told by the rector that he should not accept the invitation to Vienna because the Reich had set aside his request. Three months later, on April 1, 1936, the government returned to Krebs his request for a visa without having acting on it. The next day, the minister of justice alerted the State of Baden's minister of cult and instruction in Karlsruhe that he was investigating Krebs because of his alleged statement against Nazi officials at St. Märgen in August 1934. On April 18, Baden's minister of cult and instruction informed the University of Freiburg that he was revoking Krebs's teaching license until the theologian was cleared of the allegations against him. Archbishop Gröber intervened on Krebs's behalf without success.

At judicial hearings beginning on May 23, 1936, a prosecutor argued that Krebs was an enemy of the state on three grounds. First, he had verbally attacked the Reich's leaders in August 1934 at St. Märgen. Further, he was a communist who had assisted Freiburg's labor unions after the war and participated in the Catholic Center party.[46] Finally, he had defied civil authority by calling in 1919 for the abdication of Baden's Grand Duke of Baden. As the proceedings dragged on, the Reich revoked Krebs's passport in July 1936. Seven months later, on February 22, 1937, the government informed the University's rector that Krebs had violated the law concerning the reordering of the civil service when he had spoken against state officials in August 1934 at St. Märgen. Krebs was required to submit a written self-defense within three days. In his formal response Krebs argued that the state could not act alone on the allegations against him because the Vatican's Concordat of 1932 with the State of Baden stated that civil charges against a priest had to be reviewed by the appropriate ecclesiastical authorities as well as by the state. Tension between Krebs and the state heightened after the release of Pius XI's encyclical *Mit brennender Sorge*, on March 21, 1937. For many weeks, it appeared that the Reich would act against Krebs. However, on July 19, the Reich abruptly dropped its charges against Krebs because of a lack of witnesses and evidence. It nevertheless punished him: on August 31 Rust informed Krebs that he was henceforth "retired" from his professorship, and soon afterwards he moved Krebs's academic chair from the faculty of theology to the faculties of law and politics.[47]

In late summer 1937, Krebs turned his attention to researching and writing articles for encyclopedias on Catholicism that were being compiled for China and Japan.[48] He also lectured at St. Peter's Seminary in Freiburg at the request of Archbishop Gröber, who also named Krebs a monsignor. Gröber conferred this honor on Krebs as a sign of ecclesiastical respect, which he hoped might protect Krebs from the Reich. At the start of 1940, Krebs, at the age of fifty-nine, fell seriously ill for four months; as he recuperated, he composed an essay on sickness and death in the Christian life.[49] In the autumn of 1940, he resumed his research, his lecturing at the seminary, and his pastoral ministry.

In 1943 Krebs found himself in a theological disagreement with Archbishop Gröber. The conflict came about after Cardinal Bertram, as the president of the bishops' conference, publicly questioned the orthodoxy of the theological and liturgical renewal being promoted by Romano Guardini in Berlin and Joseph Jungmann in Innsbruck. On January 18, Gröber responded to Bertram by sending to the German and Austrian episcopate a twenty-one-page letter criticizing theologians' neglect of neo-Scholasticism and their emphasis on laity's participation in the mass. Although his letter was confidential, Gröber discussed its contents with Freiburg's priests on February 9. Troubled by Gröber's public comments, Krebs wrote him a private memorandum on March 9, arguing on the basis of scripture and tradition for a non-Scholastic theological perspective and for the retrieval of ancient modes of worship. Unknown to Krebs, his memorandum to Gröber concurred with a forty-three-page report by Karl Rahner at the request of Vienna's Cardinal Theodor Innitzer, who submitted the report to Bertram and the bishops of Germany and Austria. The Vatican eventually stepped into the fray and granted permission for judicious theological and liturgical renewal.[50]

Krebs could not dwell on this ecclesiastical conflict, however, because he was soon again at odds with the Reich. He became the focus of Nazi ire after he preached a sermon on the feast of St. James the Greater (July 25) in 1943 at a mass in the Black Forest village of Oedsdach im Renchtal. In light of the scripture readings, Krebs spoke on Christian love: "To be sure, we may fight against our enemies, but we may not hate them." This statement offended a Luftwaffe lieutenant who afterward reported the comment to his superiors. Krebs was interrogated by the Gestapo on October 20, 1943, and on November 29 watched as police searched his residence. Then he was incarcerated in Karlsruhe and, a few days later, was sentenced to imprisonment. He remained in the Karlsruhe prison for a couple of weeks and was about to be taken to a concentration camp when he was abruptly released; an influential physician had submitted an official report warning that because of Krebs's poor health, imprisonment would lead to his death. Krebs was permitted to return to his residence in Freiburg and was informed on December 28 that the government was forbidding him to say mass, to preach, or to hear confessions. After a formal appeal to the state by Archbishop Gröber, Krebs was allowed to celebrate mass in private.[51]

During 1944, while Engelbert Krebs remained under virtual house arrest in Freiburg, Romano Guardini was residing in the Allgäu village of Mooshausen. Taking refuge in this rural area, Guardini wrote his memoirs, which included his remembrance of how in 1915 he had come to write his doctoral dissertation under Krebs's direction. He had hoped to work with Freiburg's senior scholar, Carl Braig, and felt rejected after he and Braig could not agree on a dissertation topic. As Guardini recalled, "then an associate advised me to go to Engelbert Krebs who was an instructor at the time. He was known to be prudent and always ready to help and was praised for his great intellectual and spiritual openness. I did this and have never regretted it. He directed me to St.

Bonaventure whose critical edition from Quaracchi was appearing, so that the first requirement for a systematic investigation was fulfilled, and [Krebs suggested] that I should treat the Franciscan's teaching on redemption."[52] Guardini proceeded to write his dissertation on Bonaventure's theology, which shaped Gaurdini's thought for the remainder of his life.

Guardini's praise of his dissertation director probably never reached Engelbert Krebs himself, since Guardini's memoirs were not published until 1984. In 1944 Guardini's words may have helped Krebs, who had not recuperated from the trauma of his imprisonment in Karlsruhe. Having withdrawn from public life, Krebs was celebrating a mass at a side altar in Freiburg's cathedral on November 27, 1944, when Allied bombs rained down on the city. He managed to find shelter and eventually emerged to see the entire city—including the cathedral, his residence, and his possessions—in shambles. The French army occupied Freiburg in the spring of 1945, and on May 25, 1945, the provisional government reinstated Krebs in his professorship at the University of Freiburg. The theologian found, however, that he no longer had the mental focus and stamina for teaching. He resigned from the university with the rank of professor emeritus in September 1946 and died from a kidney infection on November 29, 1950.[53]

Engelbert Krebs crafted a theology that brought Catholicism into a critical dialogue with modernity. On the one hand, he retained neo-Scholasticism's use of clear, well-defined concepts, and, on the other hand, he addressed such contemporary issues as the Christian life in a religiously and morally diverse society and the enigma of evil and suffering. Recognizing the modern emphasis on human initiative and action, he highlighted the ethical orientation of Christian faith. Love of God expresses itself, he stressed, in love of neighbor, regardless of gender, race, and religion, and the church must not withdraw from world but must witness to the coming of God's new creation.[54] As we have seen, Krebs's theology shaped his social and political views. He was committed to social justice, especially for industrial workers, women, and Jews, and implicit in this commitment was an acceptance of Germany as a pluralistic society with a parliamentary democracy.[55] While he probably espoused in theory the papal teaching against the separation of church and state, he acknowledged in fact the merit of religious freedom in his defense of Jews and in his recognition of the church's success in the United States. Because Krebs did not write a retrospect on his life and thought, he never publicly commented on the evolution of his thought. If he had said after 1945 how he perceived the two world wars, he would have clarified the development of his theology as well as his politics. In any case, he demonstrated by his persistent opposition to Hitler that he was more astute in his theological and political views during the Third Reich than he had been during the First World War when he linked Catholicism and German nationalism. Commenting on Krebs's life and theology, Thomas O'Meara has rightly observed that "the variety of his writings and interests displays his intention of belonging to a dynamic church, and, unafraid of leaving antique enclosures to address contemporary issues, he aided the unfolding of German Catholicism leading to Vatican II."[56]

In publicly opposing the Third Reich, Engelbert Krebs stood beside Romano Guardini but apart from Martin Heidegger, Karl Eschweiler, Joseph Lortz, and Karl Adam. What united Krebs with Guardini and distanced him from Heidegger and the others was much more than a judgment regarding Hitler; it was the issue of the church in the modern world. Krebs was not searching for a political leader who would somehow restore Christendom. The ills of the Weimar Republic did not justify the inhuman actions of the Third Reich. While acknowledging modernity's shortcomings, Krebs saw its merits as well, including its respect for human rights and for democracy. In this recognition, he implicitly distinguished liberalism from modernity. While seeing the former as an ideology, he saw the latter as the horizon of life and thought that had emerged out of the Renaissance. Whereas Heidegger, Eschweiler, Lortz, and Adam held that the history of the West since the Middle Ages was a story of degeneration, Krebs along with Guardini judged that Western history required a much more sophisticated narrative, told in relation to a belief in the coming of God's reign.

7

Catholic Theology
in Nazi Germany

KONRAD ADENAUER COMMENTED IN 1946 THAT CHURCH LEADERS
should have done more to oppose Hitler. Cologne's former
mayor, who became the chancellor of the Federal Republic of
Germany in 1949, wrote, "I believe that if all of the bishops had
together made public statements from the pulpit on a particular
day, they could have prevented a great deal."[1] While it is debat-
able whether a public condemnation of the persecution of the
Jews would have in fact deterred Hitler, it is true—as Pope John
Paul II and the German bishops have stated in recent years—that
church officials should have done more to protest Nazi atrocities
and to protect the victims of the Third Reich.[2] Why didn't they?
In general, bishops, with their theologians, lead the church on the
basis of their ideas about what God wants the church to be and to
do in the world. Similar to actors who rely on a script and stage
direction in the theater, pastoral leaders speak and act in the public arena in light of their understanding of the church's nature
and mission. In order to understand the conduct of the bishops
and their theologians in Nazi Germany, it is necessary to tell their
story—even though this means presenting some material from
previous chapters—in relation to three distinct notions or models
of the church: church as perfect society, church as moral voice,
and church as body of Christ.[3]

Theological Models in Conflict, 1933–1945

Two distinct models of church came into conflict among the
German bishops during the 1930s and 1940s. As explained in

152

chapter 1, the bishops espoused the dominant notion of the church as a perfect society, a self-sufficient institution, within which men and women received the spiritual nourishment to sustain them in this life and to bring them into unity with God in the next. This ecclesiology had come to full elaboration during the late 1800s in neo-Scholasticism and in the documents of the First Vatican Council. While all German bishops upheld this model of church, some of them also increasingly perceived its inadequacy in the Third Reich and simultaneously acted out of an understanding of the church as a moral voice, a public advocate of basic values of human life, including civil rights. They found a basis for this servant ecclesiology in the universal social outreach of pastoral leaders like Adolf Kolping (d. 1865), who as a priest was dedicated to helping the poor, and Bishop Wilhelm Ketteler (d. 1877), who as Mainz's ordinary instituted outreach programs for the needy. They were also inspired by the social encyclicals *Rerum Novarum* (1891) of Pope Leo XIII and *Quadragesimo Anno* (1931) of Pope Pius XI.[4] These two ecclesiologies—church as perfect society and church as moral voice—manifested themselves in the diverging stances toward the Reich of Breslau's Cardinal Adolf Bertram and Berlin's Bishop Konrad Preysing. As Kurt Meier has noted, "the episcopacy was of differing minds concerning which stance should be taken toward the National Socialist regime. It fluctuated between the possibilities of public protest and the approach of negotiations and petitions. The last was favored by the president of the Fulda conference of bishops, Cardinal Bertram."[5] This tension among the bishops unfolded in four stages from 1933 into 1945.

During 1933 and 1934, the bishops decided on their goal: to preserve the church as an autonomous institution in Germany. Agreeing with Pope Pius XI and Cardinal Pacelli, they judged that the Concordat of 1933 was the best formal means for ensuring that the state would not interfere in the church's religious activities, its decision making, and the functioning of its institutions. At the same time, they agreed that Cardinal Bertram, as the president of the bishops' conference, would speak for all of the bishops on church–state matters, and that he would resolve church–state differences by means of private negotiations. The bishops publicly criticized the religious ideas associated with the Nazi party. Cardinal Faulhaber preached his Advent sermons of 1933 against the Aryan view of Christ and Christian belief promoted by the so-called German Christians. The Vatican's Holy Office placed Rosenberg's *Myth of the Twentieth Century* on the *Index of Forbidden Books* on February 7, 1934, and, a few days later, Cologne's Cardinal Schulte preached against Nazism. On April 8, 1934, Freiburg's Archbishop Gröber gave a sermon warning about "heathen" ideas. In early June, the German episcopacy issued a statement condemning neopaganism, the state's suppression of Catholic organizations, including the Catholic press, and the state's efforts to create a national church.

Consonant with the *societas-perfecta* ecclesiology, the bishops remained silent concerning the new regime's political and social actions. They did not publicly object to the Nazi party's national boycott of Jewish businesses on April 1, 1933, nor did they protest when the state dismissed Jews from civil service positions, including professorships. In early June of 1933, Cardinal Faulhaber issued no public protest after Storm Troopers in Munich assaulted Catholics who were attending the national assembly of the Kolping Society. Further, neither Faulhaber nor any of the bishops publicly protested the incarceration of leaders of the Catholic Center party and the Bavarian People's party in late June 1933, and said nothing when the state required that all civil servants belong to the Nazi party and renounce their memberships in Catholic associations. The bishops issued no public statements after Storm Troopers murdered Hitler's political enemies in the so-called Röhm *Putsch*, beginning on June 30, 1934. Among those murdered were four nationally respected Catholic lay leaders: Fritz Gerlich, Edgar Jung, Erich Klausener, and Adalbert Probst.[6]

From 1935 through 1939, the bishops maintained their defensive stance toward the Third Reich as the state intensified its persecution of the church. The state initiated judicial hearings and trials against priests, brothers, and sisters charged with pedophilia and the violation of monetary laws that prohibited religious orders from sending funds to their members engaged in missionary work. The bishops issued a pastoral letter on August

20, 1935, criticizing the state's activities against the church, including its suppression of the Catholic press, its laws against church meetings, the imprisonment of clergy, and its defamation of the character of many church leaders. In his encyclical *Mit brennender Sorge*—issued on March 14, 1937, and read at all churches on Palm Sunday, March 21, 1937—Pius XI listed the Reich's violations of the concordat, sharply criticized Nazi neopaganism, and exhorted Catholics to remain true to the Christian faith.[7] After Hitler retaliated by having the Gestapo destroy Catholic printing presses, Catholics demonstrated their ecclesial loyalty by participating in religious ceremonies; in Aachen alone, eight hundred thousand people participated in a pilgrimage.[8] In May 1938, when Hitler visited Rome, Pius XI withdrew to Castel Gandolfo and closed the Vatican's museums.

While the bishops as a group continued to remain silent during the late 1930s about Hitler's abuse of human rights, individual bishops began to protest the Reich's actions publicly. The episcopacy said nothing in public about the Reich's Nüremburg laws. Enacted on September 15, 1935, these laws excluded Jews from the professions of law, medicine, and teaching. Moreover, Cardinal Faulhaber issued a statement on January 3, 1937, declaring that the church and the Reich stood together in opposing Bolshevism, and the bishops praised the Führer in September 1938 for avoiding war during the Sudeten crisis. They issued, however, no statement after *Kristallnacht* (November 9–10, 1938)—the night on which Nazis destroyed 267 synagogues, murdered ninety-one Jews, desecrated Jewish cemeteries, and sent more than twenty thousand Jews to concentration camps. Acting on his outrage over the pogrom, Bishop Preysing provided more support for his associates Margarete Sommer and Bernhard Lichtenberg, the cathedral's vicar, in their work on behalf of Jews. He also backed Lichtenberg's public condemnations of the Jewish persecution.

Preysing's efforts for social justice had antecedents. Bishop Galen had used the commemoration of the martyrs in Xanten (near Aachen) on February 6, 1936, to praise the Catholic lay leaders who were murdered in the Röhm *Putsch,* and, on April 10, 1938, Bishop Sproll had protested the *Anschluss* ("annexation") of

Austria by refusing to vote. By their actions, Preysing, Galen, and Sproll had demonstrated that the church should be a moral advocate, indeed a servant of justice, and they would have gained greater papal support for their model of church if Pius XI (d. 1939) had lived long enough to issue his encyclical condemning racism, *Humani Generis Unitas*.[9]

Tension among the bishops increased during the early years of the war (1939–1943). While all bishops wanted to convey their patriotism, they differed among themselves concerning their public stance toward Hitler's disregard for human lives. As the Führer used the war as a pretext for closing Catholic publishing houses, eliminating religious education after the age of fourteen in public schools, monitoring priests' sermons, and seizing church property, Bertram and most bishops stiffened their resolve to protect the church by not protesting injustice. Furthermore, they authorized Bertram to settle church–state conflicts in private meetings with Nazi officials. In 1942 they felt confirmed in this strategy in light of the Nazi persecution of Holland's Jewish Catholics, after the Dutch bishops publicly protested the Reich's deportation of Jews. Furthermore, they judged that they were adhering to Pope Pius XII's understanding of the church's mission. The pontiff conveyed in private his personal disdain for the Nazi state and his disapproval of the war.[10] At the same time, Pius XII publicly declared that his primary concern was to preserve the church's ability to care for its members' spiritual needs and to maintain a neutrality among the warring nations so that he could mediate an international peace. He manifested this public orientation in his first encyclical, *Summi Pontificatus*, in which the pontiff criticized totalitarianism in abstract terms and called for reconciliation among all people through union with Jesus Christ.[11]

Germany's dire moral situation strengthened some bishops' conviction that the church must publicly speak out on behalf of the Reich's innocent victims. Bishop Galen preached during late July and August 1941 against euthanasia, the seizure of church property, and the suppression of the religious orders. Soon afterward, Bishops Franz Rudolf Bornewasser, Godehard Machens, and Preysing also spoke out against euthanasia. In November

1941, Bishops Preysing and Galen presented to the conference of bishops the draft of a letter to be issued by the episcopacy against the Reich's abuse of human rights, including the deportation of Jews. They failed, however, to win the conference's endorsement for this letter because Cardinal Bertram convinced the majority of bishops that the letter would bring harm upon the church.

The conflict among the bishops became more acute during the last two years of the war.[12] The Wehrmacht's inability to take Moscow and its defeat at Stalingrad in February 1943 indicated that Hitler was not invincible and that he might actually bring total destruction upon Germany. Since this precarious situation prompted the Reich to become more ruthless at home, Cardinal Bertram urged the bishops to be even more circumspect in their public statements and to caution their priests to say nothing that could be reported to the Gestapo. To support his position, Bertram needed only to point to those occasions when the state imprisoned a priest simply because he had included a seemingly unpatriotic comment in a sermon. A case in point was the Reich's action against Engelbert Krebs in 1943 after he preached on loving one's enemy.

Bishop Preysing persisted, however, in his efforts to get the bishops' conference to protest the state's abuse of human rights. He found an ally in Archbishop Frings, who in 1941 had succeeded Cardinal Schulte in Cologne. Frings managed to win the episcopacy's endorsement of the Decalogue Letter (August 19, 1943)—an episcopal statement drafted by Preysing that appealed to the Fifth Commandment in protesting the Reich's killing of innocent people. Gradually recognizing that the church's mission includes social justice, Pope Pius XII gave public addresses condemning the murder of noncombatants and defending human rights. Moreover, he initiated a breakthrough in the church's political thought when he affirmed the values of a parliamentary democracy in his Christmas address "Benignitas et Humanitas" (December 24, 1944). As Klaus Schatz has pointed out, in this address "there was quietly overcome the issue of democracy and also the issue of the right for forceful resistance against tyrannical state authority, thereby overcoming the anti-revolutionary fixations which were maintained [by the church] during the entire nineteenth century. The experience of the totalitarian regime and reflection [on the assassination attempt against Hitler] on July 20, 1944, had brought about a change on the Catholic side."[13]

By the time of Hitler's suicide on April 30, 1945, the bishops were clearly operating out of two distinct models of the church. The conflict between Bertram and Preysing involved more than political strategy; it was at heart theological. "What stood in the backdrop," Schatz has noted, "was surely a difference in views of the church's mission. With Bertram there existed the priority of internal pastoral care for Catholics in the strict sense. With Preysing and Galen there was stressed more strongly, beyond internal [ministry], the universal mission of the church as the advocate of natural law and human rights."[14] Each ecclesiology had its merits and limitations during the Third Reich.

Church as a Perfect Society

As discussed in chapter 1, the *societas-perfecta* ecclesiology conceives of the church as a self-sufficient institution that, having been established by Jesus Christ, rests on an authority wholly independent of human societies and their civil governments. In keeping with its origins, its structure is hierarchical: the pope, representing Jesus Christ, is the church's head, to whom the bishops are accountable; decision making is top-down. According to this conventional eccesiology, the church should be concerned primarily about the spiritual well-being of its members. It must lead the faithful to redemption in Jesus Christ. According to Donald Dietrich, "Redemption was a question of saving one's soul and not a moral commitment to the socio-political betterment of mankind."[15] For this reason, Pius XI, Pius XII, most bishops, and most theologians during the Third Reich were resolved not to say or do anything that might provoke Hitler into closing the churches. They prized the Concordat of 1933, which gave a formal assurance that the Reich would allow the parishes to administer the sacraments and to teach Christian faith and morals.[16] As long as the churches were operating, the pope and bishops were fulfilling their duty of making God's grace available to the faithful. In Victor Conzemius's view, the concordat "gave the church during this period of dictatorship a basis of existence. It was, to be sure, a precarious and ever more restricted basis, but it did make possible the Church's continued functioning."[17]

The understanding of the church as a perfect society evinced at least two strengths in Hitler's Germany. First, it fostered among German Catholics a belief in the church as a divinely established institution superior to the Reich. Thus, it generated the same solidarity among Catholics in the face of Nazi persecution as it had also done sixty years earlier during the Kulturkampf. Catholics refused to abandon the church's religious teachings for the Nazi *Weltanschauung*.[18] As the Gestapo noted in a report dated August 20, 1942, Catholics demonstrated a passive resistance to Nazism by means of their participation in the mass and in religious devotions such as processions on the feast of Corpus Christi and pilgrimages to sacred shrines.[19] Second, the conventional ecclesiology reinforced the church's organizational structure and authority. Although Hitler tried to take control of the church, he did not succeed in doing so. The church's ability to gather information, its lines of communication, and its decision making occurred outside the state's knowledge and interference. This ecclesial autonomy showed itself when the bishops clandestinely printed and distributed *Mit brenennder Sorge,* requiring that it be read at all churches on Palm Sunday. It manifested itself again in the late summer of 1941 when bishops distributed copies of Bishop Galen's sermon condemning euthanasia. The bishops succeeded in preserving the church's institutional autonomy in the Third Reich. The church was, as Kurt Meier has said, "the most important group in German society that was able to preserve its institutions and value system. Even National Socialism saw in the church an observable obstacle to its totalitarian goals."[20] Moreover, because the church as an organization was still functioning in the summer of 1945, it was able to distribute food and clothing to refugees while also offering them spiritual sustenance through the sacraments and religious devotions. In Klaus Schatz's judgment, "The total disruption of 1945 was for the churches, especially for the Catholic church, not a *Stunde Null* [zero hour]. The churches were the single large organizations that remained in tact in their inner value systems as well as in their organizational structures."[21]

Nevertheless, the perfect-society ecclesiology manifested limitations in Nazi Germany. Because it valued authoritarian governance, it blurred the differences between the church's conservative political orientation and the reactionary thrust of National Socialism. In 1933 Walter Dirks, a socialist Catholic editor, astutely observed, "While Catholicism has little understanding for each form of the [neopagan] Wotan cult and for a state church, it is situated nevertheless close to less coarse forms of fascist ideology. The words 'authority', 'trust in the leader', 'peace and order' find attentive ears [among Catholics]."[22] Church officials' disapproval of parliamentary democracy seemingly overlapped with Hitler's disdain for the Weimar Republic. Catholics and Nazis wanted an authoritarian government that would overcome individualism and build up the corporate character of society. This goal was expressed in Pius XI's encyclical *Quadragesimo Anno*.[23] Furthermore, because church officials were influenced by the conventional ecclesiology to concern themselves primarily with preserving the institution, they said little in public about Hitler's abuse of human rights. As Konrad Repgen has pointed out, "While Catholics believed that the Jews could help themselves, they did not want to damage their own interests by engaging themselves on behalf of others."[24] But this concern for institutional preservation eroded the hierarchy's moral authority. In 1943 Alfred Delp, S.J., commented at a gathering of priests "that the church's silence on the horrors perpetrated in the East was endangering its moral influence."[25] Delp himself was executed by the state on February 2, 1945, because of his participation in the Kreisau Circle, the group that met to draft a new democratic constitution for Germany. The popes and bishops paid a high moral price for their silence. According to Victor Conzemius, "[t]he tacit acceptance by many bishops and numerous Catholic laymen of the barbarous Jewish persecution by the National Socialists, especially after *Kristallnacht* 1938, revealed, however, an undeniable moral blindness."[26]

The model of the church as a hierarchical institution also had negative consequences for the laity. It excluded them from participating in the church–state decisions of the papacy and episcopacy. Bishops did not seek the advice of lay leaders, for example, from the Catholic Center party, who possessed proven competence in legal, educational, societal, and political matters. As a result, when the bishops dropped their bans against membership in the Nazi party on March 28, 1933, they may have underestimated the strong resistance among the laity to National Socialism. "Given the resistance [to National Socialism] among rank and file Catholics," Klaus Schatz has said, "it is possible and worthwhile to ask whether the German bishops could have taken a stronger stand against Hitler."[27] Further, since the papacy and episcopacy were inclined to work in secret because of the *societas-perfecta* ecclesiology, they did not inform the laity of their opposition to the Führer's policies and actions. Because of Pius XII's and Cardinal Bertam's practice of secret negotiations with the Reich, Catholics received little or no clear guidance from their highest ranking ecclesiastical leaders concerning such issues as the murder of Catholic lay leaders by Storm Troopers and the Reich's deportation of Jews. Although Cardinal Bertram "incessantly sent protests and requests to the offices of the regime," he did not tell the laity of these communications. "The members of the church who knew nothing of course of the numerous petitions had the feeling that the episcopacy had failed the people in a necessary assertion [of the church's moral voice]."[28] In not communicating sufficiently with the laity, the pope and the bishops followed the conventional ecclesiology. "Too much reliance was placed on diplomatic protests," John Jay Hughes has said; "and too little was done to acquaint rank and file Catholics in Germany with the existence and content of these protests and to mobilize them in support of church rights. The fundamental cause of this failure was theological: the view of the Church as consisting of a more or less passive laity, an obedient body of pastoral clergy, and a hierarchy that directed and led both laity and clergy, making all decisions in lonely and splendid isolation."[29]

In sum, while the ecclesiology of *societas perfecta* contributed to the church's survival in the Third Reich, it also constrained church leaders from condemning Nazi policies and actions. In

Martin Conway's words, "the Catholic experience of Nazism was more passive than active. Their stance was less one of clear-cut opposition than of surviving and getting by."[30] Although Pius XI, Pius XII, and the German bishops kept the churches operating, they neglected to publicly defend fundamental truths of human life. In short, they failed by omission, not by commission. In the judgment of Guenther Lewy, "The Church's opposition [to Hitler] was carefully circumscribed; it was rooted in her concern for her institutional interests rather than in a belief in freedom and justice for all men."[31]

Church as a Moral Advocate

On February 18, 1946, Pius XII named to the College of Cardinals three German bishops who had publicly opposed the Third Reich: Galen, Preysing, and Frings. In singling out these three leaders, the pontiff implicitly affirmed that the church's mission includes the pursuit of social justice. In effect, he acknowledged that the church is not only a *societas perfecta*; it is also a moral advocate, a servant of justice and truth for all people.

This servant ecclesiology evinced at least two merits during the Third Reich. First, it directed church leaders to use the church's resources for the well-being of all innocent victims regardless of religious belief. It conveyed the idea that the church's mission is not primarily institutional preservation but a reality beyond itself. Implicit here is the differentiation between the church and the coming reign of God. Although God's kingdom is in a limited degree present in history through the church, it is not fully realized in the church. Hence the church must witness to the advent of God's new creation. In speaking out on behalf of Hitler's victims, Galen, Preysing, and Frings demonstrated that the church's mission is congruent with Jesus' parable of the last judgment: "Inherit the kingdom prepared for you. . . . For I was hungry and you gave me food, I was thirsty and you gave me drink" (Matthew 25:34–35).

The second merit of the model of church as moral advocate is that it illuminates the significance of the suffering and death of individuals like Dietrich Bonhoeffer, Alfred Delp, Franz Jäggerstätter, Nikolaus Gross, Max Metzger, and Sophie and Hans Scholl, who out of belief in Jesus Christ labored on behalf of human rights and were executed as enemies of the state. These martyrs suffered in part because their actions were misunderstood and criticized by other Christians, especially by bishops, whose theology of the church did not include social justice.[32] They found little or no basis for their actions in church teachings that said that since every legitimate government receives its authority from God, it deserves the obedience of its citizens. The Christian martyrs under Hitler made religious sense of their actions insofar as they had developed their own theology of Christian life as witnessing to a justice and truth greater than that acknowledged by civil authorities and even by ecclesiastical authorities.

Servant ecclesiology contained, however, an ambiguity prior to the Second Vatican Council. It left unclear the ultimate aim of the church's advocacy of social justice. According to one understanding, Christians should defend human rights and work for justice in order to build a Christian society, a society explicitly founded on belief in Jesus Christ and somehow committed to the church and its tradition. Pius XI conveyed this understanding in 1925 in *Quas Primas*, which instituted the feast of Christ the King, and again in 1931 in *Quadragesimo Anno*.[33] An alternative understanding is that the church should advocate justice so that society can become more human, but not necessarily more formally Christian. In this regard, Dietrich Bonhoeffer, who was executed on April 9, 1945, spoke of the world "coming of age," and Alfred Delp envisioned the church contributing to the formation of a secular society that embraces religious, ethnic, and racial diversity. Commenting on these two views of the church's work for human rights, Martin Conway has written:

> Catholic political action during the 1920s and 1930s had focused on the twin goals of the defense of the church and the achievement of a new social and political order based on Catholic principles. But the immediate pre-war years witnessed the tentative emergence of a new perception of Catholics, not as defenders of the church or advocates of a distinctive social and political pro-

gramme, but as Christian citizens acting within society without seeking to impose their values on it. This new mentality would come to the fore after the Second World war; but it had already begun to take shape in the difficult circumstances of the pre-war years.[34]

Beginning in the 1950s, church leaders began to convey through their social and political programs an acceptance of secularization. Pius XII, John XXIII, and Paul VI set aside the ideal of Catholicism as the established religion, an ideal that the First Vatican Council had taken for granted. Thus they distanced themselves from the political stance of Pius XI, who seemingly preferred authoritarian civil leaders, such as Italy's Mussolini, Portugal's Salazar, and Spain's Franco, because of their claimed allegiance to the church. Pius XII distanced the church from the political convictions of his predecessor as well as from those of the First Vatican Council when he acknowledged the value of a parliamentary democracy in "Benignitas et Humanitas."[35] Further, John XXIII explicitly endorsed the value of religious freedom in his encyclical *Pacem in Terris*. Finally, in 1965 Pope Paul VI and the Second Vatican Council officially affirmed that the church must be an advocate of human rights in a secular world. As Cardinal Walter Kasper has pointed out, the church's acceptance of the modern notion of appropriate human autonomy and secularity was fully achieved when the Council adopted on December 7, 1965, both the Pastoral Constitution on the Church in the Modern World, *Gaudium et Spes,* and also the Declaration on Religious Freedom, *Dignitatis Humanae.*[36]

Church as Body of Christ

A third model of the church that shaped how German Catholics viewed Hitler was the metaphor of church as body of Christ. For some, like Karl Eschweiler, Joseph Lortz, and Karl Adam, the ecclesiology of mystical body warranted the church's accommodation with the Third Reich. But for others, like Romano Guardini and Engelbert Krebs, this same theology highlighted the contradiction between Catholicism and National Socialism.

During the 1920s, Catholic theologians retrieved the neglected understanding of the church as mystical body of Christ, *corpus Christi mysticum*, which had been expressed by St. Paul, for example, in 1 Corinthians 10:16–17 and Romans 12:5 and also by St. Augustine.[37] Inspired by the work of Johann Adam Möhler at Tübingen in the early 1800s, German scholars after World War I wanted to bring about a renewal in ecclesiology similar to those occurring in biblical studies and liturgy. Karl Adam, Romano Guardini, Peter Lippert, and Arnold Rademacher clarified the body-of-Christ ecclesiology for general readers as well as for bishops and theologians.[38] Using Ferdinand Tönnies's distinction between society (*Gesellschaft*) and community (*Gemeinschaft*), they explained that the church is not only a hierarchical organization with rules, formal lines of decision making, and office-holders; it is also an association of people with personal ties to one another, with a sense of themselves as a "we." To varying degrees, the theologians drew on Romanticism as they spoke of the church as an "organic unity," a human solidarity involving emotional bonds, common experiences, and shared customs. But this Romantic discourse about a community involving the whole person sounded at times similar to Nazi rhetoric about the importance of moving beyond individualism to the recovery of a national community anchored in folk traditions, family ties, and closeness to nature—hence, in an ethnic-racial (*Volk*) solidarity. Alois Baumgartner has pointed out that "[t]he organic idea of community centering itself on the mystery of the body of Christ offered finally even a basis for the acceptance of the emphasis on the ideas of race, ethnicity, and nation that came with the National Socialist seizure of power."[39]

Karl Eschweiler, Joseph Lortz, and Karl Adam were intent on overcoming modernity by fostering the idea that Germans should see themselves not primarily as discrete selves but as members of a corporate or communal reality. Given this orientation, each was attracted to Hitler's rhetoric about Germany becoming a national community united by "earth and blood." Eschweiler stressed in 1930 that Christians are not an assembly of isolated individuals but "are called the body of Christ in Holy Scripture." While Jesus' followers have subjective, religious experiences, they simultaneously participate in an objective, corporate reality. As Eschweiler put it, "Objectively true and ethically genuine Christianity is only possible when the religious subjectivity acknowledges the visible church as the definite authority in the name of Christ and forms itself through free obedience into the spirit and love of the God-man."[40] As we have seen, in 1933 Eschweiler linked the church as a supernatural or spiritual community with the state as a natural or ethnic-racial community by arguing that a supernatural solidarity is possible only insofar as there already exists a natural solidarity. The interdependence of church and state reflects "the undividable unity, established by the creator, of the spiritual soul in its body."[41] Eschweiler was supported in his view by Lortz, who declared in 1933 that Hitler was strengthening Germany's natural solidarity in such a way that the church as a spiritual body would flourish. According to Lortz, "This ethnic-racial community functions as the mother earth of the church's growth. The history of the church is the complete illustration that grace does not work magically from the outside but organically according to natural gifts."[42] In short, according to Eschweiler and Lortz, a German-speaking church as body of Christ depended on the vitality of Germany's social-political body.[43]

Karl Adam offered a similar view of church and state in 1933. Ten years earlier, he had laid out a balanced ecclesiology in *The Spirit of Catholicism*. Intent on presenting the church as more than an institution, he had explained that "because the Church is the body of Christ, she is essentially an organism, with its members purposively interrelated, and a visible organism." This visible organism, the church, is moreover universal; it rests on the common humanity that binds all peoples, the humanity that was united with the divine word in Jesus Christ. In Adam's words, "If Christ is what the Church confesses Him to be, the Incarnate God and Saviour of men—as indeed He is—then it must be His mission to reunite to God mankind as a unity, as a whole, and not this or that individual man."[44] The early emphasis on universal humanity as the basis of the church was eclipsed by 1933 in Adam's work, however, when Adam began turning to the idea that the unity in the church between Christ and human beings depends on a people's ethnic and racial character. "Human nature," he said, "exists not as humanity itself, as *natura humana,* but it exists only as *natura individua,* that is, only in the concrete person with his blood-determined condition."[45] Although all people share in the same human nature, they always embody it in ways determined by ethnicity and race. The church can flourish among a specific people only insofar as it takes on the traits of that people. It must be "the true mother of the ethnic-racial character of every people in their particularity out of the word and sacrament of the Lord." The German-speaking church must become incarnate in the German people and must encourage the strengthening of Germany's ethnic and racial identity. The church "needs an ethnic-racial people in order to be a living Catholicism. And for this reason, nationalism and Catholicism do not contradict each other. They belong together as the natural and the supernatural."

While Eschweiler, Lortz, and Adam allowed their talk about the body of Christ to become entangled with Nazi rhetoric, Guardini and Krebs had none of this. Romano Guardini refused to link body-of-Christ ecclesiology with the idea of ethnic-racial communities. As early as 1921, he maintained that the church is "the *corpus Christi mysticum* which is developed in the Epistles of St. Paul to the Ephesians and Colossians . . . . Under Christ the Head, the Church gathers together 'all which is in Heaven, on earth, and under the earth'. . . . In the Church everything—angels, men and things—are linked with God." This unity involves no essential dependence on ethnicity or race. To become a people depends on religious, not biological factors, and it leads not to nationalism but universalism. As Guardini said, "The people [*Volk*] is a human society which maintains an unbroken continuity with the roots of nature and life, and obeys their intrinsic laws. The people contains . . . the whole of mankind, in all its variety of ages, sexes, temperament, mental and physical condition; to which we must add the sum total of its work and spheres of production as determined by class and vocation."[46] This appreciation for the solidarity of all women and men in Christ equipped Guardini to maintain a critical distance from talk of an ethnic-racial people; he dedicated himself to the strengthening of European culture.

Engelbert Krebs stood with Guardini by employing the notion of the body of Christ in order to stress the church's universality. In 1925 he wrote that the church is "the mystical body of Christ," witnessing to the coming of God's reign.[47] Speaking against ethnic bias and racism in 1935, he contended that the church brings to every culture the God-given supernatural essence of the Christian religion—"an essence that exists beyond ethnicity and race, beyond culture and beyond time." The church's planting of God's word in particular cultures is "the true realization in the communion of the great organism of the church, the realization in the mystical body of Christ. There occurs the allocation of the supernatural gifts by the Holy Spirit who distributes them as the Spirit wills independent of all blood-determined differentiations." As church history shows, the Spirit draws on all racial and ethnic groups—for example, "the Jewish, Greek, Roman, German, Syrian heritages"—to enrich the church's life in particular ways. "At the same time, however, we learn to gratefully acknowledge the particular realization of other peoples, to delight in the community of our spiritual kingdom and to avoid every arrogant putting down of other peoples' special kinds of spirituality since this is a danger of the impoverishment by Ebionitism."[48] In support of his emphasis on the universality of Christian faith, Krebs appealed to St. Paul: "For just as the body is one and has many members, and all the members of the body, though many, are one body, so it is with Christ. For by one Spirit we were all baptized into one body—Jews or Greeks, slaves or free—and all were made to drink of one spirit" (1 Corinthians 12:12).

Theologians' differing views of body-of-Christ ecclesiology were assessed during the 1940s.[49] Erich Przywara gave an insightful, critical evaluation of the theology of *corpus Christi mysticum* in 1940, distinguishing between the spiritual or supernatural communion in Christ and natural forms of community.[50] Karl Rahner observed in 1943 that some theologians' emphasis on the nonrational aspects of the Christian life—for example, on ethnicity and race—was harming theological renewal in German Catholicism.[51] On June 29, 1943, Pius XII issued his encyclical *Mystici Corporis*, which deliberately set limits on the use of the notion of the body of Christ. Drawing on the work of Sebastian Tromp, S.J., the pontiff clarified that the notion of the church as body of Christ highlights the church's universality, its union with all people regardless of ethnicity and race. Pius also stressed that body-of-Christ ecclesiology should recognize the church's institutional, hierarchical, and juridical dimensions. In other words, church as community should be subordinate to church as perfect society.[52] Pius went on to claim that the mystical body of Christ on earth exists only in the Roman Catholic Church. This claim was subsequently judged by bishops and theologians as too restrictive, as ignoring Christ's presence in other churches, and it was eventually retracted by the Second Vatican Council.[53] In any case, Pius XII's emphasis on the universality of the church and his avoidance of talk about organic relationships left no conceptual room for theologians to link the church and nationalistic talk about ethnicity and race.

Body-of-Christ ecclesiology without an ethnic-racial cast strengthened the church's resistance to Nazism because it called for the deliberate nurturing of Christian solidarity by means of worship, devotions, and various forms of mutual support. Pastors looked for ways to strengthen their congregations' communal bonds and shared belief in Jesus Christ, thereby counteracting Nazi neopaganism and the state's interference in the church and in parishioners' private lives. Attendance at mass remained high during the Third Reich, and the faithful brought new energy to the singing of hymns. There was also an increase in participation in pilgrimages, religious devotions, and processions such as those for the feast of Corpus Christi; indeed, these rituals became more elaborate. The number of meetings of Catholics in Aschaffenburg, for example, was four times greater in 1937 than in 1933, and more people were attending these gatherings than previously.[54] The sense of the church as body of Christ that had begun in the 1920s because of Catholics' desire for community and because of advances in biblical and liturgical studies matured in the 1930s and 1940s as the faithful experienced a strengthening of their personal and social identities by participating in their local churches. While they assembled for mass and other religious rituals primarily for their spiritual well-being, they also found that these occasions could function as expressions of political protest against Nazism and the Third Reich. Focusing on the building up of the Christian community, body-of-Christ ecclesiology lacked, however, a clear orientation toward social justice. It did not explicitly direct Catholics to protect those outside the church.

The Inadequacy of Ecclesiology, 1933–1945

When Konrad Adenauer observed in 1946 that the bishops should have protested together against Hitler, he implicitly spoke out of a theology of church that was not then embraced by most church leaders. In assuming that the church's mission includes the defense of human rights, he conveyed an understanding of the church as a moral advocate, a servant of justice and truth. But Adenauer was ahead of most church leaders, for whom the moral-advocate ecclesiology had not attained either a clear formulation or a widespread acceptance, even though it had been expressed in *Rerum Novarum* and *Quadragesimo Anno*. Adhering to the theology of church that they had learned as seminarians, most bishops and theologians espoused the perfect-society ecclesiology, with its idea that the church's primary mission is the salvation of believers by means of the sacraments, religious instruction, and obedience to ecclesiastical authorities. They judged, therefore, that their first responsibility was to protect the institutional church and its operations. The *societas-perfecta* ecclesiology had overshadowed, however, not only the moral-advocate ecclesiology but also the body-of-Christ ecclesiology. In *Mystici Corporis*, it clearly subsumed the model of church as community. This reduction of the church's self-understanding to one model meant that most church leaders were intent on preserving the church as an institution in the Third Reich. In John S. Conway's words, "The Catholic leaders' readiness to support the nationalist and anti-Semitic goals of the Nazi regime demonstrated how unprepared they were, institutionally or theologically, to mobilize their following in any campaign beyond the defense of the immediate interests of their own community."[55]

Responsibility for the inadequacy of Catholic ecclesiology in the early twentieth century belonged, on the one hand, to the popes and bishops and, on the other, to the theologians themselves. Beginning with Pius IX, ecclesiastical officials increasingly suppressed theological inquiries that were undertaken apart from the questions and categories of neo-Scholasticism and that took seriously the issues and ideas of modernity. As noted in earlier chapters, church authorities forced Wilhelm Koch to resign from the University of Tübingen in 1917 because of his historical-critical approach to doctrine, and they excommunicated Breslau's Joseph Wittig in 1926 because of his historical reconstruction of Jesus' life and world. The Holy Office undertook formal proceedings against Karl Adam in 1910 and again in 1932 because of his reliance on phenomenology. Suspicion was even cast upon Romano Guardini, who wrote in 1944 that for over two decades "church authorities have given me no help of any kind. . . . [T]he laity immediately accepted my work [in the 1920s] with growing enthusiasm; in recent years, however, ecclesiastical officials are beginning to trust me."[56] These individual cases manifest one of the reasons for the church's inadequate response to the Third Reich: for a century, the papacy and episcopacy had stifled scholars' intellectual freedom, thereby preventing them from critically reflecting on the character of modernity and on the church's nature and mission in the contemporary world.

At the same time, the theologians themselves were also responsible for the impoverishment of their scholarship. Theologians in every age have the task of helping the believing community to articulate the truths of Christian faith in relation to the intellectual, cultural, social, and political situations in which the church finds itself. But the majority of theologians during the 1920s and 1930s failed to understand what had come about in Germany after the First World War. Instead of learning from the social sciences, they continued to think within the neo-Scholastic framework and condemned the notions of personal freedom and of parliamentary democracy as expressions of rebellion against God and the church.[57] Conceiving of the church as a medieval fortress or a Gothic cathedral under siege from liberalism and secularism, they failed to recognize the valid insights of modern thought and the constructive elements of a parliamentary democracy. "The thrust of theologians during the Weimar era and into the early Nazi Reich was," Donald Dietrich has said, "to oppose the republic rooted in liberalism and socialism as well as to repudiate democratic values shaped through nineteenth-century political experiences and not by scholasticism."[58] If the theologians had distinguished between modernity and liberalism, they could have reevaluated the conventional assumptions that modernity was an apostasy and that the state should formally recognize the Catholic church (the thesis-hypothesis theory). It was not until the Second World War that these assumptions were seriously examined—not, however, by the senior theologians but by the younger ones.

The progressive theologians whom we have discussed stood at the end of the restoration era in Catholic thought and prepared the way for the next era. Karl Eschweiler, Joseph Lortz, Karl Adam, Romano Guardini, and Engelbert Krebs contributed in their respective ways to the fermentation in Catholicism that eventually eroded neo-Scholasticism and opened the way for the next generation of scholars to think within an intellectual horizon not threatened by the Enlightenment and the post-Enlightenment. As Klaus Schatz has pointed out, "the period of spiritual upheaval after the First World War in German Catholicism led to a series of initiatives (the Catholic youth movement, the liturgical movement, the biblical movement) that broke open the restoration certainties, enlivened forgotten traditions, and became fruitful for the entire church, in part already under Pius XII but above all in the Second Vatican Council."[59] Nevertheless, most of the theologians who were born in the 1880s stood back after the Second World War while a new generation of German scholars, born in the early 1900s, adopted contemporary categories of thought and addressed urgent modern issues. Romano Guardini was one of the few theologians of his generation to contribute to theology after the war. Roger Aubert has noted that "[u]nlike the war from 1914 to 1918, the war from 1939 to 1945 led to a complete caesura in the history of theology."[60] Theologians like Mannes Dominikus Koster, O.P., Karl Rahner, Rudolf Schnackenburg, and Otto Semmelroth inquired anew into the church's nature and mission, locating the church in relation to history, culture, and the universal human aspiration for freedom.[61] Referring to the church in the late 1940s and 1950s, Klaus Schatz has said, "Primarily at the end of—but also in the course of—the experiences with totalitarian systems, the recognition gained strength that the business of the church and of Christian faith is inseparably bound up with 'human rights.'"[62]

Representative of this new theological orientation was Karl Rahner. Having lost his teaching position at the University of Innsbruck in the summer of 1938, when the Nazis closed the faculty of Catholic theology, he joined Cardinal Theodor Innitzer's pastoral institute in Vienna. In 1943, as the thirty-nine-year-old scholar lived amid horrific events, he wrote, "The church exists in relation to a new age. With respect to the overwhelming political, social, and cultural upheavals of the last thirty years it is only too clear that we are caught up in a historical process of upheaval which is going far beyond what can normally be attributed to every change in generations."[63] Rahner's experience of a radical transition in society confirmed his intuition that the church needed to undertake theology in new ways—ways that drew on existentialism and phenomenology while also returning to the Bible and patristic texts. Indeed, theologians needed to see the church anew in relation to Jesus' teachings and the testimonies of the earliest Christians. In light of his fresh perspective on theology and the church, Rahner came to see the inadequacy of the church's efforts in the Third Reich: "At that time, we priests already had enough to do in order to protect our own skins. But we should have done much more to protect also the skins of other people, of non-Christians, than we in fact did."[64]

In *Gaudium et Spes,* the Second Vatican Council embraced the notion of the church as moral advocate, thereby affirming the ecclesiology that Bishop Preysing had upheld with very limited success during the Third Reich. Paul VI and the council declared in the Pastoral Constitution on the Church in the Modern World:

> The joys and hopes, the grief and anguish of the people of our time, especially of those who are poor or afflicted, are the joys and hopes, the grief and anguish of the followers of Christ as well. . . . The church is not motivated by earthly ambition but is interested in one thing only—to carry on the work of Christ under the guidance of the holy Spirit, who came into the world to bear witness to

the truth, to save and not to judge, to serve and not to be served. (art. 1)

With these words, the pope and bishops explained in effect that the church's mission includes the promotion of justice and truth.[65] Speaking more concretely, the council asserted in its Declaration on the Relation of the Church to Non-Christian Religions (*Nostra Aetate*) that "the church reproves, as foreign to the mind of Christ, any discrimination against people or any harassment of them on the basis of their race, color, condition in life or religion" (art. 5). Undergirding these clarifications was the council's foundational statement about the church's nature. The Dogmatic Constitution on the Church (*Lumen Gentium*) attests that the church is a mystery that can be understood only by means of diverse images and models, such as people of God, sacrament, and body of Christ, as well as institution. No longer should *societas-perfecta* ecclesiology hold a hegemony over ecclesiastical officials' decisions and policies.

The story of the ecclesial experiences and theological investigations that led up to the Second Vatican Council is beyond the scope of this book. What can be noted in conclusion is, however, that an awareness of the Catholic church's inadequate response to Hitler shaped the theological orientations of the German-speaking bishops and theologians who participated in the council. Pastoral leaders such as Cardinal Joseph Frings, Cardinal Franz König, and Karl Rahner brought to the council their commitment to deepen the church's understanding of itself and its mission in the contemporary world.[66] Wanting to engage in a critical dialogue with modernity, they were intent on providing the church with a rich ecclesiology so that its pastoral leaders would never again be at a loss amid political oppression and social injustice. The German-speaking delegates at the council promoted the view that the church should be an advocate of the rights and dignity of every human being.

What Frings, König, and Rahner learned firsthand during the 1930s and 1940s can be attained today through an examination of the church in Nazi Germany. This study can generate not only an admiration for the men and women who suffered in the pursuit of justice and truth but also the resolve not to forget the lessons of the church's struggle with Hitler.

One of these lessons is that religious ideas about the church and its role in society have definite social and political implications. Bishops and theologians who operate—whether consciously or unwittingly—out of a *societas-perfecta* ecclesiology may succeed in preserving ecclesiastical structures and practices but may ignore injustice in the church and the abuse of human rights in society. Further, pastoral leaders who link the church as body of Christ and the ethnic solidarity of a specific group of believers may strengthen a sense of community while simultaneously fueling nationalism and racism. Yet a body-of-Christ ecclesiology that highlights the spiritual, or mystical, communion among all the faithful may implicitly promote an acceptance of the political and ecclesiatical status quo. Finally, church leaders may declare that they are working for the coming of God's reign, but they must also clarify their ultimate aim. On the one hand, insofar as they stand in the theological orientation of Pope Pius XI and Catholic Action, they are intent on transforming secular society into a Christian one, dedicated to Christ the King. On the other hand, to the degree that they are inspired by the Second Vatican Council, they are guided by a respect for the "rightful autonomy" of human affairs and a commitment to what Pope Paul VI identifed as "the progress of peoples," anchored in a pledge to defend human rights.[67]

A Chronology
1917—1949

1917

February   Revolution erupts in Russia.

November 1   The German bishops issue a pastoral letter on their nation's political situation; they warn against the separation of church and state.

November   Vladimir Lenin establishes a Soviet government in Russia.

1918

November 7   King Ludwig III of Bavaria abdicates in Munich; Kurt Eisner establishes a socialist republic in Bavaria.

November 9   Kaiser Wilhelm II abdicates; an interim, parliamentary government is established.

1919

January 5   The German Workers' party, the *Deutsche Arbeiterpartei* (DAP), is founded in Munich.

May 1   The German army and the Free Corps suppress the Communist revolt that began in Bavaria on April 6.

June 28   Germany signs of the Treaty of Versailles.

August 11   Germany adopts the Weimar Constitution.

1920

February 24   The DAP declares its twenty-five point political program, shaped by Adolf Hitler. Soon afterwards, the DAP is renamed the National Socialist German Workers' party, the *Nationalsozialistische Deutsche Arbeiter-partei* (NSDAP), or Nazi party.

1922

February 6   Cardinal Ambrogio Achille Ratti is elected Pope Pius XI, following Pope Benedict XV (d. January 22, 1922).

December 23   Pius XI issues *Ubi Arcano Dei*, on the peace of Jesus Christ.

1923

November 8   Hitler attempts his Beerhall *Putsch.*

1924

January 21   Lenin dies, and Joseph Stalin emerges as the Soviet Union's new leader.

1925

April 26   Paul von Hindenburg is elected the Weimar Republic's president.

July   Hitler publishes his *Mein Kampf,* volume 1.

December 11   Pius XI issues *Quas Primas,* establishing the feast of Christ the King.

1929

October 25   The crash of the New York Stock Exchange starts the Great Depression.

1931

January   Germany's unemployment reaches 6 million—more than 30 percent of all workers.

February 10   The Bavarian bishops' conference condemns Nazi ideology.

May 15   Pius XI issues *Quadragesimo Anno,* on social justice and the "corporate" state.

August 17   The Fulda bishops' conference bans membership in the Nazi party.

1933

January 30   Hindenburg appoints Hitler chancellor.

1933 (*cont.*)

February 28   Hindenburg grants Hitler dictatorial powers as a result of the Reichstag's fire.

March 5   The Nazi party wins 43.9 percent of the vote in the Reichstag elections.

March 23   The Reichstag passes the Enabling Act, which suspends the Weimar Constitution and confirms Hitler as dictator.

March 28   The Catholic bishops lift their ban against membership in the Nazi party.

April 1   The Nazi party boycotts Jewish businesses.

April 7   Hitler decrees that "untrustworthy" people and "non-Aryans" cannot hold civil service jobs, including professorships.

May 10   Nazi students burn books at universities throughout Germany.

May 30   The German bishops meet in Berlin and on June 3 approve the draft of the Reich Concordat.

July 4–5   The Catholic Center party and Bavarian People's party are dissolved.

July 9   Cardinal Pacelli and Vice Chancellor Papen initial the Reich Concordat.

July 20   Cardinal Pacelli and Vice Chancellor Papen formally sign the Reich Concordat.

September 10   Germany's unemployment drops to 3.5 million. Pius XI ratifies the Reich Concordat.

December   Cardinal Faulhaber preaches his Advent sermons.

1934

April 24   Hitler establishes the Peoples' Supreme Court, which upholds Nazi laws.

June 30   The SS and Gestapo suppress the alleged Röhm *Putsch* by murdering Hitler's political enemies, including Catholic lay leaders.

August 2   Hindenburg dies, and Hitler as the Führer unites the offices of president and chancellor; he receives the oath of loyalty from the German military.

1935
September 15   Hitler decrees the Nüremberg Race Laws, depriving Jews of their civil rights.

1937
March 14   Pius XI issues *Mit brennender Sorge,* condemning neo-paganism; it is read at Masses throughout Germany on Sunday, March 21.

1938
March 12   Germany annexes Austria.

September 29   The Munich Treaty cedes the Sudeten region to the Third Reich.

November 8   Nazis carry out a nationwide pogrom, *Kristallnacht,* against Jews.

1939
February 10   Pope Pius XI dies.

March 2   Cardinal Eugenio Pacelli is elected Pope Pius XII (d. October 9, 1958).

August 23   Hitler and Stalin sign a nonaggression pact.

September 1   Germany invades Poland, thereby igniting the Second World War.

October 20   Pius XII issues *Summi Pontificatus* on the nation-state in the modern world.

1940
June 22   France signs an armistice with Germany.

1941
June 22   Germany invades the Soviet Union.

December 7   Japan attacks Pearl Harbor, and the United States enters the war against Japan.

December 11   Hitler declares war on the United States.

1942

January 20   The Wannsee Conference decides on the "final solution" against Jews.

1943

January 31   Germany's Sixth Army surrenders at Stalingrad.

February 22   Sophie and Hans Scholl of the White Rose are executed for treason.

June 29   Pius XII issues *Mystici Corporis* on the church as body of Christ.

August 19   The German bishops issue their Decalogue Letter, condemning the murder of innocent victims.

1944

June 6   The Allied forces invade Normandy.

July 20   An attempt to assassinate Hitler fails.

December 24   Pope Pius XII acknowledges the merits of parliamentary democracy in his address, "Benignitas et Humanitas."

1945

April 30   Hitler and Eva Braun commit suicide in Berlin.

May 7   Germany accepts an unconditional surrender.

1949

May   The German Democratic Republic (DDR) is established in east Germany, and the Federal Republic of Germany (BRD) is established in west Germany.

Notes

The following abbreviations are used in the notes.

LTK 1st ed.   *Lexikon für Theologie und Kirche.* Edited by Michael Buchberger. 10 vols. Freiburg: Herder, 1929–38.

LTK 3rd ed.   *Lexikon für Theologie und Kirche.* Edited by Walter Kasper with Konrad Baumgartner et al. 11 vols. Freiburg: Herder, 1993–2001.

NCE   *New Catholic Encyclopedia.* Edited by the Editorial Staff of the Catholic University of America. 15 vols. New York: McGraw-Hill, 1967.

ThQ   *Theologische Quartalschrift*

ThS   *Theological Studies*

1. *The Bishops' Accommodation with Hitler in 1933*

1. I am grateful to Claus Arnold at the University of Münster and Kevin P. Spicer, C.S.C., at Stonehill College for making available to me the fruits of their respective historical studies on the Catholic church in Germany. I also wish to thank Steven M. Rodenborn and Sue A. Rozeboom at the University of Notre Dame for their critical readings of drafts of this book.

2. A word about the book's format is in order. I usually give the English title of a German book when the German text has been published in English. In the case of German books that have not appeared in English, I cite the German title and then put in square brackets my English translation of that title. The date of a book's publication in its original language is frequently included with the publication information. Further,

when a personal name includes the German honorific "von," the "von" is included only when the name is first mentioned, not subsequently.

3. Background literature on the German bishops' decisions in 1933 includes Konrad Repgen, "Hitlers Machtergreifung und der deutsche Katholizismus," in *Katholische Kirche im Dritten Reich* (Mainz: Matthias Grünewald, 1976), 1–34; Ludwig Volk, S.J., *Das Reichskonkordat vom 20. Juli 1933* (Mainz: Matthias Grünewald, 1972); idem, "Zur Kundgebung des deutschen Episkopats vom 28. März 1933," *Stimmen der Zeit* 173 (1963–64): 431–56; Victor Conzemius, "German Catholics and the Nazi Regime in 1933," *Irish Ecclesiastical Review* 108 (1967): 326–35.

4. Kurt Meier, "Deutschland und Österreich," in *Erster und Zweiter Krieg: Demokratien und Totalitäre Systeme* (1914–1958), ed. Jean-Marie Mayeur and Kurt Meier (Freiburg: Herder, 1992), 681–772, here 686.

5. Quoted in Klaus Scholder, *Die Kirchen und das Dritte Reich* (Frankfurt am Main: Propyläen, 1986), 1:168. Scholder's work has been continued in Gerhard Besier, *Die Kirchen und das Dritte Reich: Spaltungen und Abwahrkampfe 1934–37* (Munich: Propyläen, 2001). On the pastoral letter of 1931, see Alice Gallin, *Midwives to Nazism* (Macon, Ga.: Mercer University Press, 1986), 167.

6. Quoted in Heribert Smolinsky, "Nationalsozialismus: Römisch-katholische Kirche," in LThK, 3rd ed., vol. 7 (1998): 657. See John K. Zeender, "The Genesis of the German Concordat of 1933," in *Studies in Catholic History*, ed. Nelson H. Minnich et al. (Wilmington, Del.: Michael Glazier, 1985), 617–65, here 645.

7. Heinz Hürten, *Deutsche Katholiken 1918–1945* (Paderborn: Ferdinand Schöningh, 1992), 176–77.

8. For glimpses of life in Germany in 1933, see Sebastian Haffner, *Defying Hitler,* trans. Oliver Pretzel (New York: Farrar, Straus and Giroux, 2000); Günter Grass, *My Century,* trans. Michael Henry Heim (New York: Harcourt, 1999); Victor Klemperer, *I Will Bear Witness, 1933-1941,* trans. Martin Chalmers (New York: Random House, 1998).

9. Zeender, "Genesis of the German Concordat of 1933," 620–36. See also Joseph A. Biesinger, "The Reich Concordat of 1933," in *Controversial Concordats,* ed. Frank J. Coppa (Washington, D.C.: Catholic University of America Press, 1999), 120–81, here 124.

10. Quoted in Guenther Lewy, *The Catholic Church and Hitler's Wars* (New York: McGraw Hill, 1964), 39.

11. For the entire English text of the Reich Concordat of 1933, see *Controversial Concordats,* ed. Coppa, 205–14.

12. Biesinger, "Reich Concordat of 1933," 139–40.

13. Quoted in Karl Dietrich Erdmann, *Deutschland unter der Herrschaft des Nationalsozialismus, 1933–1939* (Munich: Deutscher, 1987), 185.

14. Lewy, *Catholic Church and Hitler's Wars*, 86.

15. Konrad Repken, "German Catholicism and the Jews: 1933–1946," in *Judaism and Christianity under the Impact of National Socialism*, ed. Otto Dov Kulka and Paul R. Mendes-Flohr (Jerusalem: Historical Society of Israel and Zaman Shazar Center for Jewish History, 1987), 197–226, here 203.

16. See Richard P. McBrien, *Catholicism*, rev. ed. (San Francisco: HarperCollins, 1994), 607–783; Avery Dulles, *Models of the Church*, rev. ed. (Garden City, N.Y.: Doubleday, 1987); Yves Congar, "Moving Toward a Pilgrim Church," in *Vatican II Revisited*, ed. Alberic Stacpole (Minneapolis: Winston Press, 1986), 129–52; idem, *L'Église de Saint Augustine à l'epoque moderne* (Paris: Cerf, 1970), which appeared in German as *Die Lehre von der Kirche von Augustinus bis zur Gegenwart* (Freiburg: Herder, 1970); Jean Frisque, "Die Ekklesiologie im 20. Jahrhundert," in *Bilanz der Theologie im 20. Jahrhundert*, vol. 3, ed. Herbert Vorgrimler and Robert Vander Gucht (Freiburg: Herder, 1970), 192–243; Roger Aubert, "Die ekklesiologische Geographie im 19. Jahrhundert," in *Sentire Ecclesiam*, ed. Jean Daniélou and Herbert Vorgrimler (Freiburg: Herder, 1961).

17. Robert Bellarmine, *Disputationes de Controversiis Christianae Fidei adversus huius temporis Haereticos*, 3 vols. (Ingolstadt, 1586–93). See Congar, "Moving Toward a Pilgrim Church," 132.

18. The council's first draft of the Constitution on the Church, entitled *Supremi Pastoris*, was distributed to the bishops on January 21, 1870. The text is quoted here from Dulles, *Models of the Church*, 36–37. See Hermann J. Pottmeyer, "Vatican Council I," in *The HarperCollins Encyclopedia of Catholicism*, ed. Richard P. McBrien (San Francisco: HarperCollins, 1995), 1296–98.

19. According to Martin Conway, the Catholic church from 1918 to 1945 was characterized by "three essential attributes": "its hierarchy, its uncompromising doctrinal stance, and its activist and associational structure" (*Catholic Politics in Europe, 1918–1945* [London: Routledge, 1997], 2).

20. Bernhard Bartmann, *Lehrbuch der Dogmatik* (Freiburg: Herder, 1911), 537.

21. Ludwig Koester, "Kirche," LThK, 1st ed., vol. 5 (1933): 968–81, here 972–73.

22. Yves Congar has noted how this notion of society, rooted in Aristotle's *Politics*, took shape in the modern period as it was used by French bishops in reaction to the French Revolution; see Congar, "Moving Toward a Pilgrim Church," 131–33.

23. Bartmann, *Lehrbuch der Dogmatik*, 542.

24. Unless otherwise noted, papal encyclicals are quoted from *The Papal Encyclicals,* ed. Claudia Carlen (Raleigh, N.C.: McGrath Publishing, 1981).

25. Vatican I schema, chapter 7, quoted in Dulles, *Models of the Church,* 41.

26. Bartmann, *Lehrbuch der Dogmatik,* 544.

27. Ibid., 537, 542. See also Koester, "Kirche," 977, 979; Dulles, *Models of the Church,* 37. Richard P. McBrien has written that "preconciliar Catholicism also tended to limit the essential, or constitutive, mission of the Church to preaching, teaching, catechesis, and worship (understood as the whole sacramental life)" ("Before and After Vatican II," *Priests and People* 10 [August–September 1996]: 297–302, here 299).

28. Vatican I schema quoted in Dulles, *Models of the Church,* 38. As Dulles notes, this notion of the "unequal society" is stated by Pius X in *Vehementer Nos* (February 11, 1906); see *Acta Sanctae Sedis* 39 (1906–7): 8–9. On the distinction between clergy and laity, see Thomas F. O'Meara, O.P., *Theology of Ministry,* rev. ed. (New York: Paulist, 1999), 172–81.

29. Bartmann, *Lehrbuch der Dogmatik,* 542, 523.

30. Medard Kehl, "Ekklesiologie," LThK, 3rd ed., vol. 5 (1996): 568–74, esp. 571–72.

31. Koester, "Kirche," 977. See Walter Kasper and Joachim Drumm, "Kirche," in LThK 3rd ed., vol. 5 (1996): 1458–65, here 1464; Congar, "Moving Toward a Pilgrim Church," 133; idem, *Die Lehre von der Kirche,* 89. On the origins of the hierarchical view of church in the thought of Pseudo-Denis, see O'Meara, *Theology of Ministry,* 104–7.

32. Quoted in *Religion from Tolstoy to Camus,* ed. Walter Kaufmann (New York: Harper & Row, 1964).

33. Klaus Schatz, *Kirchengeschichte der Neuzeit II* (Düsseldorf: Patmos, 1989), 7–8.

34. See Walter Kasper, *Theology and the Church,* trans. Margaret Kohl (New York: Crossroad, 1989), 32–73; Thomas F. O'Meara, O.P., *Church and Culture: German Catholic Theology, 1860-1914* (Notre Dame, Ind.: University of Notre Dame Press, 1991), 1–7, 187–201.

35. See J. F. Broderick, "Church, History of, IV (Late Modern: 1789–1965)," NCE 3:716–24.

36. See Gregory Baum, "Modernism," in *Encyclopedia of Catholicism,* ed. McBrien, 877–78.

37. See Schatz, *Kirchengeschichte der Neuzeit II,* 29; Jean-Marie Mayeur, "Drei Päpste: Benedikt XV., Pius XI., Pius XII.," trans. Dorothee Becker, in *Erster und Zweiter Krieg,* ed. Mayeur and Meier, 1–40; Gerald O'Collins, *Theology of Secularity* (Notre Dame, Ind.: Fides, 1974).

38. Quoted in *Religion from Tolstoy To Camus,* ed. Kaufmann, 170.

39. Schatz, *Kirchengeschichte der Neuzeit II*, 98.

40. See O'Meara, *Church and Culture*, 45–46; Schatz, *Kirchengeschichte der Neuzeit II*, 67; Gerald McCool, *Catholic Theology in the Nineteenth Century* (New York: Seabury, 1977).

41. For a Scholastic account of the *philosophia perennis*, see Maurice de Wolf, *Scholasticism Old and New*, trans. P. Coffey (Dublin: M. H. Hill and Son, 1910).

42. Joseph Kleutgen, *Die Philosophie der Vorzeit* (1878), 4; quoted in Hermann J. Pottmeyer, "Kingdom of God–Church–Society: The Contemporary Relevance of Johann Baptist Hirscher, Theologian of Reform," in *The Legacy of the Tübingen School*, ed. Donald J. Dietrich and Michael J. Himes (New York: Crossroad, 1997), 144–55, here 148. See Anthony Battaglia, "Enlightenment," in *The New Dictionary of Catholic Social Thought*, ed. Judith A. Dwyer (Collegeville, Minn.: Liturgical Press, 1999), 337–38.

43. Martin Grabmann, "Neoscholastik," in LThK, 1st ed., vol. 7 (1935): 522.

44. See Winfried Becker, "Neueste Zeit (1803/6 - 1995)," in *Die Kirchen in der Deutschen Geschichte*, ed. Winfried Becker et al. (Stuttgart: Alfred Kröner, 1996), 507–8.

45. Avery Dulles, *The Craft of Theology*, new expanded ed. (New York: Crossroad, 1995), 126.

46. Yves Congar, *A History of Theology*, trans. and ed. Hunter Guthrie (Garden City, N.Y.: Doubleday, 1968), 15. See Étienne Fouilloux, "Die Kultur der katholischen Kirche," in *Erster und Zweiter Krieg*, ed. Mayeur and Meier, 175–215, here 188; Francis Schüssler Fiorenza, "Systematic Theology: Task and Methods," in *Systematic Theology*, vol. 1, ed. Francis Schüssler Fiorenza and John P. Galvin (Minneapolis: Fortress Press, 1991), 27–34.

47. Romano Guardini, *Berichte über mein Leben* (Düsseldorf: Patmos, 1984), 92–93.

48. Kasper, *Theology and Church*, 79.

49. See Owen Chadwick, *A History of the Popes, 1830-1914* (New York: Oxford University Press, 1998); Schatz, *Kirchengeschichte der Neuzeit II*, 29; M. Conway, *Catholic Politics*, 99–101.

50. See Yves Congar, "Church: Ecclesiology," in *Encyclopedia of Religion*, ed. Mircea Eliade (New York: Macmillan, 1987), 3:480–86; idem, *Lehre von der Kirche*, 101–13; J. Bryan Hehir, "Church and State," in *Encyclopedia of Catholicism*, ed. McBrien, 314–17.

51. See Schatz, *Kirchengeschichte der Neuzeit II*, 78.

52. See Pius XII, "Lux in Tenebris Lucet" ["Benignitas et Humanitas"], *The Tablet* 184 (December 30, 1944): 316–18; also in *Acta Apostolicae*

Sedis 37 (1945): 10–23. See Mayeur, "Drei Päpste," 25–40; Schatz, *Kirchengeschichte der Neuzeit II,* 40; Paul E. Sigmund, "Democracy," in *New Dictionary of Catholic Social Thought,* ed. Dwyer, 269–75; J. N. Moody, "Church and State Since 1789," NCE 3:735–38.

53. Pius XI condemned communism in his encyclical *Divini Redemptoris* (March 19, 1937) which he issued on the heels of his encyclical *Mit brennender Sorge* (March 14, 1937), condemning Nazi neopaganism.

54. M. Conway, *Catholic Politics,* 62, 69–70.

55. John F. Pollard, "Fascism," in *Dictionary of Catholic Social Thought,* ed. Dwyer, 385–87; Roger Aubert, "Theologie während der ersten hälfte des 20. Jahrhunderts," in *Bilanz der Theologie im 20. Jahrhundert,* vol. 2, ed. Herbert Vorgrimler and Robert Vander Gucht (Freiburg: Herder, 1969), 7–70, here 21; Anthony R. E. Rhodes, *The Vatican in the Age of Dictators* (New York: Holt, Rinehart, Winston, 1973), 161–83.

56. Josef Pieper, *No One Could Have Known,* trans. Graham Harrison (San Francisco: St. Ignatius Press, 1987), 91. In May 1931, the German bishops at Fulda called for the realization in Germany of the corporate social and economic order proposed in *Quadragesimo Anno.*

57. The theory was that "what could not be held as a *thesis,* a principle intrinsically right, might be held as a *hypothesis,* allowable, and even best, in given conditions." See Cuthbert Butler, *The Vatican Council,* vol. 2 (London: Longmans, Green and Company, 1930), 23. The theory was proposed by the Jesuit Roman journal *Civiltà Cattolica,* in the turbulent wake of Pius IX's *Syllabus of Errors* and was promoted by Bishop Félix Antoine Philibert Dupanloup (d. 1878) of Orléans, France. See Schatz, *Kirchengeschichte der Neuzeit II,* 83–85, 90–91, 110–12; Hehir, "Church and State"; Moody, "Church and State."

58. See Hehir, "Church and State"; Moody, "Church and State."

59. M. Conway, *Catholic Politics,* 99-100.

60. Klaus Schatz, *Zwischen Säkularisation und Zweitem Vatikanum* (Frankfurt am Main: Knecht, 1986), 225, 273.

61. Schatz, *Kirchengeschichte der Neuzeit II,* 14.

62. M. Conway, *Catholic Politics,* 50.

63. John S. Conway, *The Nazi Persecution of the Churches 1933–45* (London: Weidenfeld & Nicolson,1968), 92.

64. See M. Conway, *Catholic Politics,* 50–51; Schatz, *Zwischen Säkularisation und Zweitem Vatikanum,* 270–71.

65. Quoted in Scholder, *Kirchen und das Dritte Reich,* 1:320.

66. Questions about the background of the concordat persist: Did the Reich or the Holy See initiate the negotiations toward a concordat? Did the Holy See suggest to the German bishops that they drop their bans against Nazi membership so that a concordat could be negotiated? Did

Monsignor Kaas prematurely disband the Catholic Center party? On the unresolved issues, see Biesinger, "Reich Concordat of 1933."

67. Peter Gay, *Weimar Culture* (New York: Harper & Row, 1968).

68. See Gallin, *Midwives to Nazism.*

69. See Schatz, *Zwischen Säkularisation und Zweitem Vatikanum,* 228–29.

70. See Hürten, *Deutsche Katholiken,* 38–40; Schatz, *Zwischen Säkularisation und Zweitem Vatikanum,* 225.

71. See Hürten, *Deutsche Katholiken,* 59–60; *Katholizismus, Verfassungsstaat und Demokratie,* ed. Anton Rauscher (Paderborn: Ferdinand Schöningh, 1988).

72. See Hürten, *Deutsche Katholiken,* 23, 59–60; Schatz, *Zwischen Säkularisation und Zweitem Vatikanum,* 224–25; Becker, "Neueste Zeit (1803/6 –1995)," 525.

73. See Wilhelm Ribhegge, "Joseph Mausbach (1860–1931) and His Role in the Public Life of the Empire and the Weimar Republic," trans. Ralph Keen, *Catholic Historical Review* 84 (1998): 11–41; Schatz, *Zwischen Säkularisation und Zweitem Vatikanum,* 234–35; Wilhelm Damberg, "Kirchengeschichte zwischen Demokratie und Diktatur: Georg Schreiber und Joseph Lortz 1933-1950," in *Zur Geschichte der theologischen Fakultäten in der Zeit des Nationalsozialismus,* ed. Leonore Siegele-Wenschkewitz and Carsten Nicolaisen (Göttingen: Vandenhoeck & Ruprecht, 1993), 145–67.

74. See Schatz, *Zwischen Säkularisation und Zweitem Vatikanum,* 227–28; Richard Grunberger, *Red Rising in Bavaria* (New York: St. Martin's, 1973).

75. José M. Sánchez, *Pius XII and the Holocaust: Understanding the Controversy* (Washington, D.C.: Catholic University of America Press, 2002), 36.

76. In *L'Osservatore Romano,* quoted in John Cornwell, *Hitler's Pope: The Secret History of Pius XII* (New York: Viking, 1999), 130–31.

77. Quoted in Sánchez, *Pius XII and the Holocaust,* 86; Hürten, *Deutsche Katholiken,* 248.

78. In Cardinal Walter Kasper's words, theology is "the reflected memory of the church" (*Theology and Church,* 6). According to Richard P. McBrien, theology is "[t]he ordered effort to understand, interpret, and systematize our experience of God and of Christian faith" (*Catholicism,* rev. ed. [San Francisco: HarperCollins, 1994], 1252).

79. On Germany's faculties of Catholic theology in the 1930s and 1940s, see the selected bibliography in the appendix. For a list of the professors of systematic theology on these faculties, see Dorothea Nebel, "Die Lehrstuhlinhaber für Apologetik/Fundamentaltheologie und

Dogmatik im deutschsprachigen Raum zwischen den Vatikanischen Konzilien," in *Die katholisch-theologische Disziplinen in Deutschland 1870– 1962*, ed. Hubert Wolf with Claus Arnold (Paderborn: Ferdinand Schöningh, 1999), 164–230.

80. See Helmut Böhm, "Die Theologische Fakultät der Universität München," in *Das Erzbistum München und Freising in der Zeit der nationalsozialistischen Herrschaft*, vol. 1, ed. Georg Schwaiger (Munich: Schnell & Steiner, 1984), 684–738.

81. I do not discuss here Protestant theologians in the Third Reich because they operated within an ecclesiastical and theological horizon that stood apart from the Catholic church and Catholic theology. See *Betrayal: German Churches and the Holocaust*, ed. Robert P. Ericksen and Susannah Heschel (Minneapolis: Fortress, 1999); Robert P. Ericksen, *Theologians under Hitler* (New Haven: Yale University Press, 1985).

82. See Kasper, *Theology and Church,* 79; Fouilloux, "Kultur der katholischen Kirche," 175–215.

83. See Georg Denzler, *Widerstand ist Nicht das Richtige Wort: Priester, Bischöfe und Theologen im Dritten Reich* (Zurich: Pendo, 2003); idem, *Widerstand oder Anpassung?* (Munich: Piper, 1984); Donald J. Dietrich, *Catholic Citizens in the Third Reich: Psycho-Social Principles and Moral Reasoning* (New Brunswick, N.J.: Transaction Books, 1988), 180–215; idem, "Catholic Theologians in Hitler's Third Reich: Adaptation and Critique," *Journal of Church and State* 29 (1987): 19–45; Hürten, *Deutsche Katholiken*, 214–30. Our study goes beyond these texts by correlating a theologian's political views of Hitler with his theological ideas.

84. Peter Eicher, "Die katholische Theologie," in *Neues Handbuch theologischer Grundbegriffe*, vol. 3, ed. P. Eicher (Munich: Kösel, 1985), 196– 235, here 198.

85. See Friedrich Wilhelm Graf, "Moderne Modernisierer, modernitätskritische Traditionalisten oder reaktionäre Modernisten?" in *Antimodernismus und Modernismus in der katholische Kirche*, ed. Hubert Wolf (Paderborn: Ferdinand Schöningh, 1998), 67–106; Wilhelm Imkamp, "Die katholische Theologie in Bayern von der Jahrhundertwende bis zum Ende des Zweiten Weltkrieges," in *Handbuch der bayerischen Kirchengeschichte*, vol. 3, ed. Walter Brandmüller (St. Ottilien: EOS, 1991), 539–651; Georg May, *Kirchenkampf oder Katholikenverfolgung* (Stein am Rhein: Christiana, 1991); Joseph Ratzinger, *The Nature and Mission of Theology*, trans. Adrian Walker (San Francisco: Ignatius Press, 1995); Thomas Ruster, *Die verlorene Nützlichkeit der Religion: Katholizismus und Moderne in der Weimarer Republik* (Paderborn: Ferdinand Schöningh, 1994).

86. On the significance of this phrase, see Hajo Holborn, *A History of Modern Germany* (New York: Alfred A. Knopf, 1969), 3:658.

2. Karl Eschweiler: Claiming the Church's Authority

1. Karl Eschweiler, "Die Kirche im neuen Reich," *Deutsches Volkstum* 15 (June 1933): 451–58.

2. Karl Eschweiler, *Die zwei Wege der neueren Theologie* (Augsburg: Benno Filser, 1926).

3. On Eschweiler's life and thought, see Joachim Drumm, "Eschweiler, Karl," in LThK, 3rd ed., vol. 5 (1996): 881; Thomas Ruster, *Die verlorene Nützlichkeit der Religion: Katholizismus und Moderne in der Weimarer Republik* (Paderborn: Ferdinand Schöningh, 1994), 293–304; Georg Denzler, *Widerstand oder Anpassung?* (Munich: Piper, 1984), 106–7; Gerhard Reifferscheid, *Das Bistum Ermland und das Dritte Reich* (Cologne: Böhlau, 1975), 34–78.

4. Karl Eschweiler, *Die ästhetischen Elemente in der Religionsphilosophie des Heiligen Augustin* (Euskirchen: Buchdruckerei der Euskirchener Volkszeitung, 1909).

5. See Alois Dempf, "Fortschrittliche Intelligenz nach dem Ersten Weltkrieg," *Hochland* 61 (1969): 234–42; Barbara Nichtweiss, *Erik Peterson* (Freiburg: Herder, 1992), 722–27.

6. Albert Ehrhard, *Der Katholizismus und das zwangzigste Jahrhundert im Licht der kirchlichen Entwicklung der Neuzeit* (Stuttgart: Joseph Roth, 1902), 348.

7. See Waldemar Gurian, *Hitler and the Christians*, trans. E. F. Peter (London: Sheed & Ward, 1936); Heinz Hürten, *Ein Zeuge der Krise unserer Welt in der ersten Hälfte des 20. Jahrhunderts* (Mainz: Matthias Grünewald, 1972).

8. Karl Eschweiler, *Der theologische Rationalismus von der Aufklärung bis zum Vatikanum* (Munich, 1920).

9. Karl Eschweiler, *Die Erlebnistheologie Johann Michael Sailers als Grundlegung des theologischen Fideismus in der vorvatikanischen Theologie: Ein ideengeschichtlicher Beitrag zur theologischen Erkenntnislehre* (University of Bonn, 1922).

10. Karl Eschweiler, "Religion und Metaphysik: Zu Max Schelers 'Vom Ewigen Leben im Menschen,'" *Hochland* 19 (1921–22): 303–13, 470–89.

11. Karl Eschweiler, "Zur Krisis der neuscholastischen Religionsphilosophie," *Bonner Zeitschrift für Theologie und Seelsorge* 1 (1924): 313–37.

12. Karl Eschweiler, "Die Herkunft des industriellen Menschen," *Hochland* 22 (1925): 378–98. See St. Thomas Aquinas, *Summa theologiae*, trans. English Dominican Fathers (New York: Benzinger, 1948), I.1, 8 ad. 2.

13. See Thomas Fliethmann, *Vernünftig Glauben* (Würzburg: Echter, 1997); Gerald A. McCool, *Catholic Theology in the Nineteenth Century* (New York: Seabury, 1977), 59–67.

14. Eschweiler, *Zwei Wege der neueren Theologie,* 29.

15. Ibid., 48.

16. Ibid., 121.

17. Ibid., 259.

18. See David Berger, "Ratio fidei fundamenta demonstrat: Fundamentaltheologisches Denken zwischen 1870 und 1960," in *Die katholisch-theologischen Disziplinen in Deutschland 1870–1962,* ed. Hubert Wolf with Claus Arnold (Paderborn: Ferdinand Schöningh, 1999), 95–128; Wilhelm Tolksdorf, *Analysis fidei* (Frankfurt am Main: Peter Lang, 2000), 78–89; Johannes Flury, *Um die Redlichkeit des Glaubens* (Freibourg, Switzerland: Universitätsverlag, 1979), 165–75. On the discussion sparked by *Die zwei Wege der neueren Theologie,* see Karl Eschweiler, "Eine neue Kontroverse über das Verhältnis von Glauben und Wissen," *Bonner Zeitschrift für Theologie und Seelsorge* 3 (1926): 260–76.

19. Thomas O'Meara has proposed that it would have been more fruitful to have compared the Idealist theology of Johann Evangelist Kuhn at the University of Tübingen and the neo-Scholastic theology of J. Lorenz Constantin von Schäzler at the University of Freiburg, since these two scholars are outstanding representatives of their respective theological orientations. See Thomas O'Meara, O.P., *Church and Culture: German Catholic Theology, 1860–1914* (Notre Dame, Ind.: University of Notre Dame Press, 1991), 213 n. 11. Eschweiler took issue with the work of Jacques Maritain; see Karl Eschweiler, *J. Maritain–J. Cocteau: Der Künstler und der Weise* (Augsburg: Benno Filser, 1927).

20. Reifferscheid, *Das Bistum Ermland,* 34–37.

21. During his first year at Braunsberg, Eschweiler saw the publication of his book *Die Philosophie der spanischen Spätscholastik auf den deutschen Universitäten des 17. Jahrhunderts* (Münster, 1928).

22. Karl Eschweiler, *Johann Adam Möhlers Kirchenbegriff: Das Hauptstück der katholischen Auseinandersetzung mit der deutschen Idealismus* (Braunsberg: Herder, 1930). See Ruster, *Verlorene Nützlichkeit der Religion,* 298–303; Roger Aubert, "Die ekklesiologische Geographie im 19. Jahrhundert," in *Sentire Ecclesiam,* ed. Jean Daniélou and Herbert Vorgrimler (Freiburg: Herder, 1961), 443 n. 39.

23. Eschweiler, *Johann Adam Möhlers Kirchenbegriff,* 85, 136–37.

24. Ibid., 158.

25. Ibid., 169–70. See Michael J. Himes, *Ongoing Incarnation: Johann Adam Möhler and the Beginnings of Modern Ecclesiology* (New York: Crossroad, 1997).

26. Karl Eschweiler, "Politische Theologie," *Religiöse Besinnung* 4, no. 2 (1931–32): 72–88, here 74.

27. Karl Muth, "Res publica 1926: Gedanken zur politischen Krise der Gegenwart," *Hochland* 24 Part 1 (1926–27): 1–14, here 13.

28. Gundlach presented his views on democracy at a seminar of the Königswinter Circle on May 12–13, 1932; see Donald J. Dietrich, "Catholic Theologians in Hitler's Third Reich: Adaptation and Critique," *Journal of Church and State* 29 (1987): 23 n. 9.

29. Kurt Ziesche, *Das Königtum Christi in Europa* (Regensburg: G. J. Manz, 1926), vii, 23, 56, 97.

30. Friedrich Muckermann, "An den Pforten des Reiches," *Der Gral* 22, no. 4 (1927–28): 208–9; idem, "Der Reichsgedanke als Kulturidee," *Schönere Zukunft* 63, no. 32 (1927–28): 700.

31. On the dream of a new German empire uniting church and state, see Klaus Breuning, *Die Vision des Reiches* (Munich: Max Heuber, 1969).

32. Damasus Winzen, "Gedanken zu einer 'Theologie des Reiches,'" *Catholica* 2 (1933): 97–116, here 116.

33. Robert Grosche, "Die Grundlagen einer christlichen Politik der deutschen Katholiken," *Die Schildgenossen* 13 (1933–34): 46–52, here 52.

34. Albert Mirgeler, "Die deutschen Katholiken und das Reich," *Die Schildgenossen* 13 (1933–34): 53–56.

35. See Heinz Hürten, *Deutsche Katholiken 1918–1945* (Paderborn: Ferdinand Schöningh, 1992), 219.

36. Vincent Berning, "Modernismus und Reformkatholizismus," in *Die Zukunft der Glaubensunterweisung,* ed. Franz Pöggler (Freiburg: Seelsorge, 1971), 22.

37. See Carl Schmitt, "Romantik," *Hochland* 22, no. 1 (1924–25): 157–71.

38. Quoted in Robert Wistrich, *Who's Who in Nazi Germany* (New York: Routledge, 1995), 225–26. See also Joseph W. Bendersky, *Carl Schmitt: Political Theorist* (Princeton: Princeton University Press, 1983).

39. Quoted in Hasso Hofmann, "Schmitt," in *Staatslexicon,* 7th ed. (Freiburg: Herder, 1988), 4:1052–55, here 1053.

40. Quoted in Wistrich, *Who's Who in Nazi Germany,* 226.

41. See Brigitte Poschmann, "Maximilian Kaller (1880–1947)," in *Zeitgeschichte in Lebensbildern,* vol. 7, ed. J. Aretz, R. Morsey, and A. Rauscher (Mainz: Matthias Grünewald, 1994), 49–62; Reifferscheid, *Das Bistum Ermland,* 276.

42. Hans Barion, "Kirche oder Partei? Der Katholizismus im neueren Reich," *Europäische Revue* 9 (1933): 401–9.

43. See Ruster, *Verlorene Nützlichkeit der Religion,* 297 n. 500.

44. Eschweiler, "Kirche im neuen Reich," 451.

45. The Nazi party's official program is available in *The Third Reich and the Christian Churches*, ed. Peter Matheson (Grand Rapids: W. B. Eerdmans, 1981).

46. Eschweiler, "Kirche im neuen Reich," 456.

47. See Reifferscheid, *Das Bistum Ermland*, 37–77.

48. See Helmut Heiber, *Universitäten unterm Hakenkreuz*, part 2, vol. 2 (Munich: K. G. Saur, 1994), 96–98; Denzler, *Widerstand oder Anpassung?* 107.

49. See *Mitteilungen zur Weltanschaulichen Lage* 2, no. 2 (October 30, 1936): 1–3; Guenther Lewy, *The Catholic Church and Hitler's Wars* (New York: McGraw Hill, 1964), 108–9, 365 n. 61.

50. See Hans-Paul Höpfner, *Die Universität Bonn im Dritten Reich* (Bonn: Bouvier Verlag, 1999), 181–217.

51. Wilhelm Neuss, "Gedanken eines katholischen Theologen zur Judenfrage," *Deutsche Zeitung* (June 1, 1933).

52. See Raimund Baumgärtner, *Weltanschauungs Kampf im Dritten Reich* (Mainz: Matthias Grünewald, 1977).

53. Rosenberg's *Myth of the Twentieth Century* sold 233,000 copies by 1935; see Denzler, *Widerstand oder Anpassung?*, 105–6.

54. Edith Stein was born into a Jewish family in Breslau in 1891, studied phenomenology with Edmund Husserl, and attained international distinction because of her philosophical writings. She converted to the Catholic faith in 1922 and became a Carmelite nun at Cologne in 1933, taking the name Teresa Benedicta of the Cross. To avoid arrest, she fled to the Carmel in Echt, Holland, on December 31, 1938. Stein and her sister, Rosa, were seized by the Gestapo on August 2, 1942, and were killed seven days later at Auschwitz. She was beatified on May 1, 1987 and canonized on October 11, 1998. See Suzanne M. Batzdorff, "Aunt Edith: Jewish Heritage, Catholic Saint," *America* 185 (February 13, 1999): 15–23; eadem, "Tracing Edith Stein's Past," *America* 181 (November 25, 1995): 12–18.

55. See Ulrich von Hehl, *Katholische Kirche und Nationalsozialismus im Erzbistum Köln* (Mainz: Matthias Grünewald, 1977), 87–88; John S. Conway, *The Nazi Persecution of the Churches 1933–45* (London: Weidenfeld & Nicolson, 1968), 172. Teusch's booklets reached approximately seventeen million readers; see Klaus Schatz, *Zwischen Säkularisation und Zweitem Vatikanum* (Frankfurt am Main: Knecht, 1986), 268.

56. See Wilhelm Neuss, *Kampf gegen den Mythus der 20. Jahrhunderts* (Cologne, 1947); Richard Grunberger, *Social History of the Third Reich* (London: Weidenfeld & Nicolson, 1971), 441.

57. These later editions omitted a chapter on the spirituality of

Meister Eckhart, whom Rosenberg had presented as a representative of the Germanic spirit. See von Hehl, *Katholische Kirche*, 86–91.

58. See Eduard Hegel, *Geschichte der katholisch-theologischen Fakultät Münster*, part 1 (Münster: Aschendorff, 1966), 484.

59. See Eduard Hegel, "Nekrologe: Wilhelm Neuss," *Historisches Jahrbuch* 87 (1967): 247–51.

60. See Bernhard Stasiewski, *Bonner Gelehrte: Beiträge zur Geschichte des Wissenschaft in Bonn. Katholische Theologie* (Bonn: H. Bouvier Verlag, 1968), 7–12.

61. O'Meara, *Church and Culture*, 66. In relying on Scheeben's interpretation of Thomas Aquinas, Eschweiler stood with other German Catholic scholars of the 1920s; see Erich Przywara, *Katholische Krise* (Düsseldorf: Patmos, 1967), 109.

62. Ruster, *Verlorene Nützlichkeit der Religion*, 297.

3. Joseph Lortz: Renewing Western Civilization

1. On Lortz's life and thought, see Hubert Wolf, "Der Historiker ist kein Prophet," in *Die katholisch-theologischen Disziplinen in Deutschland 1870–1962*, ed. Hubert Wolf with Claus Arnold (Paderborn: Ferdinand Schöningh, 1999), 71–94; Gabriele Lautenschläger, *Joseph Lortz (1887–1975): Weg, Umwelt und Werk eines katholischen Kirchenhistorikers* (Würzburg: Echter, 1987); Wilhelm Damberg, "Kirchengeschichte zwischen Demokratie und Diktatur: Georg Schreiber und Joseph Lortz in Münster 1933-1950," in *Theologische Fakultäten im Nationalsozialismus*, ed. Leonore Siegele-Wenschkewitz and Carsten Nicolaisen (Göttingen: Vandenhoeck & Ruprecht, 1993), 146–67; Erwin Iserloh, "Lortz, Joseph (1887-1975)," in *Theologische Realenzyklopädie*, ed. Gerhard Krause and Gerhard Müller (Berlin/New York: Walter de Gruyter, 1977–), 21:466–68; idem, *Kirche—Ereignis und Institution*, vol. 1 (Münster: Aschendorff, 1985), 35–37.

2. On Lortz's engagement with National Socialism, see Thomas Ruster, "Roman Catholic Theologians and National Socialism: Adaptation to Nazi Ideology," in *Christian Responses to the Holocaust*, ed. Donald Dietrich (Syracuse: Syracuse University Press, 2004), 12–23; Georg Denzler, "Katholische Zugänge zum Nationalsozialismus," in *Theologische Wissenschaft im "Dritten Reich,"* ed. Georg Denzler and Leonore Siegele-Wenschkewitz (Frankfurt am Main: Haag & Herchen, 2000), 40–67; Michael B. Lukens, "Joseph Lortz and a Catholic Accommodation with National Socialism," in *Betrayal: German Churches and the Holocaust*, ed. Robert P. Ericksen and Susannah Heschel (Minneapolis: Fortress, 1999),

149–68; Victor Conzemius, "Joseph Lortz—ein Kirchenhistoriker als Brückenbauer," *Geschichte und Gegenwart* 9 (1990): 247–78.

3. Joseph Lortz, "Tertullians Apologie des religiösen Lebens des Christen, systematisch und entwicklungsgeschichtlich dargestellt" (University of Bonn, 1920).

4. On Albert Ehrhard, see Thomas F. O'Meara, O.P., *Church and Culture: German Catholic Theology, 1860–1914* (Notre Dame, Ind.: University of Notre Dame Press, 1991), 148–55.

5. Joseph Lortz, *Tertullian als Apologet*, 2 vols. (Münster, 1927–29).

6. Joseph Lortz, *Geschichte der Kirche in ideengeschichtlicher Betrachtung: Eine Sinndeutung der christlichen Vergangenheit* (Münster: Aschendorff, 1932); English, *History of the Church*, trans. Edwin G. Kaiser (Milwaukee: Bruce, 1938). Although the English text was translated from the fourth edition of the German text (1936), it does not include that edition's appendix "National Sozialismus und die Kirche." It also does not give the full title of the German text: "History of the Church in the History-of-Ideas Perspective. An Interpretation of the Christian Past."

7. Lortz, *History of the Church*, 7.

8. Ibid., 219, 312.

9. Ibid., 444–48.

10. Ibid., 9–10.

11. Ibid., 473.

12. Ibid., 387.

13. Ibid., 463, 473.

14. Ibid., 496.

15. Joseph Lortz, *Katholischer Zugang zur Nationalsozialismus, kirchengeschichtlich gesehen* (Münster: Aschendorff, 1933).

16. Ibid., 8.

17. Ibid., 14.

18. Ibid., 23.

19. Ibid., 26.

20. Joseph Lortz, "Katholisch und doch nationalsozialistich," *Germania* 64, no. 27 (January 28, 1934). The second and third parts of this essay appeared in February and May, 1934.

21. The title of the pamphlet's third edition omits the expression, "kirchengeschichtlichen gesehen" ("in the perspective of church history"). It may be that Lortz changed the title in order to appear detached from the church; see Gerhard Reifferscheid, *Das Bistum Ermland und das Dritte Reich* (Cologne: Böhlau, 1975), 36 n. 10.

22. Joseph Lortz, *Geschichte der Kirche in ideengeschichtler Betrachung*, 4th ed. (Münster: Aschendorff, 1936), 90.

23. See Klaus Wittstadt, "Die katholisch-theologische Fakultät der Universität Würzburg während der Zeit des Dritten Reiches," in *Vierhundert Jahre Universität Würzburg: Eine Festscrift*, ed. Peter Baumgart (Neustadt an der Aisch: Verlag Degener & Co., 1982), 399–435.

24. Joseph Pascher, "Das Dritte Reich, erlebt an drei deutschen Universitäten," in *Die deutsche Universität im Dritten Reich*, ed. Helmut Kuhn et al. (Munich: R. Piper, 1966), 45–69, here 48.

25. Ludwig Ruland, "Alle Deutschen sagen 'Ja,'" *Völkische Beobachter*, Suddeutsche Ausgabe 46 (November 8, 1933): 1; see Georg Denzler, *Widerstand oder Anpassung?* (Munich: Piper, 1984), 107–8. Ruland's reasoning was similar to that of the Abbey of Beuron's abbot, Alban Schachleiter, whose public support of National Socialism led to his suspension from the Benedictine Order on February 20, 1933.

26. On Sebastian Merkle, see Wolf, "Historiker ist kein Prophet," 77–80, 82–83; Manfred Weitlauff, "Merkle, Sebastian," in *Neue Deutsche Biographie*, vol. 17 (Berlin: Duncker & Humblot, 1993), 159–61; Georg Denzler, "Kirchengeschichte als theologische Wissenschaft," in *Bilanz der Theologie im 20. Jahrhundert*, vol. 3, ed. Herbert Vorgrimler and Robert Vander Gucht (Freiburg: Herder, 1970), 435–70, here 462–64; O'Meara, *Church and Culture*, passim.

27. See Sebastian Merkle, "Gutes an Luther und Übles an seinem Tadlern," in *Luther in ökumenischer Sicht*, ed. Alfred von Marin (Stuttgart, 1929).

28. See Wittstadt, "Die katholisch-theologische Fakultät der Universität Würzburg"; Wilhelm Ribhegge, *Geschichte der Universität Münster* (Münster: Regensberg Verlag, 1985), 188. The Catholic liturgist Anton Baumstark (d. 1948) favored National Socialism; see Fritz West, *The Comparative Liturgy of Anton Baumstark* (Bramcote, Nottingham: Grove Books, 1995). The Catholic scholar Peter Wust (d. 1939), a professor in Münster's faculty of philosophy, was publicly critical of National Socialism. As previously noted, Josef Pieper, who eventually became a professor of philosophy at the University of Münster, initially held that the social, political, and economic principles presented in Pius XI's *Quadragesimo Anno* could be realized by Hitler's government; see Josef Pieper, *No One Could Have Known*, trans. Graham Harrison (San Francisco: St. Ignatius Press, 1987).

29. See Richard Heinzmann, "Die Identität des Christentums im Umbruch des 20. Jahrhunderts: Michael Schmaus zum 90. Geburtstag," *Münchener Theologische Zeitschrift* 38 (1987): 115–33; idem, "Michael Schmaus in memoriam," *Münchener Theologische Zeitschrift* 45 (1994): 123–27, 124; Pascher, "Dritte Reich," 64.

30. See Eduard Hegel, *Geschichte der katholisch-theologischen Fakultät*

Münster, part 1 (Münster: Aschendorff, 1966), 458, 469, 479, 501–3, 506, 557–58; idem, *Geschichte der katholische-theologischen Fakultät Münster,* part 2 (Münster: Aschendorff, 1971), 75–78, 416–18. According to Ernst Deuerlein, Schmaus as one of Vice Chancellor "Papen's Catholics"; see Ernst Deuerlein, "Zur Vergegenwärtigung der Lage des deutschen Katholizismus 1933," *Stimmen der Zeit* 168 (1961). Schmaus remained distant from National Socialism because of the christological focus of his theology; see Donald J. Dietrich, "Catholic Theologians in Hitler's Third Reich: Adaptation and Critique," *Journal of Church and State* 29 (1987): 35; Richard Heinzmann, "Der Gott der Philosophen und die Systembildung in der Theologie: Zur Christozentrik der Dogmatik von Michael Schmaus," in *Für euch Bischof, mit euch Christ,* ed. Manfred Weitlauf and Peter Neuner (St. Ottilien: EOS, 1998), 441–50.

31. Schmaus's *Katholische Dogmatik* was reprinted nine times and translated into numerous other languages, including English; see Peter Walter, "Die deutschsprachige Dogmatik zwischen den beiden Vatikanischen Konzilien untersucht am Beispiel der Ekklesiologie," in *Katholische-theologische Disziplinen,* ed. Wolf and Arnold, 129–63; Richard Heinzmann, "Die Identität des Christentums im Umbruch des 20. Jahrhunderts," *Münchener Theologische Zeitschrift* 38 (1987): 115–33.

32. Michael Schmaus, *Begegnung zwischen katholischem Christentum und nationalsozialistischer Weltanschauung,* 2nd printing (Münster: Aschendorff, 1934). For an analysis of this essay, see Michael Lukens, "Michael Schmaus and the Catholic Encounter with National Socialism" (unpublished manuscript).

33. Schmaus, *Begegnung zwischen katholischem Christentum und nationalistischer Weltanschauung,* 28.

34. Ibid., 42–43.

35. See Karl Müller, "Joseph Schmidlin," in *Mission Legacies: Biographical Studies of Leaders of the Modern Missionary Movement,* ed. Gerald H. Anderson et al. (Maryknoll: Orbis, 1994); Johannes Dörmann, "Joseph Schmidlin (1876–1944): Begründer der katholischen Missionswissenschaft," in *Martyria,* ed. Jörg Kniffka (Wuppertal: R. Brockhaus, 1989), 122–29; Karl Müller, *Joseph Schmidlin (1876–1944)* (Nettetal: Steyler Verlag, 1989).

36. See Damberg, "Kirchengeschichte zwischen Demokratie und Diktatur"; "Scheiber, Georg," in *Deutsche Biographische Enzyklopädie,* vol. 9 (Munich: K. G. Saur, 1998), 35; Rudolf Morsey, "Georg Schreiber, der Wissenschaftlicher, Kulturpolitiker und Wissenschaftsorganisator," *Westfälische Zeitschrift* 131–32 (1981–82): 121–59; idem, "Georg Schreiber (1882–1963)," in *Zeitgeschichte in Lebensbildern,* vol. 2, ed. Rudolf Morsey (Mainz: Matthias Grünewald, 1975), 177–85.

37. Wolf, "Historiker ist kein Prophet," 90–91.

38. Instead of assigning Lortz to Schreiber's academic chair, Rust gave him the professorship that had belonged to Schmidlin; see Damberg, "Kirchengeschichte zwischen Demokratie und Diktatur," 150.

39. See Beth A. Griech-Polelle, *Bishop von Galen: German Catholicism and National Socialism* (New Haven: Yale University Press, 2002); Ribhegge, *Geschichte der Universität Münster*; Rudolf Morsey, "Clemens August Kardinal von Galen (1878–1946)," in *Zeitgeschichte in Lebensbildern*, 2:37–47.

40. Pieper, *No One Could Have Known*, 93.

41. Rudolf Morsey, "Clemens August Kardinal von Galen," *Internationale katholische Zeitschrift* 7 (1978): 429–42.

42. Ulrich von Hehl, "Galen, Clemens August Graf von," in *Deutsche Biographische Enzyklopädie*, vol. 3 (Munich: K. G. Saur, 1996), 560; Max Bierbaum, "Galen, v." in *Neue Deutsche Biographie*, vol. 6 (Berlin: Duncker & Humblot, 1964), 41–42.

43. Joseph Lortz, *The Reformation in Germany*, trans. Ronald Walls (New York: Herder & Herder, 1968), 22. On the revisionist work of Greving, Mauert, and Merkle, see Wolf, "Historiker ist kein Prophet," 77, 80–83. On Lortz and the beginning of ecumenism, see Leonard Swidler, *The Ecumenical Vanguard: The History of the Una Sancta Movement* (Pittsburgh: Duquesne University Press, 1966), 17–24.

44. Lortz, *Reformation in Germany*, 216.

45. Ibid., 186.

46. According to Otto Pesch, "This is precisely the change in style which Lortz brought about, and which has been, in spite of a few later regressions into the old 'style', irreversible" ("Twenty Years of Catholic Luther Research," *Luther World* 13 [1966]: 303–16, here 304).

47. See Conzemius, "Joseph Lortz," 264.

48. See Joseph Lortz's letter of explanation (1945), in Conzemius, "Joseph Lortz," 274.

49. Pieper, *No One Could Have Known*, 137.

50. See Erwin Iserloh, "Joseph Lortz, Leben und ökumenische Bedeutung," in *Zum Gedenken an Joseph Lortz (1887–1975)*, ed. Rolf Decot and Rainer Vinke (Wiesbaden: Franz Steiner, 1989), 3–11, here 10–11.

51. Joseph Lortz, *Die Reformation: Thesen als Handreichung bei ökumenischen Gesprächen*, 2nd ed. (Meitingen: Kyrios, 1945); idem, "The Reformation: Theses Put Forward as a Friendly Approach for Oecumenical Conversation," *Eastern Churches Quarterly* 7 (1947): 76–91. See also Swidler, *Ecumenical Vanguard*, 33.

52. See Hugo Ott, "Metzger, Max Josef," in *Badische Biographien*,

vol. 4, ed. Bernd Ottand (Stuttgart: W. Kohlhammer, 1996), 206–10; Leonard Swidler, *Bloodwitness for Peace and Unity* (Philadelphia: Ecumenical Press, 1977); Max Metzger, "Testament to Peace," *Jubilee* 9 (March 1962): 22–25; Heinz Kühn, *Blutzeugen des Bistums Berlin* (Berlin: Morus, 1950), 133–46.

53. See "Laros, Matthias," in *Deutsche Biographische Enzyklopädie*, vol. 6 (Munich: K. G. Saur, 1997), 254; Viktor Conzemius, "Laros, Matthias," in *Neue Deutsche Biographie*, vol. 13 (Berlin: Duncker & Humblot, 1982), 641–42.

54. Joseph Lortz, *Die Reformation als religiöses Anliegen heute* (Trier, 1948); English, *The Reformation: A Problem for Today*, trans. Lewis W. Spitz (Westminster, Md.: Westminster Press, 1964). See Lewis W. Spitz, "Die Wirkung des historiographischen Werkes von Joseph Lortz in den USA," in *Zum Gedenken an Joseph Lortz (1887–1975)*, ed. Decot and Vinke, 207–16.

55. Matthias Laros, "Was ist zu tun?" *Begegnung* 4 (1949): 123; quoted in Swidler, *Ecumenical Vanguard*, 34.

56. See Winifried Schulze and Corine Defrance, *Die Gründung des Instituts für europäische Geschichte Mainz* (Mainz: Philipp von Zabern, 1992).

57. See "Ausgewählte Bibliographie von Joseph Lortz," in *Joseph Lortz: Erneuerung und Einheit*, ed. Peter Manns (Wiesbaden: Franz Steiner, 1987), 893–95.

58. Quoted in Georg Denzler, "Wenn Gottesgelehrte völkisch denken," *Süddeutschen Zeitung* 295 (December 21–22, 1996): 1.

59. Joseph Lortz, *Mein Umweg zur Geschichte: Ein besinnlicher Rückblick auf der Journée des Anciens d'Echternach* (Wiesbaden: Franz Steiner, 1960), 45; quoted in Conzemius, "Joseph Lortz," 248.

60. Wolf, "Historiker ist kein Prophet," 90.

61. Lukens, "Joseph Lortz and a Catholic Accommodation with National Socialism," 156.

62. Conzemius, "Joseph Lortz," 260.

63. Lortz, *History of the Church*, 1.

64. Iserloh, "Joseph Lortz—Leben und ökumenische Bedeuting," 6.

65. Lukens, "Joseph Lortz and a Catholic Accommodation with National Socialism," 157.

66. Hans Küng, *The Council, Reform and Reunion*, trans. Cecily Hastings (New York: Sheed & Ward, 1961), 104.

67. Otto Pesch, "Theologische Überlegungen zum 'Subjektivismus' Luthers," in *Zum Gedenken an Joseph Lortz (1887–1976)*, ed. Decot and Vinke, 106–40.

68. Conzemius, "Joseph Lortz," 263.

4. Karl Adam: Searching for a National Community

1. On Karl Adam's life and thought, see Hans Kreidler, *Eine Theologie des Lebens* (Mainz: Matthias Grünewald, 1988); Walter Kasper, "Karl Adam," ThQ 156 (1976): 251–58. This chapter also draws on Robert A. Krieg, "Karl Adam, National Socialism, and Tradition," ThS 60 (1999): 432–56; idem, *Karl Adam: Catholicism in German Culture* (Notre Dame, Ind.: University of Notre Dame Press, 1992).

2. See Manfred Weitlauff, "Reformkatholizismus," in LThK, 3rd ed., vol. 8 (1999): 957–59; Roger Aubert, "Reform Catholicism in Germany," in *History of the Church*, vol. 9, ed. Hubert Jedin and John Dolan, trans. Margit Resch (New York: Crossroad, 1981), 422–30; T. Mark Schoof, *A Survey of Catholic Theology, 1800– 1970*, trans. N. D. Smith (New York: Paulist Newman Press, 1970), 72–76.

3. See Otto Weiss, "Der Katholische Modernismus," in *Antimodernismus und Modernismus in der katholische Kirche*, ed. Hubert Wolf (Paderborn: Ferdinand Schöningh, 1998), 107–43; idem, "Modernismus," in LThK, 3rd ed., vol. 7 (1998): 367–70; idem, *Der Modernismus in Deutschland* (Regensburg: Friedrich Pustet, 1995); Thomas Loome, *Liberal Catholicism, Reform Catholicism, Modernism* (Mainz: Matthias Grünewald, 1979). Weiss has defined modernism so that it includes reform Catholicism. By contrast, Loome differentiates between modernism and reform Catholicism. See Peter Hünermann, "Antimodernismus und Modernismus," in *Antimodernismus und Modernismus in der Katholischen Kirche*, ed. Wolf, 367–76.

4. See *Der Rheinische Reformkreis: Dokumente zu Modernismus und Reformkatholizismus in Deutschland 1942–1955*, ed. Hubert Wolf and Claus Arnold, 2 vols. (Paderborn: Ferdinand Schöningh, 2001); Lucia Scherzberg, *Kirchenreform mit Hilfe des Nationalsozialismus* (Darmstadt: Wissenschaftliche Buchgesellschaft, 2001).

5. Karl Adam, "Der Antimodernisteneid und die theologische Fakultäten," *Katholische Kirchenzeitung für Deutschland* 1 (1910): 83–85.

6. See Friedrich Heiler, "Zum Tod von Karl Adam," ThQ 146 (1966): 257–60.

7. René Wellek, "Romanticism Re-examined," in *Concepts of Criticism*, ed. S. G. Nichols (New Haven: Yale University Press, 1963), 199–221, here 221. See Thomas F. O'Meara, O.P., *Romantic Idealism and Roman Catholicism* (Notre Dame, Ind.: University of Notre Dame Press, 1982).

8. Friedrich Nietzsche, *Thus Spoke Zarathustra* (1891), in *The Portable Nietzsche*, trans. and ed. Walter Kaufmann (New York: Viking, 1954), 238; Stefan George, "Kingdom Come" (1928), in idem, *Poems*, trans. and ed. C. N. Valhope and E. Morwotz (New York: Pantheon, 1943), 223.

9. Reported by Paschal Botz, O.S.B., St. John's Abbey, Collegeville, Minnesota, in an interview with Thomas F. O'Meara.

10. See Kasper, "Karl Adam."

11. Edward Schillebeeckx, O.P., *God Is New Each Moment*, trans. David Smith (New York: Seabury, 1983), 12.

12. Heinrich Fries, "Lebensgeschichte im Dialog mit Kardinal Newman," in *Sinnsuche und Lebenswenden*, ed. Günther Biemer (New York: Peter Land, 1992), 133.

13. See Herbert Spiegelberg, *The Phenomenological Movement*, 3rd rev. ed. (The Hague: Martinus Nijhoff, 1982).

14. Max Scheler, *On the Eternal in Man*, trans. Bernhard Noble (New York: Harper, 1961).

15. See Heinrich Fries, *Die katholische Religionsphilosophie der Gegenwart* (Heidelberg: F. H. Kerle, 1949).

16. Karl Adam, *The Spirit of Catholicism*, trans. Dom Justin McCann (New York: Crossroad, 1997), 95.

17. Ibid., 156.

18. Karl Adam, *Christ and the Western Mind*, trans. E. Bullough (New York: Macmillan, 1930), 38.

19. Karl Adam, "Glauben und Glaubenswissenschaft im Katholizismus" (1920), retitled "Theologischer Glaube und Theologie," in idem, *Glaube und Glaubenswissenschaft im Katholizismus*, 2nd rev. ed. (Rottenburg: Bader, 1923), 17–43, here 32.

20. Friedrich Heiler (d. 1967) studied theology at the University of Munich, attending Adam's lectures. Although he subsequently converted to the Lutheran church, he remained in contact with Adam; see Heiler, "Zum Tod vom Karl Adam."

21. Adam, *Spirit of Catholicism*, 31–36.

22. Karl Adam, *The Son of God*, trans. Philip Hereford (Garden City, N.Y.: Doubleday, 1964), 9.

23. Adam contributed to the renewal of Christology by highlighting the salvific significance of the incarnation; he did not, however, give a satisfactory account of the hypostatic union; see Aloys Grillmeier, "Zum Christusbild der heutigen katholischen Theologie," in *Fragen der Theologie Heute*, ed. J. Feiner, J. Trutsch, and F. Böchle (Einsiedeln: Johannes, 1957), 265–99, here 275.

24. See O'Meara, *Romantic Idealism and Roman Catholicism*, 94–110; Karl Adam, "Die katholische Tübinger Schule," *Hochland* 24, no. 2 (1926–27): 581–601.

25. See Uwe Dietrich Adam, *Hochschule und Nationalsozialismus* (Tübingen: J. C. B. Mohr [Paul Siebeck], 1977), 38.

26. See Theodor Eschenburg, "Aus dem Universitätsleben vor 1933," in *Deutsches Geistesleben und Nationalsozialismus*, ed. Andreas Flitner

(Tübingen: Rainer Wunderlach, 1965), 40. See Georg May, *Mit Katholiken zu Besetzende Professoren an der Universität Tübingen von 1817 bis 1945* (Amsterdam: B. R. Grüner, 1975), 669–86.

27. See Bernhard Hanssler, *Bischof Johannes Baptista Sproll* (Sigmaringen: Thorbecke, 1984); Paul Kopf, "Johannes Baptista Sproll (1870–1949)," in *Zeitgeschichte in Lebensbildern,* vol. 5, ed. J. Aretz, R. Morsey, and A. Rauscher (Mainz: Matthias Grünewald, 1982), 104–17.

28. Quoted in Ludwig Volk, "Nationalsozialistischer Kirchenkampf und deutscher Episkopat," in *Die Katholiken und das Dritte Reich,* ed. Klaus Gotto and Konrad Repken (Mainz: Matthias Grünewald, 1980), 49–92, here 58.

29. Quoted in Klaus Scholder, *Die Kirchen und das Dritte Reich,* vol. 2 (Frankfurt am Main: Ullstein, 1985), 142.

30. See Bernhard Stasiewski, "Die katholisch-theologischen Fakultäten und philosophisch-theologischen Hochschulen von 1933 bis 1945," in *Seminar und Hochschule in Eichstätt unter dem Nationalsozialismus,* ed. Hermann Holzbauer (Eichstätt: Universitätsbibliothek, 1984), 23–48; idem, "Zur Geschichte der Katholisch-Theologischen Fakultäten und der Philosophisch-Theologischen Hochschulen in Deutschland 1933–1945," in *Die Kirche im Wandel der Zeit,* ed. Franz Groner (Cologne: J. P. Bachem, 1971), 169–85. An entire issue of the *Theologische Quartalschrift* is dedicated to the history of the Catholic Tübingen School; see ThQ 150 (1970).

31. See Erich Przywara, *Logos* (Düsseldorf: Patmos, 1963), 169; Thomas F. O'Meara, O.P., *Erich Przywara, S.J.* (Notre Dame, Ind.: University of Notre Dame Press, 2001).

32. See Roman Bleistein, *Alfred Delp* (Frankfurt am Main: Josef Knecht, 1989).

33. See *Kardinal Michael von Faulhaber, 1869–1952,* ed. Albrecht Liess and the Staatliches Archiv Bayern (Neuburg: Danuvia Druckhaus Neuburg, 2002).

34. See Hajo Holborn, *A History of Modern Germany* (New York: Alfred A. Knopf, 1969), 3:663.

35. Michael von Faulhaber, *Judaism, Christianity and Germany,* trans. George D. Smith, with an introduction by George N. Schuster (New York: Macmillan, 1935).

36. See Manfred Heim, "Die Theologische Fakultät der Universität München in der NS Zeit," *Münchener theologische Zeitschrift* 48 (1997): 371–87; Helmut Böhm, "Die theologische Fakultät der Universität München," in *Das Erzbistum München und Freising in der Zeit der nationalsozialistichen Herrschaft,* vol. 1, ed. Georg Schwaiger (Munich: Schnell & Steiner, 1984), 684–738.

37. See Johannes Neuhäuser, *Kreuz und Hakenkreuz* (Munich: Katholische Kirche Bayerns, 1946).

38. Joseph Pascher, "Das Dritte Reich, erlebt an drei deutschen Universitäten," in *Die deutsche Universität im Dritten Reich,* ed. Helmut Kuhn et al. (Munich: R. Piper, 1966), 60. On April 20, 1940, Pascher was assigned by Rust to the University of Münster. After the war, he taught at the University of Munich.

39. Karl Adam's brother, August Adam, was a critic of Hitler's regime; see Ulrich Lehner, "'Geistige Denazifizierung,'" *Kirchliche Zeitgeschichte* 14 (2001): 1-25.

40. Quoted in U. Adam, *Hochschule und Nationalsozialismus,* 24.

41. Karl Adam, "Deutsches Volkstum und katholisches Christentum," ThQ 114 (1933): 40–63.

42. Ibid., 53.

43. Ibid., 59.

44. Ibid., 60. There were ninety Jews who were permanent residents of Tübingen in 1933; see David Fiensey, "Relations between Jews and Christians in Tübingen, West Germany," *Explorations* 2 (1988): 2.

45. See Scholder, *Kirchen und das Dritte Reich,* 1:100–105.

46. Karl Adam, "Vom gottmenschlichen Erlöser," in *Glaubenstage und Glaubenswallfahrten,* ed. Central Committee of German Catholics (Paderborn: Bonifacius, 1934), 11–24. For the unabridged text, see idem, "Christus und das deutsche Volk," *Deutsches Volksblatt* (Stuttgart Edition) 18 (January 23, 1934): 5; and idem, "Der Erlösungstat Jesu Christi," *Deutsches Volksblatt* (Stuttgart Edition) 19 (January 24, 1934): 5–6. The original manuscript is available in the Berlin Archives: Barch Berlin R53 198, 90–91. I am grateful to Kevin Spicer for making this text available to me. For an abridged English translation of Adam's address, see Karl Adam, "In the Jubilee Year," trans. George N. Shuster, *Commoneal* 19 (August 10, 1934): 361–63.

47. See Hans Kreidler, "Karl Adam und Nationalsozialismus," in *Rottenburger Jahrbuch für Kirchengeschichte,* vol. 3, ed. Geschichtsverein der Diözese Rottenburg-Stuttgart (Sigmaringen: Jan Thorbecke, 1983), 129–40; Scholder, *Kirchen and das Dritte Reich,* 2:140–42.

48. Karl Adam, "Jesus Christ and the Spirit of the Age," in *Germany's New Religion,* trans. and ed. T. S. K. Scott-Craig and R. E. Davies (New York: Abingdon, 1937), 117–68.

49. See Karl Adam, "Die geistige Lage des deutschen Katholizismus" (December 10, 1939), in Bundesarchiv NS 43 20, 230–41. I am indebted to Kevin Spicer for making the original text available to me. On this speech, see Kreidler, "Karl Adam und der Nationalsozialismus," 136–38.

50. For Adam's subsequent comments on this speech, see *Rheinische Reformkreis*, ed. Wolf and Arnold, 100; Scherzberg, *Kirchenreform*, 255.

51. See Josef Joos, *Am Räderwerk der Zeit* (Augsburg: Winifried Werk, 1951); Erich Kock, *Er widerstand—Bernhard Lichtenberg* (Berlin: Morus, 1996); Scherzberg, *Kirchenreform*, 267–75. On the conflict between Adam and Lichtenberg, see Kevin Spicer, C.S.C., *The Catholic Clergy of Berlin and the Third Reich* (DeKalb, Ill.: Northern Illinois University Press, 2004); idem, "Last Years of a Resister in the Diocese of Berlin: Bernhard Lichtenberg's Conflict with Karl Adam and his Fateful Imprisonment," *Church History* 70 (2001): 248–70; idem, "The Provost from St. Hedwig: Bernhard Lichtenberg as a Paradigm for Resistance," in *The Burdens of History*, ed. Sharon Leder and Milton Teichman (Merion Station, Pa.: Merion Westfield, 2000), 25–40.

52. See Kreidler, "Karl Adam und Nationalsozialismus," 138.

53. Karl Adam, "Jesus, der Christus und Wir Deutsche," Parts 1 and 2, *Wissenschaft und Weisheit* 10 (1943): 73–103, here 91. See Hans Küng, *Judaism: Between Yesterday and Tomorrow*, trans. John Bowden (New York: Continuum, 1996), 678 n. 29.

54. Karl Adam, "Jesus, der Christus und Wir Deutsche," Part 3, *Wissenschaft und Weisheit* 11 (1944): 10–23, here 21.

55. See Kathleen Cahalan, *Formed in the Image of Christ: The Sacramental-Moral Theology of Bernard Häring* (Collegeville, Minn.: Liturgical Press, 2004).

56. See *Rheinische Reformkreis*, ed. Wolf and Arnold, 114–19.

57. Karl Adam, "Das Problem der Entmythologisierung und die Auferstehung des Christus," ThQ 132 (1952): 385–410.

58. Karl Adam's contributions to theology have been highlighted by Heinrich Fries, *Wegbereiter und Wege* (Olten-Freiburg: Walter, 1968), 25–37; Bernard Häring, "In Memory of Karl Adam," *Ave Maria* 103 (June 11, 1966): 6; Karl Rahner, "Theologie in der Welt," *Frankfurter Allgemeine Zeitung* 256 (October 20, 1956): 10.

59. Donald Dietrich has made a general observation that applies to Karl Adam: "With both conservatives and Nazi radicals using the same terms, the ultimate effect was an inability to clarify the political values upon which the state was thought to rest" ("Catholic Theologians in Hitler's Third Reich: Adaptation and Critique," *Journal of Church and State* 29 [1987]: 21).

60. Klaus Schatz, *Zwischen Säkularisation und Zweitem Vatikanum* (Frankfurt am Main: Knecht, 1986), 218.

61. Kreidler, "Karl Adam und Nationalsozialismus," 138.

62. Schoof, *Survey of Catholic Theology*, 88. Schoof adds: "Even a man who was as little concerned with politics as Karl Adam, following his

predecessors at Tübingen and influenced, as they were, by Romanticism, believed that the 'spirit of the people' was a pillar of the church and hoped, together with many others, that the Nazis would be able to exert a healthy influence." Calling attention to Romanticism's dark side, Victor Klemperer noted that "National Socialism adapts Fascism, Bolshevism, Americanism, [and] works it all into Teutonic Romanticism" (*I Will Bear Witness 1942–1945*, trans. Martin Klemperer [New York: Random House, 1999], 124).

5. Romano Guardini: Respecting the Human Person

1. On Guardini's life and thought, see Romano Guardini, *Berichte über mein Leben* (Düsseldorf: Patmos, 1984); Josef Kreiml, *Die Selbstoffenbarung Gottes in Jesus Christus* (Regensburg: S. Roderer, 2001); Alfons Knoll, *Glaube und Kultur bei Romano Guardini* (Paderborn: Ferdinand Schöningh, 1993); Arno Schilson, *Perspektiven theologischer Erneuerung: Studien zum Werk Romano Guardinis* (Düsseldorf: Patmos, 1986); Hanna-Barbara Gerl, *Romano Guardini 1885–1968* (Mainz: Matthias Grünewald, 1985). This chapter also draws on Robert A. Krieg, "Romano Guardini's Theology of the Human Person," ThS 59 (1998): 457–74; idem, *Romano Guardini: A Precursor of Vatican II* (Notre Dame, Ind.: University of Notre Dame Press, 1997).

2. See Guardini, *Berichte über mein Leben*, 72–73, 90–93.

3. Romano Guardini, *Die Lehre des heiligen Bonaventura von der Erlösung* (Düsseldorf: Schwann, 1921).

4. Romano Guardini, *Gegensatz und Gegensätze* (Freiburg: Caritas, 1914).

5. Romano Guardini, *Systembildende Elemente in der Theologie Bonaventuras* (Leiden: Brill, 1964).

6. See *Adolf Kardinal Bertram*, ed. Bernhard Stasiewski (Cologne: Böhlau, 1992).

7. Michael Phayer, *The Catholic Church and the Holocaust, 1930-1965* (Bloomington, Ind.: Indiana University Press, 2000), 10–11.

8. The University of Breslau saw a turnover of only approximately 22 percent of its faculty from 1933 to 1945 because of retirements and interventions by the Reich's minister of education. This change was a smaller percentage than at most other German universities. See Uwe Dietrich Adam, *Hochschule und Nationalsozialismus* (Tübingen: J. C. B. Mohr [Paul Siebeck], 1977), 39.

9. See Erich Kleineidam, *Die katholisch-theologische Fakultät der Universität Breslau 1811–1945* (Cologne: Wienand, 1961).

10. Josef Wittig, "Die Erlösten," *Hochland* 19 part 2 (1922): 1–24; idem, *Leben Jesu in Palästina* (Munich: Kempten, 1925, 1927). See Otto Weiss, *Der Modernismus in Deutschland* (Regensburg: Friedrich Pustet, 1995), 514–26.

11. See Hubert Jedin, *Lebensbericht* (Mainz: Matthias Grünewald, 1984); John W. O'Malley, *Trent and All That* (Cambridge, Mass.: Harvard University Press, 2000), 46–60. Jedin edited the multivolume *Handbook of Church History* (New York: Herder & Herder, 1962–79).

12. See Antonia Leugers, *Gegen eine Mauer bischöflichen Schweigens* (Frankfurt am Main: Josef Knecht, 1996); Manfred Weitlauff, "Preysing, Konrad Graf von," in *Biographisch-Bibliographisches Kirchenlexikon,* ed. F. W. Bautz, vol. 7 (Herzberg: Traugott Bautz, 1994), 941–48; Ludwig Volk, "Konrad Kardinal von Preysing (1880–1950)," in *Zeitgeschichte in Lebensbildern,* vol. 2, ed. R. Morsey (Mainz: Matthias Grünewald, 1975), 88–100.

13. See Phayer, *Catholic Church and the Holocaust, 1930–1965,* 44–48, 79–81.

14. See Michael Phayer, *Protestant and Catholic Women in Nazi Germany* (Detroit: Wayne State University Press, 1990).

15. See Ernst Christian Helmreich, *The German Churches under Hitler* (Detroit: Wayne State University Press, 1979), 133–56.

16. See Romano Guardini, *Der Heilbringer in Mythos, Offenbarung und Politik* (Stuttgart: Deutsche Verlagsanstalt, 1946); reprinted in idem, *Unterscheidung des Christlichen,* 2nd ed. (Mainz: Matthias Grünewald, 1963), 411–58.

17. Guardini, *Berichte über mein Leben,* 41.

18. See Klaus P. Fischer, *Nazi Germany* (New York: Continuum, 1995), 130, 343. *"Das Heil"* can mean something natural such as health, or it can mean something from God such as blessings. Hence, "der *Heilbringer"* can refer to any human being who brings about something beneficial for people, or it can designate Jesus Christ. These two distinct meanings of "das *Heil"* are evident in Richard Wagner's *Die Meistersinger von Nürnberg* (1862–67). The opera opens with the church choir singing: "Da zu dir der Heiland [Jesus Christ] kam, . . . gab er uns des Heils Gebot." That is: "When the savior [Jesus Christ] came to you, . . . he gave us the message of salvation." However, the opera ends with the townsfolk applying "*Heil"* not to Jesus Christ but to the opera's hero; they sing: "Heil Hans Sachs!," meaning "Health to Hans Sachs" and "Health to all people through Hans Sachs." In other words, Hans Sachs is a "Heiland," or bearer of grace, though not in the same way that Jesus Christ is the "Heiland."

19. Romano Guardini, "Der Heiland," in idem, *Unterscheidung des Christlichen* (Mainz: Matthias Grünewald, 1935), 362–88. See also Knoll, *Glaube und Kultur bei Romano Guardini*, 382–87.

20. The moral theologian Gustav Gundlach voiced a similar concern about Germany in the 1930s. See Donald J. Dietrich, "Catholic Theologians in Hitler's Third Reich," *Journal of Church and State* 29 (1987): 19–45, here 40; Johannes Schwarte, *Gustav Gundlach S.J. (1892–1963)* (Munich: Ferdinand Schöningh, 1975).

21. See Gerl, *Romano Guardini*, 317.

22. See Heinz Hürten, *Deutsche Katholiken 1918–1945* (Paderborn: Ferdinand Schöningh, 1992), 455–56; Heinz Robert Schlette, "Romano Guardini—Versuch einer Würdigung" (1969), in idem, *Aporie und Glaube* (Munich: Kösel, 1970), 247–87, 263–66.

23. See Eugene O'Sullivan, *In His Presence: A Book on Liturgy and Prayer* (Wilmington, Del.: Michael Glazier, 1980); Karl Frölich, "Das Volksliturgie Apostolat von St. Paul in München," in *Das Erzbistum München und Freising in der Zeit der nationalsozialistischen Herrschaft*, vol. 1, ed. Georg Schwaiger (Munich: Schnell & Steiner, 1984), 122–30. That the religious and political orientation, which Guardini inspired, strengthened opposition to Hitler is evident in the life of Hans A. Reinhold (d. 1968); see Jay P. Corrin, *Catholic Intellectuals and the Challenge of Democracy* (Notre Dame, Ind.: University of Notre Dame Press, 2002), 238–73.

24. Walter Ferber, "Romano Guardini (1885–1968)," in *Zeitgeschichte in Lebensbildern*, vol. 1, ed. Rudolf Morsey (Mainz: Matthias Grünewald, 1973), 293.

25. Guardini, *Berichte über mein Leben*, 52.

26. Ibid., 54.

27. See Douglas Auchincloss, "Romano Guardini and the New Age," *Catholic Digest* 25 (November 1960): 35–40.

28. See *Begegnungen in Mooshausen*, ed. Hanna-Barbara Gerl et al. (Weissenhorn: Anton H. Konrad, 1990). Regarding life in Berlin for Guardini and those associated with him, see Heinz R. Kuehn, *Mixed Blessings: An Almost Ordinary Life in Hitler's Germany* (Athens, Ga.: University of Georgia Press, 1989).

29. While chapters 2, 3, and 4 of *Der Heilbringer* repeat "Der Heiland," chapters 1, 5, 6, and 7 are new, making explicit what was implicit in Guardini's article of 1935.

30. Guardini, *Heilbringer*, 79. Guardini elaborated on this idea in his address upon receiving the Erasmus Prize (April 28, 1962); see R. Guardini, "Europa: Wirklichkeit und Aufgabe," in idem, *Sorge um den Menschen*, vol. 1 (Würzburg: Werkbund, 1962), 238–53.

31. See Romano Guardini, "Warum so viele Bücher?" (1955), in idem, *Stationen und Rückblicke* (Würzburg: Echter, 1965), 30.

32. Commenting on Guardini's political outlook, Felix Messerschmid has noted, "The personal and spiritual strengths and the political weaknesses of the conservative position have become clear in an impressive manner in the figure of Romano Guardini. Conservative thought necessarily leads to solitude. When it expresses itself politically, it easily becomes conservativist or even reactionary. In the last years of his life, this experience came to Guardini in full consciousness; in his writings, however, it is not very evident" (see F. Messerschmid, "Vorwort zu den Guardini-Aufsätzen," *Geschichte in Wissenschaft und Unterricht* 21 [1970]: 709–10). Also see Ulrich Bröckling, *Katholische Intellektuelle in der Weimarer Republik* (Munich: Wilhelm Funk, 1993), 44–55.

33. On April 18, 1948, in Paris, Guardini gave a public lecture on peace to the "Semaine des Intellectuels catholiques francais"; see R. Guardini, *A la Recherche de la Paix* (Strasbourg: Éditions F.-X. Le Roux & Cie, 1948). One year later, he published "Introduction à Jean-Pierre de Caussade," trans. Claire C. Lossey, *Dieu Vivant* 13 (1949): 83–96. For the German text, see R. Guardini, "Einführung," in *Jean Pierre de Caussade,* ed. Wolfgang Rüttenauer (Freiburg: Herder, 1940), 1–20.

34. Karl Rahner, "Thinker and Christian, Obituary of Romano Guardini," in idem, *Opportunities for Faith,* trans. Edward Quinn (New York: Seabury, 1975), 127–31. Referring to Guardini, Roger Aubert has observed: "In all of his works there is a concern to describe the situation of human beings before God not from a static but from an existential and dramatic viewpoint and to remember unceasingly that God is not only an omnipotent 'he' but also a living 'you'" ("Theologie während der ersten Hälfte des 20. Jahrhunderts," in *Bilanz der Theologie im 20. Jahrhundert,* vol. 2, ed. Herbert Vorgrimler and Robert Vander Gucht [Freiburg: Herder, 1969], 24).

35. On Guardini's theological anthropology, see Knoll, *Glaube und Kultur bei Romano Guardini,* 338-73; Gunda Böning, "Strukturen der Freiheit," in *Konservativ mit Blick nach vorn,* ed. Arno Schilson (Würzburg: Echter, 1994), 49–68; Schilson, *Perspektiven theologischer Erneuerung,* 158–96; Jörg Splett, "Zum Person-Begriff Romano Guardinis," in *"Christliche Weltanschauung,"* ed. Walter Seidel (Würzburg: Echter, 1985), 80–109; Schlette, "Romano Guardini"; Ursula Berning-Baldeaux, *Person und Bildung im Denken Romano Guardinis* (Würzburg: Echter, 1968); Helmut Kuhn, "Romano Guardini: Christian Existence," *Philosophy Today* 4 (1960): 158–71.

36. Romano Guardini, *Welt und Person* (Würzburg: Werkbund, 1939), 2; idem, *The World and the Person,* trans. Stella Lang (Chicago: Henry

Regnery, 1965), viii. The translation from the German text is my own. In subsequent notes, the citation from the English edition is in parentheses.

37. Ibid., 105 (128). The German language distinguishes between the formal "you," *Sie,* and the personal or intimate "you," *Du.* A person uses *Du* when addressing family and close friends. Guardini with Buber maintained that personal existence requires *Du* relationships with a few other people and also with God.

38. Ibid., 109 (135).

39. Ibid., 113–14 (141).

40. Ibid., 93 (114).

41. Romano Guardini, *Verantwortung: Gedanken zur Jüdischen Frage* (Munich: Kösel, 1952), 17. The essay under this title also appeared in *Hochland* 44 (1952): 481–93.

42. Guardini, "Verantwortung," 21.

43. See Robert Krieg, "Martin Buber and Romano Guardini," in *Humanity at the Limits,* ed. Michael A. Signer (Bloomington, Ind.: Indiana University Press, 2000), 138–47.

44. Rainer Maria Rilke, "First Elegie," verses 9, 13–15, in idem, *Duino Elegies and the Sonnets to Orpheus,* trans. A. Poulin, Jr. (Boston: Houghton Mifflin, 1977), 4–11.

45. Romano Guardini, *Rainer Maria Rilkes Deutung des Daseins* (Mainz: Grünewald, 1996), 374–75; idem, *Rilke's Duino Elegies,* trans. K. G. Knight (Chicago: Henry Regnery, 1961), 305.

46. Romano Guardini, *Das Ende der Neuzeit* (Mainz: Matthias Grünewald, 1989), 55; English, *The End of the Modern World,* trans. J. Theman and H. Burke (New York: Sheed & Ward, 1956), 81. The translation from the German text is my own; in subsequent notes, the citation from the English edition is in parentheses.

47. Ibid., 56–57 (82–83).

48. The Scholls were put to death by the Reich on February 22, 1943. Along with the six martyrs, ten other members of the White Rose were arrested and imprisoned. See Annette Dumbach and Jud Newborn, *Shattering the German Night* (Boston: Little, Brown, 1986); Hermann Vinke, *The Short Life of Sophie Scholl,* trans. Hedwig Pachter (New York: Harper & Row, 1984).

49. Romano Guardini, *Die Waage des Daseins* (Tübingen: Rainer Wunderlich, 1946), 18; reprinted in *Deutsche Stimmen 1945–1946,* ed. Carl Georg Heise et al. (Hamburg: Maximilian-Gesellschaft, 1948).

50. Ibid., 26–27.

51. Romano Guardini, "Burg Rothenfels: Rückblick und Vorschau" (1949), in *Angefochtene Zuversicht,* ed. Ingeborg Klimmer (Mainz:

Matthias Grünewald, 1985), 224–30, here 225; see Gerl, *Romano Guardini,* 199–202.

52. Romano Guardini, "Zum Problem der Demokratie" (1946), *Geschichte in Wissenschaft und Unterricht* 21 (1970): 711–16, here 712.

53. Romano Guardini, *Letters from Lake Como,* trans. Geoffrey W. Bromiley (Grand Rapids: William B. Eerdmans, 1994), 84.

54. Guardini, *Berichte über mein Leben,* 86.

55. Guardini, "'Europa,'" 20–21.

56. Romano Guardini, "Wahrheit und Ironie," in idem, *Stationen und Rückblicke,* 43.

57. Guardini, *Ende der Neuzeit,* 84–85.

58. Entry for September 6, 1953, in Guardini's diary; see Romano Guardini, *Wahrheit des Denkens und Wahrheit des Tuns* (Paderborn: Ferdinand Schöningh, 1980), 56. On Guardini's understanding of democracy, see Michele Nicoletti, "La democrazia e i suoi presuppositi in Romano Guardini," *Communio* (1993): 109–22.

59. See Guardini's diary entry for January 12, 1964, in Guardini, *Wahrheit des Denkens und Wahrheit des Tuns,* 132–33.

60. The Protestant theologian Wolfhart Pannenberg has observed that the attraction to Hitler's National Socialism was not "the logical outcome of the history of modern [liberal] Protestantism." On the contrary, Protestants joined Hitler's "German Christian" movement because it was "another form of revolt against modernity." Indeed, it was "a romantic reaction to modernity, and that was also its affinity with the Nazis." See W. Pannenberg, "The Christian West?" in *First Things* 7 (November 1990): 24–31. Pannenberg's assessment is corroborated by Gordon Craig, *The Germans* (New York: Meridian/Penguin, 1991), 290; Peter Gay, *Weimar Culture* (New York: Harper & Row, 1968), 96. On the appeal of Hitler's movement to Catholics who had rejected modernity, see Rainer Bucher, *Kirchenbildung in der Moderne* (Stuttgart: W. Kohlhammer, 1998); idem, "Das deutsche Volk Gottes," in *Das Volk Gottes—ein Ort der Befreiung,* ed. Hildegund Keul and Hans Joachim Sander (Würzburg: Echter, 1998), 64–82.

6. Engelbert Krebs: Witnessing to God's Kingdom

1. See Rüdiger Safranski, *Martin Heidegger: Between Good and Evil,* trans. Ewald Osers (Cambridge, Mass.: Harvard University Press, 1998); Hugo Ott, *Martin Heidegger: A Political Life,* trans. Allan Blunden (New York: Basic Books, 1993).

2. See Martin Heidegger, *Introduction to Metaphysics,* trans. Gregory

Fried and Richard Polt (New Haven: Yale University Press, 2000), 48, 213.

3. On the life and thought of Engelbert Krebs, see Claus Arnold, *Katholizismus als Kulturmacht: Der Freiburger Theologe Joseph Sauer (1872-1949) und das Erbe des Franz Xaver Kraus* (Paderborn: Ferdinand Schöningh, 1999), passim; Peter Walter, "Die deutschsprachige Dogmatik zwischen den beiden Vatikanischen Konzilien untersucht am Beispiel der Ekklesiologie," in *Die katholisch-theologische Disziplinen in Deutschland 1870– 1962,* ed. Hubert Wolf with Claus Arnold (Paderborn: Ferdinand Schöningh, 1999), 144–52; Thomas F. O'Meara, "The Witness of Engelbert Krebs," in *Continuity and Plurality in Catholic Theology,* ed. Anthony J. Cernera (Fairfield, Conn.: Sacred Heart University Press, 1998), 127–53; Thomas Ruster, *Die verlorene Nützlichkeit der Religion: Katholizismus und Moderne in der Weimarer Republik* (Paderborn: Ferdinand Schöningh, 1994), 312–19; Erich Naab, "Krebs, E.," in *Biographisch-Bibliographisches Kirchenlexikon,* ed. F. W. Bautz, vol. 4 (Herzberg: Traugott Bautz, 1994), 632–33; Albert Junghanns, *Der Freiburger Dogmatiker Engelbert Krebs (1881–1950)* (Ph.D. dissertation, Freiburg im Breisgau, 1980). This chapter also draws on Robert A. Krieg, "The Conflict Between Engelbert Krebs and the Third Reich," in *Christian Responses to the Holocaust,* ed. Donald J. Dietrich (Syracuse: Syracuse University Press, 2003), 24–37.

4. See Rudolf Morsey, "Georg Hertling," LThK 3rd ed., 5 (1996): 46–47; Thomas F. O'Meara, O.P., *Church and Culture: German Catholic Theology, 1860-1914* (Notre Dame, Ind.: University of Notre Dame Press, 1991), 155–60; Ernst Deuerlein, "Hertling," in *Neue Deutsche Biographie,* vol. 8 (Berlin: Duncker & Humblot, 1969), 702–4.

5. Engelbert Krebs, *Meister Dietrich: Sein Leben, seine Werke, seine Wissenschaft* (Münster, 1906).

6. Thomas O'Meara has located Krebs's life and work in the heritage of Joseph Görres; see O'Meara, "Witness of Engelbert Krebs," 128–30. On Görres, see Bernd Wacker, "Johann Joseph von Görres," in LThK 3rd ed., 4 (1995): 841–42; Georg Schwaiger, "Görres, Joseph von," in *Theologische Realenzyklopädie,* ed. Gerhard Krause and Gerhard Müller (Berlin/New York: Walter de Gruyter, 1977–), 13:550–52; Thomas F. O'Meara, O.P., *Romantic Idealism and Roman Catholicism* (Notre Dame, Ind.: University of Notre Dame Press, 1982), 126–33.

7. Engelbert Krebs, *Der Logos als Heiland im 1. Jahrhundert* (Freiburg, 1910).

8. Engelbert Krebs, *Theologie und Wissenschaft nach der Lehre des Hochscholastik anhand der bisher ungedruckten Defensio doctrinae Thomas des Hervaeus Natalis, O.P.* (Münster, 1912).

9. Krebs was offered the chair in pastoral theology held by Cornelius Krieg (d. 1911) but turned it down because he wanted to teach dogmatic theology.

10. Engelbert Krebs, ed., *Tage des Ernstes: Auswahl aus Hirschers Fastenbetrachtungen* (Kempten, 1912, 1923); idem, "Hirscher und die Wiedergebuhrt des katholischen Lebens in Deutschland," *Freiburger Diözesan-Archiv* 41 (1913): 170–86. See Hermann J. Pottmeyer, "Kingdom of God–Church–Society: The Contemporary Relevance of Johann Baptist Hirscher, Theologian of Reform," in *The Legacy of the Tübingen School*, ed. Donald J. Dietrich and Michael J. Himes (New York: Crossroad, 1997), 144–55.

11. Engelbert Krebs, "Die Wertprobleme und ihre Behandlung in der katholischen Dogmatik," *Oberrheinische Pastoralblatt* 19 (1917): 215–25, 247–55.

12. Engelbert Krebs, "Cardinal Merciers offentliches Wirken," *Hochland* 15 (1917–18): 188–205, 332–48.

13. Engelbert Krebs, "Vom Priestertum der Frau," *Hochland* 19 (1922): 196–215; idem, "Frauenleben und Frauenfragen in Fernasien," *Die christliche Frau* 26 (1928): 169–77; idem, "Lebensfragen der katholischen Akademikerin," *Stimmen der Zeit* 117 (1929): 100–110.

14. Engelbert Krebs, *Das Kennzeichen seiner Jünger* (Freiburg: Herder, 1921, 1923); idem, *A Little Book on Christian Charity*, trans. Isabel Garahan (St. Louis, Mo.: B. Herder, 1927).

15. Engelbert Krebs, *Die Protestanten und wir: Einigendes und Trennendes* (Munich, 1922). For Krebs's writings on Judaism, see notes below.

16. Engelbert Krebs, "Joseph Wittigs Weg aus der kirchlichen Gemeinschaft," *Der Katholische Gedanke* 1 (1928): 237–88; idem, "Eine Selbstkritik Joseph Wittigs," *Literarische Handweiser* 64 (1928): 257–66.

17. See O'Meara, "Witness of Engelbert Krebs," 135–40; Safranski, *Martin Heidegger: Between Good and Evil*, 43, 46, 64; Ott, *Martin Heidegger: A Political Life*, passim.

18. Engelbert Krebs, *Dogma und Leben*, vol. 1 (Paderborn: Bonifacius, 1920), 11–12.

19. Karl Eschweiler, *Die zwei Wege der neueren Theologie* (Augsburg: Benno Filser, 1926), 10.

20. Engelbert Krebs, *Dogma und Leben*, vol. 2 (Paderborn: Bonifacius, 1925), 25.

21. Thomas O'Meara has noted an ambiguity in Krebs's thought on the universality of grace; see O'Meara, "Witness of Engelbert Krebs," 149 n. 18.

22. See Pottmeyer, "Kingdom of God–Church–Society," 151–53. On the origins of this view of the church, see Johannes Brosseder, "Möhler's

Romantic Idea of the Church: Its Problem in the Present," *Philosophy and Theology* 3 (1988–89): 161–71; idem, "Romantisches Ekklesiologie-konzept und dessen Problematik im gegenwärtigen ökumenischen Gespräch," in *Biotope der Hoffnung: Zu Christentum und Kirche heute*, ed. Nikolaus Klein, Heinz Robert Schlette, and Karl Weber (Olten: Walter, 1988), 78–89.

23. Krebs, *Dogma und Leben*, 2:701.

24. See Winfried Becker, "Neueste Zeit (1803/6 - 1995)," in *Die Kirchen in der Deutschen Geschichte*, ed. Winfried Becker et al. (Stuttgart: Alfred Kröner, 1996), 559; Peter Gay, *Weimar Culture* (New York: Harper & Row, 1968), 140.

25. Engelbert Krebs, "Katholische Studenten und Juden," *Badische Beobachter* (May 26, 1922).

26. Engelbert Krebs, "The Primitive Church and Judaism," *Thought* 1 (March 1927): 658–75.

27. Engelbert Krebs, "Judentum und Christentum," in LThK 1st ed., vol. 5 (1933): 678–79.

28. See Hugo Ott, "Conrad Gröber (1872–1948)," in *Zeitgeschichte in Lebensbildern*, vol. 6, ed. Jürgen Aretz, Rudolf Morsey, Anton Rauscher (Mainz: Matthias Grünewald, 1984), 64–75.

29. In the mid-1930s, Gröber was known as the "brown [Nazi] bishop"; see Gordon Zahn, *German Catholics and Hitler's Wars* (New York: Sheed & Ward, 1962), 119–42.

30. See Remigius Bäumer, "Die theologische Fakultät Freiburg und das Dritte Reich," *Freiburger Diözesan-Archiv* 103 (1983): 265–89; idem, "Die AKD im Erzbistum Freiburg," *Freiburger Diözesan-Archiv* 104 (1984): 281–313.

31. Quoted in Ott, "Conrad Gröber," 73.

32. On Gertrud Luckner, see Michael Phayer, *Protestant and Catholic Women in Nazi Germany* (Detroit: Wayne State University Press, 1990). The Archdiocese of Freiburg was home to Constantin Noppel, S.J., who was dismissed as the rector of Rome's Germanicum in 1936 because he publicly criticized Hitler's regime; see Thomas O'Meara, "Constantin Noppel, S.J." (unpublished manuscript).

33. Zahn, *German Catholics and Hitler's Wars*, 136.

34. See Bäumer, "Theologische Fakultät Freiburg und das Dritte Reich."

35. Ludwig Andreas Veit, *Kirche im Zeitalter des Individualismus*, 2 vols. (Freiburg: Herder, 1931, 1933). See Hubert Wolf, "Der Historiker ist kein Prophet," in *Die katholisch-theologischen Disziplinen in Deutschland 1870–1962*, ed. Hubert Wolf with Claus Arnold (Paderborn: Ferdinand Schöningh, 1999), 89–92.

36. In the summer of 1935, Martin Heidegger sharply criticized

Theodor Haecker's book *Was ist der Mensch?* (1933) because of its critique of National Socialism; see Heidegger, *Introduction to Metaphysics,* 151–52.

37. Quoted in Junghanns, *Freiburger Dogmatiker,* 129.

38. Engelbert Krebs, "Die Aufgabe der Universität im neuen Reich," *Freiburger Tagespost* 173 (1933).

39. Engelbert Krebs, *Vom Wesen der Authorität im Lichte des christlichen Glaubens* (Freiburg: Herder, 1933).

40. Engelbert Krebs, "Gedanken zum Reichskonkordat," *Freiburger Tagespost* 173 (July 22, 1933).

41. See Ruster, *Verlorene Nützlichkeit der Religion,* 312–13; Helmut Heiber, *Universitäten unterm Hakenkreuz,* Part 1 (Munich: K. G. Saur, 1991), 280–81.

42. Engelbert Krebs, *Jesuitischer und deutscher Geist* (Freiburg: Waibel, 1934).

43. Quoted in Bäumer, "Theologische Fakultät Freiburg und das Dritte Reich," 279.

44. Engelbert Krebs, "Arteigenes Christentum," *Stimmen der Zeit* 129 (1935): 81–93.

45. Engelbert Krebs, "Möhlers Athanasius," *Hochland* 32, Part 2 (1934–1935): 385–98.

46. In 1921 Krebs gave a public lecture on the social values that Catholicism and socialism hold in common; see Engelbert Krebs, "Christentum und Sozialismus," *St. Blasier Zeitung* 106 (1921).

47. See Bäumer, "Theologische Fakultät Freiburg und das Dritte Reich," 280.

48. See Junghanns, *Freiburger Dogmatiker,* 179–92.

49. Engelbert Krebs, "Dogma und Sterben," *Oberrheinische Pastoralblatt* 52 (1951): 88–98, 113–18.

50. Pius XII issued his encyclical *Mediator Dei* (November 20, 1947). See Karl Rahner, *Theologische und philosophische Zeitfragen im katholischen deutschen Raum* (1943), ed. Hubert Wolf (Ostfildern: Schwabenverlag, 1994); Herbert Vorgrimler, *Karl Rahner: His Life, Thought and Works,* trans. Edward Quinn (Glen Rock, N.J.: Paulist Press, 1966), 32–40; Junghanns, *Freiburger Dogmatiker,* 197–210.

51. See Junghanns, *Freiburger Dogmatiker,* 211–14; Bäumer, "Theologische Fakultät Freiburg und das Dritte Reich," 280–81. According to Bäumer, in 1944 the rector of the University of Freiburg submitted to Bernhard Rust a formal complaint against the editor of *Theologische Revue* because in 1943 the journal wrongly listed Engelbert Krebs as still a professor at the University of Freiburg when it published a book review by Krebs.

52. Romano Guardini, *Berichte über mein Leben* (Düsseldorf: Patmos, 1984), 26.

53. See Junghanns, *Freiburger Dogmatiker,* 215–44.

54. See Engelbert Krebs, *Die Kirche und das neue Europe* (Freiburg: Herder, 1924), 29–68.

55. As Peter Walter has noted, Krebs stressed in 1925 the compatibility between the Catholicism and parliamentary democracy. In doing so, Krebs implicitly voiced his support for the Weimar Constitution during the constitution controversy (Walter, "Die deutschsprachige Dogmatik," 146–47; Krebs, *Dogma und Leben,* 2:534–37).

56. See O'Meara, "Witness of Engelbert Krebs," 147. Thomas O'Meara's assessment coincides with an observation that Hermann Pottmeyer made concerning the work of J. B. Hirscher. According to Pottmeyer, the dominant ecclesiology of the Second Vatican Council was anticipated by the theologians of the 1800s and early 1900s who, distinguishing between the church and the kingdom of God, presented the church's mission in relation to the coming of God's reign ("Kingdom of God–Church–Society," 151–53).

7. Catholic Theology in Nazi Germany

1. Konrad Adenauer's letter of February 23, 1946, to Pastor Dr. Bernhard Custodis in Bonn is printed in Georg Denzler and Fabricius Volker, *Christen und Nationalsozialisten* (Frankfurt am Main: Fischer Taschenbuch, 1993), 349–50.

2. See *Catholic Jewish Relations* (London: Catholic Truth Society, 1999); John Paul II, *Spiritual Pilgrimage: Texts on Jews and Judaism, 1979–1995,* ed. Eugene Fisher and Leon Klenicki (New York: Crossroad, 1995). For the German bishops' statement of January 23, 1995, see *Catholics Remember the Holocaust,* ed. Eugene Fisher (Washington, D.C.: United States Catholic Conference, 1998).

3. See Avery Dulles, *Models of the Church,* rev. ed. (Garden City, N.Y.: Doubleday, 1987); Michael A. Fahey, "Church," in *Systematic Theology,* ed. Francis Schüssler Fiorenza and John P. Galvin, vol. 2 (Minneapolis: Fortress Press, 1991), 1–74.

4. See Paul Misner, *Social Catholicism in Europe* (New York: Crossroad, 1991); Dulles, *Models of the Church,* 89–102.

5. Kurt Meier, "Deutschland und Österreich," in *Erster und Zweiter Krieg: Demokratien und Totalitäre Systeme* (1914–1958), ed. Jean-Marie Mayeur and Kurt Meier (Freiburg: Herder, 1992), 697, 699.

6. See John S. Conway, *The Nazi Persecution of the Churches 1933–45*

(London: Weidenfeld & Nicolson, 1968), 92; Ernst Christian Helmreich, *The German Churches under Hitler* (Detroit: Wayne State University Press, 1979), 264–70.

7. See Jean-Marie Mayeur, "Drei Päpste: Benedikt XV., Pius XI., Pius XII.," trans. Dorothee Becker, in *Erster und Zweiter Krieg*, ed. Mayeur and Meier, 1– 40.

8. See Klaus Schatz, *Zwischen Säkularisation und Zweitem Vatikanum* (Frankfurt am Main: Knecht, 1986), 261–68.

9. See Georges Passelecq and Bernard Suchecky, *The Hidden Encyclical*, trans. Steven Rendall (New York: Harcourt Brace and Company, 1997).

10. See Charles R. Gallagher, "'Personal Private Views,'" *America* 189 (September 1, 2003): 8–10.

11. Martin Conway, *Catholic Politics in Europe, 1918–1945* (London: Routledge, 1997), 80.

12. Schatz, *Zwischen Säkularisation und Zweitem Vatikanum*, 274–75; Meier, "Deutschland und Österreich," 699.

13. Klaus Schatz, *Kirchengeschichte der Neuzeit II* (Düsseldorf: Patmos, 1989), 145.

14. Schatz, *Zwischen Säkularisation und Zweitem Vatikanum*, 279.

15. Donald J. Dietrich, "Catholic Theologians in Hitler's Third Reich: Adaptation and Critique," *Journal of Church and State* 29 (1987): 19–20.

16. See Konrad Repgen, "Foreign Policy of the Popes in the Epoch of the World Wars," in *History of the Church*, vol. 10, ed. Hubert Jedin et al., trans. Anselm Biggs (New York: Crossroad, 1981), 35–95, here 70.

17. Victor Conzemius, "[Germany] Since 1789," NCE 6:447.

18. Winfried Becker, "Neueste Zeit (1803/6 - 1995)," in *Die Kirchen in der Deutschen Geschichte*, ed. Winfried Becker et al. (Stuttgart: Alfred Kröner, 1996), 512.

19. Schatz, *Zwischen Säkularisation und Zweitem Vatikanum*, 263–67.

20. Meier, "Deutschland und Österreich," 704.

21. Schatz, *Zwischen Säkularisation und Zweitem Vatikanum*, 286.

22. Quoted in Schatz, *Zwischen Säkularisation und Zweitem Vatikanum*, 240. As Donald Dietrich has noted, "With both conservative Catholics and Nazi radicals using the same terms, the ultimate effect was an inability to clarify the political values upon which the state was thought to rest." See Dietrich, "Catholic Theologians in Hitler's Third Reich," 21. Ernst Wolfgang Böckenförde has argued that an "affinity" existed between the authoritarianism of the Third Reich and the authoritarian attitude of the Catholic Church; see E. W. Böckenförde, "Der deutsche Katholizismus I, Jahre 1933," *Hochland* 53 (1961): 215–39; reprinted, along with critical essays, in idem, *Der deutsche Katholizismus im Jahre*

1933 (Freiburg: Herder, 1988). For the English text, see *Cross Currents* 11 (1961): 283–304.

23. Guenther Lewy has noted that "[i]n the failure to recognize the totalitarian goals of Hitler's state, which was regarded by the Church, as by many other Germans, as just another anti-Communist authoritarian regime that had its good as well as its bad sides, lay the basic error and tragedy of the leadership of German Catholicism" (*The Catholic Church and Hitler's Wars* [New York: McGraw Hill, 1964], 53).

24. Konrad Repgen, "German Catholicism and the Jews: 1933–1945," in *Judaism and Christianity under the Impact of National Socialism,* ed. Otto Dov Kulka and Paul R. Mendes-Flohr (Jerusalem: Historical Society of Israel and Zaman Shazar Center for Jewish History, 1987), 197–226, here 223. Gorden Craig has made a similar point: "In the Catholic church the argument that the important thing was to maintain the 'internal cohesion' of the church (a legacy from the Kulturkampf) was used to discourage political activism" (*The Germans* [New York: Meridian/ Penguin Books, 1982], 97).

25. Quoted in *Judaism and Christianity under the Impact of National Socialism,* ed. Kulka and Mendes-Flohr, 279. On Alfred Delp, see Mary Frances Coady, *With Bound Hands* (Baltimore: Loyola Press, 2004).

26. Conzemius, "[Germany] Since 1789," 447.

27. Schatz, *Kirchengeschichte der Neuzeit II,* 143.

28. Meier, "Deutschland und Österreich," 697.

29. John Jay Hughes, "The Pope's 'Pact With Hitler'": Betrayal or Self-Defense?" *Journal of Church and State* 17 (1975): 63–80, here 77–78.

30. M. Conway, *Catholic Politics,* 67.

31. Lewy, *Catholic Church and Nazi Germany,* 326.

32. See Alexander Gross, *Gehorsame Kirche—ungehorsame Christen im Nationalsozialismus* (Mainz: Matthias Grünewald, 2000).

33. See Gerald O'Collins, *Theology of Secularity* (Notre Dame, Ind.: Fides, 1974), 34; M. Conway, *Catholic Politics,* 48.

34. M. Conway, *Catholic Politics,* 74. See Enda McDonagh, "The Church in the Modern World (*Gaudium et Spes*)," in *Modern Catholicism: Vatican II and After,* ed. Adrian Hastings (New York: Oxford University Press, 1991), 96–112.

35. See M. Conway, *Catholic Politics,* 6–9.

36. Walter Kasper, *Theology and the Church,* trans. Margaret Kohl (New York: Crossroad, 1989), 55.

37. See Rudolf Michael Schmitz, *Aufbruch zum Geheimnis der Kirche Jesu Christi* (St. Ottilien: EOS, 1991); Avery Dulles, "A Half Century of Ecclesiology," ThS 50 (1989): 419–42; Dulles, *Models of the Church,* 47–62; Roger Aubert, "Theologie während der ersten Hälfte des 20. Jahrhun-

derts," in *Bilanz der Theologie im 20. Jahrhundert*, vol. 2, ed. Herbert Vor-grimler and Robert Vander Gucht (Freiburg: Herder, 1969), 30–39; Yves Congar, *Die Lehre von der Kirche von Augustinus bis zur Gegenwart* (Freiburg: Herder, 1970), 119–23.

38. See Karl Adam, *The Spirit of Catholicism*, trans. Dom Justin McCann (New York: Crossroad, 1997); Romano Guardini, *The Church and the Catholic, and The Spirit of the Liturgy*, trans. Ada Lane (New York: Sheed & Ward, 1935); Peter Lippert, *Die Weltanschauung des Katholizismus* (Leipzig: E. Reinicke, 1927); Arnold Rademacher, *Die Kirche als Gemeinschaft und Gesellschaft* (Augsburg: Haas & Grabherr, 1931). On the Romantic understanding of the "organic" character of life, see Thomas F. O'Meara, O.P., *Romantic Idealism and Roman Catholicism* (Notre Dame, Ind.: University of Notre Dame Press, 1982), 1–15; Thomas Ruster, *Die verlorene Nützlichkeit der Religion: Katholizismus und Moderne in der Weimarer Republik* (Paderborn: Ferdinand Schöningh, 1994), 138–44.

39. Alois Baumgartner, *Sehnsucht nach Gemeinschaft* (Paderborn: Ferdinand Schöningh, 1977), 164.

40. Karl Eschweiler, *Johann Adam Möhlers Kirchenbegriff*, 136–37.

41. Karl Eschweiler, "Die Kirche im neuen Reich," *Deutsches Volkstum* 15 (June 1933): 455.

42. Joseph Lortz, *Geschichte der Kirche in ideengeschichtlicher Betrachtung: Eine Sinndeutung der christlichen Vergangenheit* (Münster: Aschendorff, 1932), 4:89. This section of the German text was not included in the English edition.

43. Joseph Lortz, *History of the Church*, trans. Edwin G. Kaiser (Milwaukee: Bruce, 1938), 555.

44. Adam, *Spirit of Catholicism*, 31–32.

45. Karl Adam, "Deutsches Volkstum und katholisches Christentum," ThQ 114 (1933): 56.

46. Romano Guardini, *The Church and the Catholic, and The Spirit of the Liturgy*, trans. Ada Lane (New York: Sheed & Ward, 1935), 23, 19. Guardini worked with more than one model of the church. See Robert A. Krieg, *Romano Guardini: A Precursor of Vatican II* (Notre Dame, Ind.: University of Notre Dame Press, 1997), 46–69; Arno Schilson, *Perspektiven theologischer Erneuerung: Studien zum Werk Romano Guardinis* (Düsseldorf: Patmos, 1986), 199–216.

47. Engelbert Krebs, *Dogma und Leben*, vol. 2 (Paderborn: Bonifacius, 1925), 11. Krebs employed various notions of the church to supplement the model of institution; see Rudolf Michael Schmitz, *Aufbruch zum Geheimnis der Kirche Jesu Christi* (St. Ottilien: EOS, 1991), 187 n. 65.

48. Engelbert Krebs, "Arteigenes Christentum," *Stimmen der Zeit* 129 (1935): 81–93.

49. The period from 1918 to 1943 was a distinct phase in the unfolding of German Catholic theology and contributed to the major transition in Catholic theology after 1945. See Giacoma Martina, "The Historical Context in which the Idea of a New Ecumenical Council was Born," in *Vatican II: Assessment and Perspectives*, ed. René Latourelle, vol. 1 (Mahwah, N.J.: Paulist, 1988), 3–73, here 16; Schmitz, *Aufbruch zum Geheimnis der Kirche Jesu Christi;* Karl Rahner, *Karl Rahner in Dialogue* (New York: Crossroad, 1986), 258; Robert Grosche, *Et Intra et Extra* (Düsseldorf: Patmos, 1958), 7–19.

50. See Erich Przywara, "Corpus Christi mysticum: Eine Bilanz," *Zeitschrift für Aszese und Mystik* 15 (1940): 197–215; idem, "Das Dogma von der Kirche—Ein Aufbau," *Scholastik* 19 (1944): 81–83; Louis Bouyer, "Où en est la théologie du Corps mystique," *Revue des Sciences religieuses* 22 (1948): 313–33; Joseph J. Bluett, "The Mystical Body of Christ, 1890–1940," ThS 3 (1942): 261–89; Grosche, *Et intra et extra*, 219–37.

51. See Karl Rahner, *Theologische und philosophische Zeitfragen im katholischen deutschen Raum* (1943), ed. Hubert Wolf (Ostfildern: Schwabenverlag, 1994), 135–41.

52. See Sebastian Tromp, *Corpus Christi quod est ecclesia*, 4 vols. (Rome: Gregorian University, 1937–72); Emile Mersch, *Le Corps mystique du Christ* (Paris: Desclée De Brouwer, 1933); idem, *La théologie du Corps mystique*, 2 vols. (Paris: Desclée De Brouwer, 1944).

53. See Leo Scheffczyk, "Main Lines of the Development of Theology between the First World War and the Second Vatican Council," in *History of the Church*, vol. 10, ed. Jedin et al., 260–98, here 270; Jerome Hamer, *The Church Is a Communion*, trans. Ronald Matthews (New York: Sheed & Ward, 1968).

54. J. S. Conway, *Nazi Persecution of the Churches 1933-45*, 172. See Eugene O'Sullivan, *In His Presence: A Book on Liturgy and Prayer* (Wilmington, Del.: Michael Glazier, 1980); Karl Frölich, "Das Volksliturgie Apostolat von St. Paul in München," in *Das Erzbistum München und Freising in der Zeit der nationalsozialistischen Herrschaft*, vol. 1, ed. Georg Schwaiger (Munich: Schnell & Steiner, 1984), 122–30.

55. John S. Conway, "Coming to Terms with the Past," *German History* 16 (1998): 337–96, here 386.

56. Romano Guardini, *Berichte über mein Leben* (Düsseldorf: Patmos, 1984), 116, 119.

57. See Kasper, *Theology and Church*, 55, 46; idem, *Theologie und Kirche*, vol. 2 (Mainz: Matthias Grünewald, 1999), 218.

58. Dietrich, "Catholic Theologians in Hitler's Third Reich," 28. See Schatz, *Zwischen Säkularisation und Zweitem Vatikanum*, 238; Alice Gallin, *Midwives to Nazism* (Macon, Ga.: Mercer University Press, 1986), 17.

According to Thomas Mann, the Germans of the 1930s were "a people of the Romantic counter-revolution against the philosophical intellectualism and rationalism of the Enlightenment." See T. Mann, "Deutschland und die Deutschen" (1945), in idem, *Reden und Aufsätze* 3 (1960): 1143; quoted in Hans Küng, *Judaism: Between Yesterday and Tomorrow,* trans. John Bowden (New York: Continuum, 1996), 231.

59. Schatz, *Zwischen Säkularisation und Zweitem Vatikanum,* 238. See Joseph A. Komonchak, "Theology and Culture at Mid-Century: The Example of Henri de Lubac," ThS 51 (1990): 579–602.

60. Aubert, "Theologie während der Ersten Hälfte des 20. Jahrhunderts," 39. According to Karl Rahner, a new kind of theology "came into existence and was accepted between 1940 and 1965." See Karl Rahner, *Theological Investigations,* vol. 21, trans. Hugh Riley (New York: Crossroad, 1988), 72–73.

61. See Robert Grosche, *Pilgernde Kirche* (Freiburg: Herder, 1938); Johannes Pinsk, *Die sakramentale Welt* (Düsseldorf: Patmos, 1938), Constantin Noppel, *Die neue Pfarrei* (Freiburg: Herder, 1939); Mannes Dominikus Koster, *Ekklesiologie im Werden* (Paderborn: Bonifacius, 1940); Karl Rahner, *Hörer des Wortes* (Munich: Kösel-Pustet, 1941); Otto Semmelroth, *Die Kirche als Ursakrament* (Frankfurt: J. Knecht, 1953); Rudolf Schnackenburg, *Gottes Herrschaft und Reich* (Freiburg: Herder, 1959).

62. Schatz, *Kirchengeschichte der Neuzeit II,* 140.

63. Quoted in Hubert Wolf and Claus Arnold, "Einleitung," in *Die katholisch-theologische Disziplinen in Deutschland 1870– 1962,* ed. Hubert Wolf with Claus Arnold (Paderborn: Ferdinand Schöningh, 1999), 9.

64. Karl Rahner, *Karl Rahner, Bilder eines Lebens* (Freiburg: Herder, 1985), 37.

65. The overwhelming majority of bishops at the council recognized that they could no longer equate the church and the reign of God, and that the church is "at best the sacrament and witness to the reign of God"; see Charles E. Curran, *The Catholic Moral Tradition Today* (Washington, D.C.: Georgetown University Press, 1999), 166; Richard P. McBrien, *Church: The Continuing Quest* (Paramus, N.J.: Newman, 1970), 33; idem, "Vatican Council II," in *The HarperCollins Encyclopedia of Catholicism,* ed. Richard P. McBrien (San Francisco: HarperCollins, 1995), 1306.

66. See Roland Götz, "Die Rolle der deutschen Bischöfe auf dem Konzil," in *Die deutschsprachigen Länder und das II. Vatikanum,* ed. Hubert Wolf and Claus Arnold (Paderborn: Schöningh, 2000), 17–52; Franz Xaver Kaufmann, "Das II. Vatikanische Konzil als Moment einer Modernisierung des Katholizismus," in *Der Beitrag der deutschsprachigen*

und osteuropäischen Länder zum Zweitem Vatikanischen Konzil, ed. Klaus Wittstadt and Wim Verschooten (Louvain: Bibliotheck van de Faculteit Godgeleerdheid, 1999), 3–24.

67. The notion of the "rightful autonomy" of human affairs is presented in *Gaudium et Spes,* arts. 36, 41. The idea of the "progress of peoples" is communicated in Paul VI, *Populorum Progressio* [On the Progress of Peoples] (1967).

Selected Bibliography
German Faculties of Catholic Theology, 1933–1945

Adam, Uwe Dietrich. *Hochschule und Nationalsozialismus: Die Universität Tübingen im Dritten Reich.* Tübingen: J. C. B. Mohr (Paul Siebeck), 1977.

Bäumer, Remigius. "Die 'Arbeitsgemeinschaft katholischer Deutscher' im Erzbistum Freiburg: Der Versuch eines 'Brückenschlages' zum Nationalsozialismus," *Freiburger Diözesan-Archiv* 104 (1984): 281–313.

———. "Die theologische Fakultät Freiburg und das Dritte Reich," *Freiburger Diözesan-Archiv* 103 (1983): 265–89.

———. *Weltanschauungs Kampf im Dritten Reich.* Mainz: Matthias Grünewald, 1977.

Böhm, Helmut. "Die theologische Fakultät der Universität München." In *Das Erzbistum München und Freising in der Zeit der nationalsozialistischen Herrschaft,* edited by Georg Schwaiger, 1:684–738. Munich: Schnell & Steiner, 1984.

Bucher, Rainer. "Das deutsche Volk Gottes." In *Das Volk Gottes—ein Ort der Befreiung,* edited by Hildegund Keul and Hans Joachim Sander, 64–82. Würzburg: Echter, 1998.

———. *Kirchenbildung in der Moderne.* Stuttgart: W. Kohlhammer, 1998.

Damberg, Wilhelm. *Der Kampf um die Schulen in Westfalen 1933–1945.* Mainz: Matthias Grünewald, 1986.

———. "Kirchengeschichte zwischen Demokratie und Diktatur: Georg Schreiber und Joseph Lortz in Münster." In *Theologische Fakultäten im Nationalsozialismus,* edited by Leonore Siegele-Wenschkewitz and Carsten Nicolaisen, 146–67. Göttingen: Vandenhoeck & Ruprecht, 1993.

Denzler, Georg. "Katholische Zugänge zum Nationalsozialismus." In *Theologische Wissenschaft im "Dritten Reich,"* edited by Georg Denzler and Leonore Siegele-Wenschkewitz, 40–67. Frankfurt am Main: Haag & Herchen, 2000.

———. *Widerstand ist nicht das richtige Wort: Priester, Bishöfe und Theologen im Dritten Reich.* Zurich: Pendo, 2003.

———. *Widerstand oder Anpassung? Katholische Kirche und Drittes Reich.* Munich: Piper, 1984.

Dietrich, Donald J. *Catholic Citizens in the Third Reich.* New Brunswick, N.J.: Transaction Books, 1988.

———. "Catholic Theologians in Hitler's Third Reich: Adaptation and Critique." *Journal of Church and State* 29 (1987): 19–45.

Eschenburg, Theodor. "Aus dem Universitätsleben vor 1933." In *Deutsches Geistesleben und Nationalsozialismus: Eine Vortragsreihe der Universität Tübingen,* edited by Andreas Flitner, 24–46. Tübingen: Rainer Wunderlich, 1965.

Fouilloux, Étienne. "Die Kultur des katholischen Kirche." In *Erster und Zweiter Krieg: Demokratien und Totalitäre Systeme (1914–1958),* translated by Dorothee Becker, 175–215. Herder: Freiburg, 1992.

Gallin, Alice. *Mid-Wives to Nazism.* Macon, Ga.: Mercer University Press, 1986.

Grunberger, Richard. *Social History of the Third Reich.* London: Weidenfeld & Nicolson, 1971.

Hegel, Eduard. *Geschichte der katholisch-theologischen Fakultät Münster 1773–1964.* 2 parts. Münster: Aschendorff, 1966, 1971.

Heiber, Helmut. *Universität unter dem Hakenkreuz:* Part 1: *Der Professor im Dritten Reich. Bilder aus der akademischen Provinz.* Munich: K. G. Saur, 1991.

———. *Universität unter dem Hakenkreuz:* Part 2, Volume 1, *Die Kapitulation der Hohen Schulen. Das Jahr 1933 und seine Themen.* Munich: K. G. Saur, 1992.

———. *Universität unter dem Hakenkreuz:* Part 2, Volume 2, *Die Kapitulation der Hohen Schulen.* Munich: K. G. Saur, 1994.

Heim, Manfred. "Die theologische Fakultät der Universität München in der NS-Zeit." *Münchener theologische Zeitschrift* 48 (1997): 371–87.

Höpfner, Hans-Paul. *Die Universität Bonn im Dritten Reich.* Bonn: Bouvier, 1999.

Hürten, Heinz. *Deutsche Katholiken 1918–1945.* Paderborn: Ferdinand Schöningh, 1992.

Imkamp, Wilhelm. "Die katholische Theologie in Bayern von der Jahrhundertwende bis zum Ende des Zweiten Weltkrieges." In *Handbuch der bayerischen Kirchengeschichte,* 3:539–651. St. Ottilien: EOS, 1991.

Jedin, Hubert. "Popes Benedict XV, Pius XI, and Pius XII: Biography and

Activity within the Church." In *History of the Church:* Volume 10, *The Church in the Modern Age,* translated by Anselm Biggs, 21–34. New York: Crossroad, 1981.

Jens, Walter. *Eine deutsche Universität: 500 Jahre Tübinger Gelehretenrepublik.* Munich: Kindler, 1977.

Kleineidam, Erich. *Die katholisch-theologische Fakultät der Universität Breslau.* Cologne: Wienand, 1961.

Kolping, Adolf. *Katholische Theologie: Gestern und Heute.* Bremen: Carl Schünemann, 1964.

Lindner, Dominikus. "Die philosophische-theologische Hochschule Freising in der NS Zeit." In *Das Erzbistum München und Freising in der Zeit der nationalsozialistischen Herrschaft:* Volume 1, edited by Georg Schwaiger, 639–56. Munich: Schnell & Steiner, 1984.

Maier, Hans. "Nationalsozialische Hochschulpolitik." In *Die deutsche Universität im Dritten Reich,* edited by Helmut Kuhn et al., 71–102. Munich: Piper, 1966.

May, Georg. *Kirchenkampf oder Katholikenverfolgung: Ein Beitrag zu den gegenseitigen Verhältnis von Nationalsozialismus und christlichen Bekenntnissen.* Stein am Rhein: Christiana, 1991.

Meier, Kurt. "Deutschland und Österreich." In *Erster und Zweiter Krieg: Demokratien und Totalitäre Systeme (1914–1958),* edited by Kurt Meier, 681–772. Freiburg: Herder, 1992.

Mussinghoff, Heinz. *Theologische Fakultäten im Spannungsfeld von Staat und Kirche.* Mainz: Matthias Grünewald, 1979.

Nebel, Dorothea. "Die Lehrstuhlinhaber für Apologetik/Fundamentaltheologie und Dogmatik im deutschsprachigen Raum zwischen den Vatikanischen Konzilien." In *Die katholisch-theologische Disziplinen in Deutschland 1870–1962,* edited by Hubert Wolf with Claus Arnold, 164–230. Paderborn: Ferdinand Schöningh, 1999.

O'Meara, Thomas F. *Church and Culture: German Catholic Theology, 1860–1914.* Notre Dame, Ind.: University of Notre Dame Press, 1991.

Pascher, Joseph. "Das Dritte Reich, erlebt an drei deutschen Universitäten." In *Die deutsche Universität im Dritten Reich,* edited by Helmut Kuhn et al., 45–69. Munich: Piper, 1966.

Reifferscheid, Gerhard. *Das Bistum Ermland und das Dritte Reich.* Cologne: Böhlau, 1975.

Reiter, Ernst. *Die Eichstätter Bischöfe im Dritten Reich.* Regensburg: F. Pustet, 1982.

Ribhegge, Wilhelm. *Geschichte der Universität Münster: Europa in Westfalen.* Münster: Regensburg, 1985.

Ruster, Thomas. *Die verlorene Nützlichkeit der Religion: Katholizismus und*

Moderne in der Weimarer Republik. Paderborn: Ferdinand Schöningh, 1994.

Schatz, Klaus. *Kirchengeschichte der Neuzeit II.* Düsseldorf: Patmos, 1989.

———. *Zwischen Säkularisation und Zweitem Vatikanum: Der Weg des deutschen Katholizismus im 19. und 20. Jahrhundert.* Frankfurt am Main: Josef Knecht, 1986.

Scheffczyk, Leo. "Main Lines of the Development of Theology between the First World War and the Second Vatican Council." In *History of the Church:* Volume 10, *The Church in the Modern Age,* edited by Hubert Jedin, Konrad Repgen, and John Dolan, translated by Anselm Biggs, 260–98. New York: Crossroad, 1981.

Schmitz, Rudolf Michael. *Aufbruch zum Geheimnis der Kirche Jesu Christi: Aspekte der katholischen Ekklesiologie des deutschen Sprachraumes von 1918 bis 1943.* St. Ottilien: EOS, 1991.

Schoof, T. Mark. *A Survey of Catholic Theology, 1800-1970,* translated by N. D. Smith. New York: Paulist Newman, 1970.

Stasiewski, Bernhard, ed. *Bonner Gelehrte: Beiträge zur Geschichte des Wissenschaft in Bonn. Katholische Theologie.* Bonn: H. Bouvier, 1968.

———. "Die katholisch-theologischen Fakultäten und philosophisch-theologischen Hochschulen von 1933 bis 1945: Ein Überblick." In *Seminar und Hochschule in Eichstätt unter dem Nationalismus,* edited by Hermann Holzbauer, 23–48. Eichstätt: Universitätsbibliothek, 1984.

———. "Zur Geschichte der katholisch-theologischen Fakultäten und der philosophisch-theologischen Hochschulen in Deutschland 1933-1945." In *Die Kirche im Wandel der Zeit,* 169–85. Cologne: J. P. Bachem, 1971.

Wittstadt, Klaus. "Die katholisch-theologische Fakultät der Universität Würzburg während der Zeit des Dritten Reiches." In *Vierhundert Jahre Universität Würzburg,* edited by Peter Baumgart, 399–435. Neustadt an der Aisch: Degener & Co., 1982.

Index